here's your island paradise..

by

C.M.Hartwell

WOTS HOT? Publishing

First Edition

Published by WOTS HOT? Publishing

September 2013

Copyright © C.M.Hartwell 2013

www.the-hyip.com

To everyone who supported me throughout the process, before, during and hopefully after - thank you.

And especially to Katia, for the proof reading.

No matter the struggle, continue the climb; in the darkness you may only be one step from the summit.

*A word about spelling.
Anglo-Saxon spelling these days has become not just trans-Atlantic in its scope, but trans-global.
I have used modern English mainly in this book, so if in doubt, I meant to do it.
That's my story and I'm sticking to it.

My jaw jerked open and I began gasping for air.

I noticed that I was choking now as my throat seemed to be blocking up with something, my left cheek pressing heavily with the full weight of my head into a warm sticky substance on the floor.

As I watched, the ground in front of me changed colour as a fast-growing circle of black centred at my chest began spreading out across the tiles. A sweet salty sensation filled the air like a fresh slab of meat being sliced open at a butcher's, as the dark liquid at first fully encompassed then quickly surpassed my entire stretched-out frame.

I was transfixed by this rapidly moving pool as it raced over the smooth ceramic then touched and bounced back off the bar panels like a wave hitting a sea wall.

It reminded me of hot black treacle, and I began to think rather worryingly that it looked a lot like blood.

I put the facts together and with horror grasped that it was mine.

It felt as though a violation had taken place upon me that I had been powerless to control or stop, and for the first time in my life I really understood the word violation and what it meant, and all the horrible connotations it holds.

It was 10.30pm, Wednesday the 2nd of February 1994.

Great. I wish I'd stayed in bed.

Table of Contents

PART I
Life Is What Happens When You Are Making Other Plans

PART II
The Dissection of the Consequences of a Crime

PART III
Trial and Tribulation
(The sun is always shining somewhere in the world)

Aftermath

PART I - Life Is What Happens When You Are Making Other Plans

Chapter 1 - Paradise found

In the late autumn of 1993 through a series of unforeseen events, I found myself at the age of twenty four stepping from a plane onto a hot dusty tropical runway to start a new life in the Caribbean. Looking back my life always seemed to have been slightly disjointed and off balance virtually since birth, and when I arrived on the tiny island of Virgin Gorda in the British West Indies it was running true to form.

Earlier that year I had been having one of those rare moments you experience where everything appears to come together. I had a beautiful wife, was dabbling in the property market in my home county of Kent in southern England, and had just finished renovating my first house with the help of my older brother. Already at that tender age I'd spent a year and a half travelling and seeing much of the world, was a qualified and keen carpenter and shop fitter, and at last was putting my life-long fear of failure firmly into the background as something for once actually seemed to be working out as planned.

I'd fallen into a relationship and recently married the younger sister of an old school friend, and I really have nothing bad to say about Jenny. She was and is a bubbly, kind, attractive person inside and out, one of those people that you just instantly warm to and enjoy being in their company. For me and my awkward ways she turned out to be a real bonus as not only did we make a pretty good team, she brought to my life a sense of acceptance and belonging that I had never before felt, and I was grateful for that. It was Jenny that had secured a job working as a beautician and massage therapist to wealthy tourists in that rich little enclave of the Caribbean, and it was together that we had set off on that cold wet Tuesday morning from London, and now fifteen or so hours later had arrived cramped and creased in the British Virgin Islands about to embark on our latest adventure.

Being the middle son of an insecure sea captain, I'd had the kind of mischievous rebelliousness that only a father who lives strictly by the rules and has achieved great things through doing just that, could really grow to dislike. As such things had not exactly run smoothly in my house as a child. I'm sure he loved me, in the peculiar way that some people scared stiff of real human contact define love, but to say that he didn't show it would be an understatement.

In a house of three children I always seemed to be the one at the wrong end of the frustrated fury of a large man in a white string vest and one eye shut, the other angrily wide open, as was my father's way when awoken from his slumber by my exuberant games of toy soldiers and superheroes.

My memories of my father back then are mostly of him sleeping, or else shouting at me or another member of the family in his underwear, interspersed with images of a seemingly completely unconnected upstanding figure in a pristine black uniform with gold braid above several shiny stripes at his shoulder. He usually wore a white peaked officer's cap that sat

2

perfectly square on his round head, and he would stand proudly at the front door of our house as my mother inspected him before he went out to sail his ship or attend a high powered merchant navy meeting, or whatever it was he did when he left the house.

Keeping up appearances is very important I was frequently told.

My parent's lack of understanding of teen angst and my subsequent but by no means unusual young male enthusiasm for experimenting with the new and exciting (to me at any rate) adult world of petrol engines, sex, and alcohol, was the main reson I left behind a promising academic career in a posh grammar school at the age of sixteen for a life dedicated to a search for excitement, and finding ever-impending poverty.

There was always another crazy scene to live out, another party to go to, another new place to visit. Another person to meet and try to impress with my endless plans and another dream to dream but never quite see to fruition through a haze of hash smoke and hair gel. Like most young men I had a belief that just by charm, some wit and a cocky smile you could conquer the world, and growing up in Thatcher's Britain in the late 1980's not only did this seem possible but almost inevitable, and besides, everyone was doing it.

From the fifty year old council worker with grown up kids to the young upwardly mobile middle class loudmouth, everyone was suddenly an entrepreneur. It was the time when Alan Sugar first put a few cheap electronic components together and sold bargain transistor radios from his local East London market, and Freddie Laker took on the big boys and started the first trans-Atlantic shuttle service, doomed to failure and succumbing eventually to the dirty tricks of the multi-national airlines, who themselves didn't see why Thatcher's Britain meant that playing fair should be any more a part of the new world than it had been for the old.

This was the era of late 1980's Britain in which I grew up and was thrust out into the world, under prepared, mis-qualified, and if it wasn't for a certain speed of thought I think that would have been the end of my story. However I was nothing if not adaptable, and this product of the antiquated grammar school system which either set you up for a life of civil service drudgery, a military career or a bank job in the City, or else left you discarded and rootless, never quite being in the regimented camp of the system and never truly at home with the ranks of the working classes, survived.

At the age of seventeen after extended periods on the dole and hanging around with shifty characters in seedy pubs and clubs in the seaside provincial town where I spent my youth, I finally decided to work for a living. A novel concept to someone who until that point believed that all I had to do was turn up at the front door of life, ring the doorbell, and it would immediately spring open and invite me through to a world of riches, women, fast cars and easy living.

Unfortunately my co-ordination was a little off, and I could no more ring that bell than I could kick a football, which for today's youth along with reality TV fantasies of superstardom has replaced the yuppie dream of the eighties. Different era, similar dreams, similar likelihood of success.

Having left school early and lost the chance of a university education and the more normal and well-trodden paths to employment that would entail, I tried various jobs and studies to keep me busy and find something that I both enjoyed doing and could bring in some badly needed cash, and maybe even lead to a career somewhere down the line. From starting and dropping out of courses in Travel and Tourism and accountancy at college, to working as a farm labourer, greengrocery delivery driver, and even door to door oil-painting salesman, I experimented with many things with differing levels of success.

Eventually a friend of mine in a similar situation - an ex-grammar school kid with family problems and a slight belief that the world owed him a living, just like me - explained one stoned day his ideas of 'starting at the bottom in a blue-collar job and working your way up', and so building a grass-roots business and becoming that elusive millionaire which everyone in the Eighties desperately wanted to be. I liked the sound of this; of being your own boss, not taking any crap, not playing the 'game', and most importantly not going anywhere near an office. Invigorated I began to seek out a platform which would suit me and get me on the first rung of life's ladder.

I settled on becoming a bricklayer, or else a plumber as a possible back-up plan, but when I went to my local jobcentre to enquire what training was available, the only thing remotely close to those options that was recruiting at the time was a course in Carpentry and Joinery. This was not my first, or even second choice, but I had made up my mind to do 'something', and having got this far I thought I may as well take a look at the prospectus while I was here; after all, what did I have to lose? It was billed as a modern apprenticeship, which usually meant a less than satisfactory education with an even less satisfactory pay packet at the end of it, and often became little more than a source of cheap labour for unscrupulous employers who benefited from tax breaks and incentives to try to get people off the unemployment lines, and thus make the government of the day look good, or at least better than it should.

I had always been good with my hands and enjoyed woodwork at school - before Health and Safety got involved and closed down such 'dangerous' pastimes for children on school premises. (If children aren't allowed to try different things, how on Earth will they ever find what they want to do with their lives? Anyway, moving on...) So I figured, 'I'll give it a go!' It was creative which was something that I liked the idea of, and could stimulate a career in property development or real estate. There was one potential problem in that the minimum starting age for this course was eighteen, and I was still some way off that, whereupon with what some would call ingenuity and others just plain lying, I faked an ID, signed up and after some it has to be said pretty lacklustre checking on behalf of the jobcentre, was accepted and invited to begin studying a few weeks later.

Soon I began classes while working on the side as an 'improver' with a local construction firm, and I took to it all quite well. Within a short period of time I'd picked up papers and experience in joinery, cabinet making, site management and concrete formworking, and armed with these new skills at the age of nineteen I set off out into the world to make my fortune.

To bring me from those turbulent teen years to arriving that late afternoon on Virgin Gorda is a story in its own right of travel, adventures, a few small successes and several noteworthy failures. I'd mixed with the highest, and lowest, of society on four continents, had many jobs and faltered careers, and countless scrapes which I had fallen into and thus far managed to climb out of again alive and with little more than a few scars and lessons hopefully learned to show for it. Thankfully at that point I had no kids, and on St Patrick's day 1993 for reasons which were not even entirely clear to me at the time, I found myself getting off a cruise ship in the United States Virgin Islands port of Charlotte Amalie, appropriating a ship's captain, and marrying Jenny in a hillside bar overlooking the harbour before returning to our vessel and continuing the vacation now surprisingly hitched.

I think it's fair to say we were actually living the term 'Yes Man!' twenty years before it became a Hollywood catchphrase. If it seemed fun and quirky and something that others may balk at, we just went for it and did it, and to hell with the consequences.

It was during this spring Caribbean cruise on the Holland America liner Westerdam which had seen me board single and disembark two weeks later not, that my new wife and I stumbled upon a wonderful piece of paradise known as the British Virgin Islands or BVI. Superlatives come thick and fast in this tiny group of four main islands - Tortola, Virgin Gorda, Jost Van Dyke and Anegada. Blue sky, bluer sea, tropical vegetation, curious smooth rocky caves and grottos waiting to be discovered, and beaches that I hesitate to describe because if I did two things would happen - firstly I would fail in adequately explaining their beauty, and second you would stop planning your next holiday to wherever and immediately go to the BVI, and the secret would be out. Sufficc to say in exploring dozens of countries and ten times that of sandy shores that claim to be the best, the BVI has none better, and few equals.

Two words I shall give you to sum up the subject of British Virgin Island beaches before I move on; Valley Trunk.

Enjoy.

And so the impetuous newlyweds returned to a damp grey England, and immediately made plans to leave again. A quick scout of the jobs pages revealed a small but elite beauty therapy business servicing the great and the good on Virgin Gorda, with the added bonus of the contract to serve the multi-millionaire guests on Sir Richard Branson's private island hideaway of Necker, also a part of the Virgin Islands and serviced through the northern second port of Gorda, Leverick Bay. Jenny secured an interview with the petite female English company owner in the posh Lanesborough Hotel off Hyde Park one drizzly July day, and as I had total faith that she would, indeed got the job.

I had been putting my carpentry and general building skills to use buying and renting/selling properties in England, and was happy to head over to the other side of the Atlantic for pastures new with my young wife, confident that our small investments back in the UK would tick over nicely during my absence, and certain that upon arrival in the Caribbean, something, as Mr. Micawber might say, would turn up.

So on December 14th 1993 we flew out, Jenny to her new position as assistant manager in the beauty therapy company which now employed her, and me to read my Dickens and Frank Herbert on the beach and to see what I could see.

Chapter 2 - Sundowners with Heather

Heather was the widowed wife of an American electronics magnate, who like many people had planned their joint retirement without the slightest thought that it would not unfold exactly as they had envisaged. Then just before his early and well-earned lucrative final departure from the workplace her husband died, and Heather suddenly found herself approaching sixty and unexpectedly alone.

They had bought a wonderfully ramshackle holiday home on Virgin Gorda at the top of a hill overlooking the Valley, which was the main settlement on the southern part of the island. Also known as Spanish Town, the Valley was the commercial centre and the location of the main ferry port, a dirt runway airstrip onto which we had just stepped, Virgin Gorda's one bank and the majority of the bars and restaurants which serviced both the local population and the long and short-term tourist trade alike.

There were few hotels, with the exception of a small number of ultra-exclusive resorts, and many hundreds of holiday villas as well as several charter yacht companies and the businesses that supported them dotted around the coastline.

As is common with most ex-colonies from the old European imperial overlords there was also a thriving and vociferous ex-pat community, supplemented by a large batch of rich American retirees for whom Florida was too loud and Tuscany too far from their investments and grandkids, and so the better parts of the Caribbean suited them just fine. Heather fell nicely into both sections of the long-term foreign residents, being born and raised in England then moving to and marrying in America.

Through the grapevine and with the help of a mutual friend we had been introduced by letter to Heather, who had generously offered for us to stay at her large holiday home until we got settled into our new life on the island. I think this was partly due to Heather's innate sense of kindness, and partly due to some measure of loneliness, as being on her own in paradise in the run up to Christmas 1993, she would be vacationing there alone, as she always did to escape the cold North American snows of New England where she and her late husband had set up base many years earlier.

So, after clearing immigration and armed with an address and a 'pay no more than' note from Heather to aid us in negotiations with the airport taxi driver, we headed out and drove down palm tree lined roads and into the unknown once again in our lives.

The cab was driven by a friendly West Indian chap who swore that he had seen us before the 'last time' we were there (most unlikely) and cheerfully and without prompting gave us a commentary on everything from the weather forecast (hot) to local politics during the ten minute drive to Heather's winter retreat. As we zigzagged up the hill past humming cicadas and whirling dragon flies which raced with the car along the road, life felt good.

We decanted our luggage from the people carrier and rung a bell attached to the side of a large imposing hardwood door, surrounded by thick vines which obscured the view of the rest of the house to the left and right of us from the position where we stood. Eventually the door opened to reveal a diminutive, fit looking fifty-something woman, with sandy shoulder length hair, a big smile and a warm welcoming handshake for both Jenny and I.

We were shown to the lower level of the four storey wooden house which had been built up the side of a red rocky hill, with lush vegetation that crept over the balconies and up around the window frames as if the house was part of the jungle and vice versa. Wandering termite trails snaked up many of the building's wooden supports, and looking out from our balcony we could see masses of hermit crabs that constantly scavenged on the warm rocks below when the sun was not too hot for their meanderings, adding to the exotic feel of the place. It was a wonder to us how hermit crabs could possibly live the half-mile or so from the seashore where the house was situated, but all the same there they were, busy and permanently hungry. We watched in quiet fascination as they each slowly individually picked their way around the pitted surface and clung to the crevices, stopping every now and then to investigate a likely tasty snack or morsel, paying no attention to the many other crabs they shared the space with until they occasionally inadvertently bumped shells with one another on the rock face. Whereupon they would stop, size each other up tentatively with a couple of their delicate front legs, then as if on a mutually agreed cue both would turn and scuttle off again in the opposite direction.

Is it strange that the first thing one often does when high up is to look down rather than outwards? Nevertheless this is what we did, and then together after a few moments watching with interest the foraging of the out of place crabs, we raised our gaze and surveyed the Caribbean scene laid out before us.

As Jenny and I were both seasoned travellers having back-packed around the world together as teenagers, it would be overstating it to say when we looked out from our wicker-framed balcony that we shared a 'we have arrived' moment. But still it was quite spectacular.

We embraced and silently took in the late afternoon view. A huge eternally blue sky unconcerned with the trivialities of man's travails below, gave the upper frame to what seemed like hundreds of charter yachts sailing to and fro, up to and in between several dark sheer islands which reared up out of the plate flat turquoise sea stretching away into the distance. Closer to us on dry land the odd open-topped jeep or pick-up truck popped into and out of view through the trees under our hill as they rounded corners on the jungle-encroached roads below, going about their business and oblivious to us watching from our viewpoint above.

Not bad. Not bad at all.

However a view is just a view, and no matter how glorious there is only so long one can stand and stare before you have to put it away and carry on with your day. And so we unpacked a few things, showered and changed, then climbed the cast-iron spiral staircase which rose through a large hole in the ceiling up into the main living area of the house. Here we found Heather watering some plants and generally busying herself about the room, dressed in a white slightly stained t-shirt, khaki shorts and open-toed sandals, which is the common uniform of ex-pats in warm climes everywhere.

Tropical living is not quite the same as the hustle and bustle of city life, and the first thing one notices when casually observing people in such places is the slight lack of attention to detail in the area of grooming that they acquire, as opposed to those passing through on fleeting holiday visits.

Nail polish is usually the first to fall by the wayside for women, followed swiftly by coiffured hair and finally fashionable clothing. It's not that people don't care about their appearance in hot countries, it's just that one quickly finds there are simply more important and necessary things to do with your time.

Take eating for example. In the developed world, whether in a big city or the smallest village you can generally find a well-stocked supermarket open at all hours, a pizza delivery service or two, and the security of knowing that when you go to the fridge, light the grill and turn on the tap, the fridge will be cold, the oven hot and the water wet. However in the far-flung corners of the world where some of the more adventurous live, this is not always the case.

Buying groceries in out of the way places such as Virgin Gorda can be a hit and miss affair at best. Fresh fruit and vegetables are at the end of a very long and tenuous supply chain, which gets progressively more expensive and unreliable the farther from the mainstream market you get. Virtually everything arrives by boat and being in the tropics food spoils easily, so fresh commodities are snapped up quickly by eager buyers almost as fast as they can be dropped in boxes on the shore. Electricity and water supplies are inevitably at the mercy of small provincial utility companies, who tend to have a slightly more laid back approach to customer service than they do in the highly competitive markets of major population areas. All this combines to make just the basic tasks of eating and food preparation, as well as cleaning and looking ones best, much more time consuming and thoughtful a process than it otherwise would be.

Ditto for car servicing and dealing with mechanical problems that may arise with whichever modes of transport one uses. House maintenance, a sore tooth or a trip to the bank to order a new cheque book, all takes far longer and with twice as much frustration to deal with than it does 'back home'. Naturally something's got to give, and in this environment a trip to the beauty parlour descends inexorably down the list.

A few do take this to the extreme and for these folks showering becomes a thing of the past, as after all there is always the beautiful Caribbean Sea to take a quick dip in on the way home from work. And for that matter why wash clothes? They will only get dirty again...

Thankfully such people, although not uncommon, are in the minority.

Some on the other hand work even harder to maintain the routines and conventions of modern life, no matter how much effort and however long it takes them. These stalwarts paint their nails in humid sticky air which means that they never seem to dry, or religiously don a smart shirt and a nice pair of shoes when out for a spot of shopping or having coffee with friends, or just running a casual errand across town.

However most people find themselves happily slipping somewhere between the two extremes and into 'Caribbean time', and just take it a little bit easier on the sartorial front than they would ordinarily do.

Heather was a perfect example of the final set; in terms of London or New York she could be said to be making slightly less than the expected effort of a woman of her station in life, but on Caribbean time, she had it just about right.

We could tell immediately on sitting down at the ornate ceramic conservatory table on the main balcony which served as the breakfast nook, afternoon tea dispenser, dining table and sundowner social setting, that Heather was not the most adept of homemakers. We deduced early into our conversation that back in the States and most recently in Boston where she had set up base after her husband died, Heather had a lady who 'did'. That in all probability meant cooked, cleaned, bought the groceries and pretty much did everything except pay the bills. On Virgin Gorda Heather had a regular cleaner but other than that was more self-sufficient, and today pulled out the stops to make us feel welcome. As we sank into the balcony chairs she served us up a plate of fish fingers and a simple salad comprising two halves of a whole cucumber and a handful of cherry tomatoes. This did seem a little at odds for a woman who obviously ordinarily had high standards of etiquette and very substantial means, but it was tasty and appreciated and the company was great, and with jet lag and after airline food there were no complaints from Jenny and me as we happily tucked into our impromptu supper.

We sat the three of us and chatted, and soon began to relax in each other's company. Heather quickly turned out to be a genuinely charming and funny person with a twinkle in her eye and a sharp mind. She made several references during our conversation to the new church which sat on an adjacent hilltop on what was probably the best piece of real estate on the entire island of Virgin Gorda. This nearby artificially flattened peak overlooked the Valley and north towards the small mountain which split the island in two. From its lofty position the church peered majestically out across the sea, with only a winding coast road and a thin swathe of bush between it, the rise of the hill, and the ocean. This canny choice of location stopped any chance of a future development springing up along the shore and spoiling the wonderful unbroken view from the small ecclesiastical collection of buildings, which also contained the residence of the elderly Irish-American Catholic priest from where he oversaw his mixed flock of ex-pats and locals.

In talking we got the feeling that Heather had donated quite substantially to the Church coffers, including as we understood it helping with funds to build the obviously brand new and gleaming place of worship which stood impressively silhouetted against the setting sun not far from us in the fading light. Although traditional in layout, we could see that it had a distinctly modern and sassy outer design, with whitewashed and crazy paving walls and a green angular roof. There was a certain vagueness however about Heather's motivations for doing this and she left an impression with us that religion had only recently come into her life, and perhaps was a crutch and source of solace in her time of need rather than being a true god-fearing believer.

As dusk fell and the lights down in Spanish Town began to blink on, the creaking high-pitched cicadas were replaced by the accelerated hum of mosquitos zipping past our ears, just out of sight but unmistakably and worryingly very much present in their droves. A scented insect repellent coil was lit and placed in the middle of the table, and the dishes cleared away to be washed up by us later before retiring as a sort of thank you to our genial host. Heather then stood and gave a half-guilty half-anticipatory smile.

'Time for a sundowner', she said.

We couldn't tell if it was a question or a statement, but either way without waiting for a reply Heather left the table and went inside through the French windows into the now dark living room. We heard a cupboard door being opened and the chink of what sounded like glasses being gathered together, and she returned with a bottle of Pusser's Navy Rum in one hand and three chipped white coffee mugs surprisingly in the other.

Jenny wasn't usually much of a drinker, but the moment was there and no-one could deny it, so we all sat and continued to chat into the blackening night with periodic half-inch refills of neat rum keeping the bottom of our cups wet. Buzzing insects incessantly tried to join in our conversation, only to lose interest and bite my ankles and feet in annoyance that I didn't offer them a drop of liquor and invite them to pull up a pew.

Once or twice I caught my wife's eyes sparkling in the moonlight and she suppressed a giggle when she saw me looking inquisitively at her, but she looked away and didn't explain. Only later when Heather had raised herself very wobbly and sweetly slurring said goodnight, and Jenny and I jointly decided to clear up a little, as we stood at the kitchen sink cleaning the dishes did she divulge the reason for her secretive giggles earlier.

'Did you hear Heather fart?'

She had a beaming smile on her face as she asked me.

'No way!' I replied.

'She kept doing it, you listen the next time. She shifts herself sideways slightly in her chair, lets it out, then runs her tongue around the top of her cup, every time! I couldn't stop myself laughing!'

I wasn't sure if Jenny was joking as I had heard nothing untoward in the gas department during the evening, but I had noticed Heather absentmindedly testing the rim of her cup with the tip of her tongue on occasion throughout the sundowner session, with a very slight upturning at the corners of her mouth in a 'I know something that you don't know' kind of cheeky grin to no-one in particular as she did so. At the time I had taken this oft-repeated expression by her to be nothing more than a pondering gesture such as pursing one's lips in contemplation. It seemed on reflection however that this might have been more of a subconscious pressure-releasing ritual by our slightly inebriated host, if of course my wife wasn't pulling my leg. But Jenny wasn't taken to being dishonest even in jest, so I made up my mind to keep my ears primed the next time we shared a suppertime drink and smiled as I washed up at the thought of this refined trans-Atlantic socialite behaving in such an unladylike way once the rum had begun to settle in of an evening.

We then began to wonder at the significance of the china cups as opposed to the more normal glasses which one would expect for neat alcohol, and we realised with more merriment that this was probably a subtle way to hide how much booze is being consumed, and we suspected now that we were probably quite heavily outdrank by our happy host.

There was not a bad bone in Heather's body and we thought nothing whatsoever unpleasant nor unwholesome of our new friend and landlady, but the comedy of the situation was unavoidable, as the juxtaposition of the staid and the carefree and being presented with the unexpected in life is always funny, and knowing Heather I don't think she would have begrudged us a little smile before bed at her expense.

Chapter 3 - Island life

The next morning I counted forty-two mosquito bites on one ankle and forty-five on the other. Those Caribbean mozzies really do like fresh meat.

Heather had pointedly not discussed breakfast the night before, and so we assumed that after our first initial welcoming meal we were on our own when it came to preparing our food from then on.

We did make ourselves a cup of tea in our host's kitchen before she got up, and after washing our cups said good morning to Heather and asked where the shops were so that we could get stocked with some basic provisions. She was going into town on an errand shortly we were told, and we would be welcome to join her. Jenny had her induction at her new job later that morning, so she arranged to meet her boss close by the shops where we were headed, and I would return home alone later with our supplies.

The next few days passed with us easily slipping into our new schedule - it's amazing how quickly you get used to an unfamiliar environment once the novelty wears off.

Jenny rose each day at 7.30am, and donning her thick white knee-length cotton dress which served as her beautician's overalls, she prepared a healthy light packed-lunch and placed it with her appointments book in a beauty case which doubled as a shoulder bag. This she took and climbing into a battered open-topped Suzuki jeep provided by her boss, would clatter off down the hill to one of the two salons which the company leased on the island, depending which clients were booked where on any given day. I would get up at the same time, see my wife off to work and after breakfast pick a book to read, take a bottle of water, and set off to explore.

I had a loose plan to find some work on the island, possibly as a carpenter or some other thing which took my fancy and I seemed employable for, but for now I was happy to relax and take it easy. I had worked very hard in the run-up to leaving the UK preparing a flat which my wife and I had recently bought for renting out, and felt that a break was due, even if not necessarily deserved.

There was another background task for me to fulfill, that of trying to find us some more permanent accommodation, and so with this in mind whenever I stopped to chat with someone or an opportunity presented itself, I would raise the subject with the various people who crossed my path on my survey of the island. I could be quite a naturally chatty person, and held little fear of walking up to and talking with perfect strangers and chewing the fat, so as the days went by in this way I began to know and be known by many of the folk in that part of the Valley.

The final occupying thought for me in those early days was that I liked to keep fit, and exercise in some form or other was an important part of both our lives, so looking for a gym to use whilst on the island was quite a high priority. Asking in some of the five star hotels to see if I could use their facilities, I found firstly that the fitness suites of the main resorts were sadly lacking in quality which was strange for such high priced developments, and that there was no such thing as an independent health club anywhere on the island.

I was told of a local man by the name of George Tyson who might be able to help as he was known to be a bit of a bodybuilding enthusiast. This seemed hopeful and so with some difficulty I eventually tracked him down at the back of a run-down garage off a grassy side road on the outskirts of town.

The unit consisted of several weather-beaten barns set in a loose circle around a central yard, all of them in a slight state of disrepair and unevenly patched with corrugated iron and mismatching wooden planks. The doors to each barn were either non-existent and the barn wide open for all to see, or else heavily padlocked with no seeming pattern to either, and the rough ground in between was liberally scattered with various engine parts, vehicle chassis, broken tools and enormous mechanical fixings that would not have looked out of place securing a propeller shaft to an ocean liner, much more so than serving a small island community's less significant vehicular needs. In between the scattered junk and everywhere that did not have regular foot-traffic was overgrown with what appeared to be several years' buildup of old weeds and long dry grass.

As I entered the clearing a muscly dog with matted white and brown fur of no breed that I could determine, stood up and growled menacingly at me from the end of a loose chain made of links so large that the aforementioned ocean liners could probably have made good use of them. The other end of the chain was hidden from view and I nervously hoped that it was secured to something substantial. The eyes of the hound seemed shrewd and Machiavellian, with a touch of Zoltan thrown in, and I had the distinct feeling that it kept the chain purposefully slack to lull any unwelcome visitor to the yard into thinking that they were safely out of reach of those long brown teeth. I suspected however that the dog knew exactly how long the leash was and precisely where someone would have to stand to be within range of its jaws with one swift leap from its scarred and scratched hind legs, which at first glance appeared loose and unconcerned, but looking more closely I could see the rippling muscles shivering with tension awaiting an opportunity to jump and strike. I looked the mongrel in the eye as I slowly walked past just (I hoped) out of its farthest reach, and peered into each unlit barn in turn, eyeing periodically the chain and more importantly what both ends were attached to. Unsure if anyone was home I called out the name 'George' a few times, and listened for a response.

I was about to give up and thankfully leave the unsettling presence of the very scary junkyard dog, when right past the spitting snarling animal a huge man with a smile to match appeared from between two of the buildings and walked towards me. He seemed totally unconcerned as he brushed past the mutt's snout casually knocking it to one side as he passed. The creature evidently knew who was boss and resumed its lowered head stance without so much as a flicker of recognition of the man, instead staring with venom at me and returning in earnest to growling after a momentary pause, which it then continued to do for the entire next five minutes that I stood there talking with George. For it was indeed Mr. Tyson, and although no relative to the former heavyweight champ (I asked) might just have been capable of giving him a run for his money. Like the boxer he was not excessively tall, perhaps five feet ten, not more than five eleven (175 to 180cms), and although not as defined as a professional bodybuilder, had a thick strong body that I imagined would require an actual impact from a car to knock off his stride, and even then it would not be a foregone conclusion as to which would come off worst.

I introduced myself and explained that I was looking for somewhere to do some weight training and general exercise, and already assuming apparently that I would want to use his gym before I had even seen it, George explained without ever actually explaining much at all, which is a common Caribbean trait, that his brother or uncle or nephew ran the small automotive unit behind which we now stood and to which the barns belonged. He never quite said what his job was there, if anything, but whatever the circumstances of his presence he'd at some point converted one of the empty barns into a gym for his personal use, as well as for friends and relatives and anyone who he chose to let work out.

Telling me that there was no club as such and therefore no organised system of membership, when I enquired as to how one such as myself could actually use these facilities and still quite curious to see exactly what they were, never stopping smiling that same broad smile George looked up into the air for a few seconds in an exhibition of false-pondering, then dropped his eyes back to me and offered 'life membership' for the princely sum of one hundred and fifty U.S. dollars.

(The American dollar is the currency of choice in the BVI for day to day transactions. Officially it's the Caribbean dollar, but no-one ever uses that outside of Government budgetary meetings and official documentation, and literally the entire state runs on the greenback from top to bottom.)

I guessed that not many people used the gym regularly as there was certainly no-one else there that day and all was quiet and locked-up. Perhaps he thought quite rightly that I was probably going to move on and leave Virgin Gorda at some point in the not too distant future, so another hundred and fifty dollars in his wallet for not a lot of extra inconvenience would probably suit both parties well enough.

I questioned George briefly and tested the waters of negotiation as we walked towards one of the padlocked barns, explaining that I would only be around for a couple of months and so may not actually require a full 'life membership', thus raising the possibility of some sort of a discount. Without answering he unlocked and swung a squeaking metal door wide open, and gesturing me inside we stepped into the hot gloom.

I saw before me a single room which encompassed the entire barn. It had a high, pitched roof of old black timbers with dusty cobwebs hanging from every corner and angle. Shafts of spinning dust particles suspended in the air were illuminated by sunlight streaking in through gaps in some of the poorly fitting planks of wood which covered the outside of the building, and filling almost every square inch of the space haphazardly spread around on an impacted dirt floor, were dozens of contraptions which resembled home-made weight machines of every size and description.

I say 'home-made' because that's for the most part what they were. Some I could see from rusty and half-missing labels were originally famous brand-name items, which had either been discarded broken or sold off cheap at the end of their useful life, only find their way here by some means or other to be recycled and used again in this most unlikely of places. Whether they had at one time belonged to the fitness centre of a passing cruise ship and for some reason been dismantled and removed while in port, or were from private residences or holiday homes on the local islands and were now surplus to requirements I cannot say, but probably a little of both was true.

Some of the more ingenious devices comprised of complex systems of cables and weights, utilising truck wheels and lumps of concrete with sturdy hooks buried deep within and attached to wire lines. These via convoluted routes through pulleys and eyes securely fixed to the wooden pillars supporting the roof, would inevitably end in a rudimentary pull-up bar or dumbell hanging loosely above a particularly hard and indented area of the floor, no doubt due to a heavy man standing there endlessly lifting and dropping the weight from that spot.

Forget stretching mats and posing mirrors, sauna and steam rooms. This was raw, basic, and actually kind of charming. There was one light which had to be switched on from an industrial sized old-fashioned toggle switch on the wall by the open door, and when on, this single lightbulb hanging from a high rafter in the ceiling gave little more illumination than the glowing end of a cigarette. Even in that darkened place it could barely be seen or picked out amongst the multiple rays of light streaming in from every angle from the bright day outside, the stark contrasts of these laser-beam shafts streaking across the room making it difficult to focus and see clearly the farthest extremities of the interior.

It took a while for my eyes to adjust, but after a minute or two I got used to the mixed darkness somewhat and could just about make out where the various cables started and finished, which peg went into which weight to alter the tension on each pulley, and not really having much choice in the matter I agreed to George's price and house rules. I promised to return with the designated fee forthwith, and trusting me enough to hand me the strangely miniature key to the Fort Knox sized entrance padlock, we shook on the deal and parted.

A pair of canine eyes warily followed my progress until I passed the last barn and stepped out onto the road, gratefully surrendering the territory once more to the warrior beast.

Chapter 4 - Bathing Trunks

There is no faster way to get to know a place than by walking around and aimlessly exploring, and this suited my inquisitive nature just fine as in those first few weeks I discovered all the nooks and crannies of Virgin Gorda that most visitors probably never cared to investigate. It was all learning as far as I was concerned, and one can frequently find more fascinating people and wonderful nuggets of information studying where the locals and real people live and work rather than by sticking endlessly to the tourist haunts. Often this isn't possible and when on a fleeting visit constraints of time limit you to 'doing the tourist bit', but when you have a little more freedom, just wandering and letting life unfold is as enriching a process as any university degree and in some ways more so.

I was fairly tall (and haven't shrunk yet) and could generate an imposing presence when I had to, so rarely felt nervous straying down what to others might appear foreboding dark alleys or at first glance unwelcoming side roads in out of the way areas. I felt I could get out of a scrape quite well if I inadvertently found myself in an awkward or potentially dangerous situation, and there was always the option of running away as fast as my long legs could carry me should it become necessary. So I walked and explored and looked and thought, and took in all the wonderful people and places and lives that were so alien to me and yet not.

My immediate locale was the old settlement of Spanish Town, set in a long low hollow of land on the southern part of the island, and which topographical feature gave the area its other name - the Valley. This was bordered to the north with Gorda

Peak, to the west with the yacht harbour and ferry port, south to the beaches, and east to a continuous ridge of green hills, on the other side of which running parallel to the sea was Virgin Gorda's only airstrip. This much could be gleaned from any map, but as I got my bearings I began to paint a picture in my mind and would eventually be able to describe the place in greater detail, and here is a snapshot as best as I can relate it now as I write. I will use the past tense but if you happened upon there today I don't think you will find all that much has changed since.

Starting with the first thing that greeted most new arrivals on Virgin Gorda, there was the main ferry dock and yacht harbour. This accommodated two medium sized concrete jetties where one could hop on a Speedy Boat or Smith's Ferry for the forty minute ride to the Virgin Islands' capital of Road Town in Tortola, or the nearer Beef Island.

The strangely named Beef Island was the only part of the BVI flat enough to fit a runway of sufficient length to take jet aeroplanes. For this reason Beef Island had been joined to the principal island of Tortola via a causeway, to ease traffic flow and make it more convenient to travel between the capital and the airport. From there tourists disgorged hourly and filtered out to their various destinations around the BVI either by road or boat, or else stayed at the airport as we had, to catch a smaller propeller-driven aeroplane for the short flight to Virgin Gorda or Anegada. These alternative provincial airstrips were restricted to daytime use, as only Beef Island was equipped with radar or landing lights.

Near to the yacht harbour at the heart of Spanish Town lay the municipal square, which comprised an open area about the size of two tennis courts, surrounded and enclosed by commercial units and shops overlooking a central plaza. The southern end contained a bank and a coffeehouse/bakery, and the two longer sides were filled with various travel agencies, charter yacht companies, diving schools, boutiques selling curios and knick-knacks and one small business hotel. A covered walkway linked all the establishments around the edge of the open space so that one could visit every store in turn and get back to your starting point without ever once leaving the shade.

The portion of the square nearest the bank was embellished with some small palm trees and shrubs, and several benches which few people ever cared to sit in. It wasn't particularly pleasant being baked by hot paving slabs at your feet, looking at shop windows on every side with little protection from the scorching Caribbean sun beating down from above, so quite understandably those seats more often than not remained empty during the day. From time to time a tourist unused to the area would pass a few minutes sitting there whilst a significant other was browsing in a store or collecting a snack from the bakery, but more usually it was devoid of people until dusk fell.

The best known business here and the social hub of the entire Valley was without doubt the Bath and Turtle Bar and Restaurant. The 'B & T' (or just 'the pub' as it was the only one) took up the whole of the northern parade, which contained the main saloon and kitchens.

The inner bar was decorated in a mix of modern American and traditional English styles, with ornate mirrors behind a long oak counter, and tall thin bar stools and tables arranged around a smooth grey-tiled floor.

Running the full length of the tavern and spilling out onto the square was the outer dining area, with a vine-covered wooden pergola overhead providing solar relief. Beyond the verandah and taking up about half of the plaza was an open-air dance floor, encircled with plastic tables and chairs, and on the far side of this in more or less the middle of the square was a part-time satellite bar. This opened in the evenings when the pub got very busy to save customers having to go inside and queue for a drink or wait to be served at one of the tables.

The owner of the pub was an American ex-pat in her thirties, who was well-known in the community and mixed easily with the West Indian business people and merchants of Virgin Gorda and Tortola. Under her keen stewardship this had become the place to be in Spanish Town, no more so than on Wednesday and Sunday nights when local bands were invited to play on the square to entertain diners and patrons. At these times the farthest tables and chairs were either cleared away or moved closer to the main bar area, to create what would invariably be a packed large outdoor dance floor resounding with booming Calypso music beneath the stars.

Farther afield, past the ferry port to the north of Spanish Town was a small mountain, Gorda Peak, which also provided Virgin Gorda and some say the whole group with its name - literally the 'Fat Virgin'. When I learnt the translation I tried looking at this geological formation from various angles and vantage points, and honestly if that's what Christopher Columbus saw in the shape of those rocks, then all I can say is people must have looked very different in the fifteenth century.

This mini mountain was home to a nature reserve called Gorda Peak National Park, traversed by a scenic road through a low pass to Leverick Bay and the northern resorts.

In the opposite direction just to the south of the Valley was a small collection of hills, where could be found Heather's home and the Catholic Church.

Finally when describing those parts of Virgin Gorda which formed the boundaries of my knowledge at the time, like all the BVI, there was one major attraction and the reason this miraculous place is such a mecca for tourists worldwide - the ocean.

The sea here is a rich deep blue, lapped by gentle winds which tumble through the high island peaks, creating an immense bowl of light choppy water which is pure bliss for sailors. From a distance the ocean appears flat, and some days it is. If it was always still and calm it would look nice no doubt, but soon become a little monotonous. Mundane this is not. The wind blows but rarely too strong. The water chatters and ripples with a million multi-faceted waves racing along chased by the breeze, sometimes breaking over into little white horses which roll out left and right stretching ever thinner until they blend into the wave behind, then move together in the direction of their comrades to an unknown destination far away.

Non-sailors fear not, for the BVI holds another secret. There are no private beaches on the main islands. Let me say that again; if you can get there, you can swim off it, sunbathe on it, or melt into it, with white tropical sun baking your body and sparkling coarse sand sticking to the perspiration on your skin like a glistening diamond coat. Palm trees on one side of you, the purest azure blue sea on the other. Fierce sun above you, hot crunchy silica below.

If there is a heaven on earth, it is here. Even the sand which in some places in the world is annoyingly fine and gets everywhere, or frustratingly scalding making every trip to the sea a dash for survival for the delicate soles of your feet, is just perfect. In fact the only slight annoyance is actually on reflection a bonus. I refer to the conspicuous lack of snack bars and drinks vendors endlessly patrolling the shore plying their wares. Yes, a cold beer or soft drink and possibly a hot snack in the middle of a hard day's roasting would not go amiss, but then think of the disturbance it would bring; the noise, the interruptions. On a good day in the BVI you can find a beach that would not look out of place adorning the pages of a glossy magazine, and have it all, totally, completely and luxuriously to yourself.

As the days went by and I saw my wife in her sexy white uniform drive off in her battered red jeep each morning, after I had pottered around and done the few chores assigned to me, I invariably found an excuse to go to the beach, and who wouldn't?

Soon I had discovered all the stretches of sand within easy walking distance of our home, and having narrowed it down to three of the best, a routine began to evolve.

The three nicest beaches by reputation on the south of Virgin Gorda were The Baths, Mini Trunk and the mysterious Valley Trunk, which people would mention in passing but few seemed to have ever actually visited, or else they were being deliberately vague for some reason, I could not tell. By all accounts Valley Trunk was supposed to be incredible, but in paradise appreciation of beauty often fades, and possibly also due to its out of the way location the locals seemed uninterested. Tourists seldom went as most didn't know of its existence, being superseded by other better known and serviced hotspots.

The foremost of these and the first I explored were The Baths.

The Baths are world renowned, being an extraordinary array of huge boulders and prehistoric rock formations laid out along the shore. Worn smooth by millennia of moving seawater, one could explore them and pick your way through, around, over, sometimes under, finding secret halls of stone open to the sky above, or caves where only footprints in the sand betrayed someone's passing, soon to be washed away with all evidence that they had ever stopped in that spot. Your feet whenever they touched the ground would be instantly enveloped by the Caribbean Sea, cooled by virtue of the fact that it had lapped gently under the rocks and out of direct sunlight for a few moments before it crept up and encircled your ankles. You would invariably linger there a moment longer than necessary to revel in the cold silky touch of the mix of sand and saltwater invading the crevices between your toes, gently exfoliating the skin. Every now and then a rippling reflection in the water would give away the location of a secret pool, concealed among the rocks, where you could imagine coming to and bathing alone or with company, surrounded only by echoes off the grey walls and the sun or stars above, hence the name given to this magical place.

The Baths however, being very famous as well as very beautiful, did have a noisy snack bar breaking the serenity of the scene high up on the rocks overlooking the main bay, and it was on every tourist's 'must do' of the island, so was always teeming with scantily dressed vacationers and scattered yachts bobbing up and down at anchor.

I considered the pros and cons of The Baths as my regular place of repose, and passed.

My ongoing quest for the ideal spot on Virgin Gorda to chill out next led me to a secluded beach just to the north called Mini Trunk.

This was less well-known and less used - by holidaymakers at least - and had a few of the boulders and something of the character of its illustrious neighbour, but wasn't quite as pretty. Anywhere else in the world Mini Trunk would be the stuff of fantasy, but compared to The Baths it just lacked that certain spark, and so the majority of travellers simply bypassed it altogether and carried on a mile or two down the coast to wander and swim in the more famous caves and grottos nearby.

To get to Mini Trunk an unmarked dirt track led off the main coast road which ended at some rough ground with several parking spaces, a single litter bin, and a halved oil drum on rusty legs next to a sign saying; '4 Bar-B-Q'.

Pine trees and some scrub lined the car park, on one side a couple of white goats on tethers stood and bleated at visitors between chewing mouthfuls of dry grass. To finally get to the beach one had to step over a few low rocky ridges interspersed with patches of red dusty soil, and sadly in one or two places the odd piece of carelessly discarded litter.

At first glance not too promising. Then you see it. That same cauldron of turquoise water that can be viewed from the Baths. Those same fragile white crests gently falling from slow-moving waves just off the shore. One or two boats passing by, to or from The Baths no doubt. A couple of locals lazing on towels on the dazzling sand, and you are immediately hooked.

No noise except the teasing of the ocean and a few gulls mewing overhead. Few distractions, fewer people. Just you, and the gloriously predictable sunny day stretching out before you.

Yep, sometimes life is just plain good, and that is all you need to say or think about it. No further analysis required.

Just when I was beginning to wonder whether life could get any better, the near perfection of Mini Trunk was breathtakingly surpassed.

Heather had told me how to make my way here in the first instance, and I eventually worked out the quickest route taking perhaps twenty minutes to walk from our house. I got used to packing some snacks, a bottle of mineral water, a towel, some sunscreen and a good book to pass the time, and going to stretch out on the sands of Mini Trunk as often as I could, which rapidly came to mean virtually every day. For physical activity at least once during each visit I would swim a quarter of a mile in one direction, then back to my starting point and without stopping a quarter of a mile in the other before returning to my towel, making one unbroken mile. I would swim a hundred feet (thirty metres) or so off shore parallel to the coast, and look across at the features of the land slowly passing by with each stroke and at the boulders the size of small houses which marked both extremities of the beach.

One day whilst climbing and exploring the rocks at the northern end, jumping from one to another, climbing down and then back up the next when the distance between them was too great, I came across a hidden path between two large outcrops standing like ancient sentinels.

I could see that the trail beyond was scattered with leaves and flotsam and jetsam washed up during the occasional storm surge, but there were also unmistakable signs of regular human passage. Here and there a crisp packet or plastic bottle. A footprint in some dried sand, a scratch on a soft part of the rock from a camera case or backpack slung carelessly over someone's shoulder, a broken branch of a bush clinging to life on the rocks, all betrayed recent inadvertent human contact.

So I followed. Up and over, through and around obstacles of granite and limestone, until I found a patch of enclosed sand, half in shadow, half-bathed in bright sunlight despite the high walls. I had almost resolved to stop there and relax a while in this private grotto, when I saw that the path didn't end here but continued on the other side through a shadowy hole in the wall.

I made my way through, and rounding the last boulder the view opened up to reveal the most beautiful beach I had ever seen to that point in my life or still. I had discovered the elusive Valley Trunk.

Two hundred meters of pure platinum sand, thirty meters across at its widest point and bound at either end by huge rocks, the southern of which I had just negotiated. West to my left out towards the island of Tortola was the clean, shimmering Caribbean Sea. Jungle entirely covered the eastern side of the beach, broken only by a single overgrown trail leading inlnd blocked by a gate upon which was painted; 'Private, Keep Out'. I knew that this warning had to refer to the land behind and not the beach itself, which was as public as the pavement in the precinct of Spanish Town - remember all beaches on the larger islands are public, no matter how much the no doubt extremely wealthy owners of the adjacent land would choose not to have it so, and perhaps even attempt to beguile the unknowledgeable visitor into thinking that they had stepped onto a private area. Feeling that they are possibly trespassing, a chastised passerby might then leave with their tail between their legs feeling a little disappointed that they cannot enjoy this incredible place.

Well in the BVI they can. I am all for capitalism, as long as it is not unfettered, but we all own the world, it is not a haven for the wealthy alone, and we have the right to share the marvels that Earth holds in trust for every single one of us. From the instant I laid my eyes upon it, this beach now belonged to me as much as it belongs to you, dear reader, if you are ever lucky enough to find your way there. But at that moment it was only me, and unless you are reading this by some strange coincidence on that very same stretch of white-golden sand, you cannot see what I saw and experience the feeling of exhilaration that I felt at that moment, but I wish it for you all the same.

Peering down the lane a little way inland I could just about make out one or two houses on raised ground amongst the trees, but neither saw nor heard any sign of life, and aside from a floating tethered diving platform which rocked up and down gently on the waves nearby, it was empty and I was alone.

One thought came to my mind as I stood there, feeling the sun on my back and listening to the ocean gently, slowly, methodically caress the crystal shore.

'Here's your island paradise. You found it.'

Chapter 5 - My first less than pleasurable encounter with a German sea captain

I don't know why, but I seem ordained to run into sea captains at every turn in my life. First there was my father, and in the annals of our family trees on both parents' sides there were other skippers, all the way back to the days of sailing ships and Indian tea clippers which plied the trade routes between England, the Asian sub-continent and as far as New Zealand and Australia. It might go back even further still, as with fair height and hair in the multifarious race that the Brits are and to which I belong, it's more than possible I have a touch of Viking blood in me so maybe it's my destiny never to escape seafaring no matter where I go or what I do.

My wife and I were married almost a year earlier by an American skipper in Charlotte Amalie - not the commander of our particular ship - and in January 1994 a month after arriving on Virgin Gorda, I came across another of Teutonic origin.

Christmas had come and gone along with New Year celebrations, and found us still at Heather's home on the hill. Jenny had settled well into her job, and on her days off we explored the island together in her jeep, including of course me excitedly showing her the marvellous Valley Trunk. I had spoken to a few local property developers about the possibility of working on Virgin Gorda, and it became very clear early on that manual labour was almost always carried out by cheaper to employ down-islanders, and the only role suited for me that paid enough would be as a site manager or foreman. This would entail lots of paperwork, visa applications, and more commitment than I was prepared to accept at that moment.

Jenny and I in the meantime had met and befriended a couple from Chicago who offered us the opportunity to go and work for them in America. The husband was an extraordinarily successful insurance broker, and although it was never made exactly clear to us the extent of their wealth, their fortune was not measured in single digit millions and may have been way higher. They were in their mid-forties, and very sadly the husband had contracted hepatitis from I believe a contaminated blood supply. This was slowly poisoning his liver, and there was nothing that their great wealth and the best doctors in the world could do about it. He was in fact slowly dying. We met several times for dinner and drinks, and spent a whole day with them on the beach at Mini Trunk, where he and I left the girls to sunbathe whilst us boys went climbing near the northern route to Valley Trunk. I was impressed and inspired watching him leap with me from boulder to boulder with quiet determination and an impish grin on his face as we clambered up and down the rock faces. Looking back I could see concern on his wife's face as we scaled one particularly sheer monolith, which told me without words that he was more ill than he let on. Seeing her worried expression I made some excuses to turn back and we never actually made it to our paradise beach that day.

This lovely couple lived on the shores of Lake Michigan on what sounded like a huge gated estate, for which they required a live-in housekeeper and maintenance man/estate manager, and their preference was that the two employees be husband and wife. Jenny was very enthused, and although the idea of being a glorified caretaker didn't exactly fit into my life plan as it was then, it was very tempting. Green Cards, connections, Chicago lifestyle. It could have been amazing, and plus we were a confident young couple and after getting to know each other better, there may even have been an opportunity to deepen our friendship as opposed to simply being employees. What would have come of this we will never know, as fate intervened a short while later before we could take it any further.

In the meantime there was a life to lead here in the Virgin Islands, and moreover a permanent base to secure so that we could leave our temporary accommodation with Heather. No matter how perfect it was, we needed to find our own space to be comfortable in. It wasn't that we hadn't tried to find an apartment, but in the run up to Christmas the strongly religious BVI had become very preoccupied with Christian affairs, and the yuletide season also signalled the start of the tourist rush. These two factors combined to result in a situation where virtually all available properties were booked solid for months to come, and few new rentals would be coming onto the market until Christmas was well and truly over and community business and life in general returned to normality.

I had been looking however, despite my month of rest at either one of the two Trunk bays, at one point having a strange rendezvous with a man called Ralph who showed me around a block of six newly-built apartments he owned in a less than salubrious part of Spanish Town.

I'd been running about ten minutes late for the appointment which was arranged after I chanced upon an ad in the local newspaper. Telephoning a number in Road Town, a gruff West Indian chap on the other end of the line had described the apartments for rent, the range of costs depending on the individual abode, and a little about their layout and facilities.

I assumed that he was a property developer as he immediately proposed to meet me in person the next day to show me around, and employed no agency or personal assistant to do the viewings. This meant a forty minute ferry ride each way for him from the main island of Tortola, and would take him the better part of half a day after taking into consideration the trip from the ferry dock to the apartments, showing me around, and then returning home, and a busy man would surely have asked a surrogate to carry out this menial task in his stead.

However he chose to come himself, and as I sauntered along the street a few minutes after the allotted time, I saw a tall heavily set man in a dark suit standing with his hands twitching impatiently in his pockets and staring at the corner of the road about which I appeared.

I strolled up the garden path to greet him. 'Are you Ralph?' I enquired casually.

'Mr. O'Neal, yes', was his stern and somewhat chastening reply. He was obviously a little put out at being kept waiting.

Okay, I thought, maybe I was a little rude. But I was a landlord myself, and in the property business a little healthy disinterest is not a bad thing, especially if you end up liking a certain property and then enter into negotiations to secure it. Estate agents and property developers can smell genuine interest a mile off, and prices and terms are often set to match the perceived circumstances of the customer, so applying some feigned indifference in such situations can rarely be a bad thing.

In truth I had taken an instant dislike to the location of the apartment block, which was not in a particularly good area (I knew the Valley quite well by now) and the flats themselves were pretty basic as well as being at the top end of what we were prepared to pay. On the other hand Jenny and I were very much aware that the generosity of our host was not limitless, and although we were paying a nominal rent to Heather it was plain that she did not need the money, and the token amount which we gave her each week was no substitute for the privacy she was losing by us being there. We had no desire to outstay our welcome with our gracious host so even though I didn't want to live in any of these flats around which Mr. O'Neal was currently showing me, I made certain to pay attention to what I was seeing and could relate it to Jenny later just to make sure I didn't discount an opportunity too hastily.

The meeting concluded after I had looked around three of the apartments. Two were empty, one had a tenant in who I was assured was soon to depart as her husband and she were down-islanders, the term for someone originally from one of the other Caribbean states working itinerantly from place to place as necessary and visa requirements allowed. His work contract was up and they were about to return to their place of origin.

I told Mr. O'Neal that I would think about it, which in reality I already had and decided in the negative, and by this time 'Ralph' had softened a bit and we shook hands and exchanged a few pleasantries as we parted. I asked if he had come all the way from Tortola just to show me these apartments, and he answered that he had some other business to attend to on Virgin Gorda; relatives to visit and suchlike. My slight guilt assuaged at possibly wasting a large chunk of his day, I left.

I later found out, and was to encounter again under very different circumstances, that this initially gruff property developer was none other than the Honourable Mr. Ralph O'Neal OBE, Chief Minister of the British Virgin Islands, and effectively the ruler of this small nation.

Technically the BVI is a self-governing dependency of the United Kingdom, which means that it is autonomous but still retains a Governor appointed by Her Majesty's Government in London to oversee Island affairs. This position is largely ceremonial but does have some legislative authority, which although diminished since the days of colonial empire can still carry some weight. There had been debates ongoing within the BVI for many years since gaining virtual independence in the 1960's as to whether they should move towards total severance with Great Britain and become a fully-fledged republic, but this was usually dismissed fairly quickly by members of the legislative assembly as there are many perks and few disadvantages to being connected, however loosely, to Britain for a nation as small as the BVI.

The Mother country still retains some rights of dubious importance to moor warships in the surrounding waters in times of conflict, and that's about it for England. This dates back to the times when the Spanish and Portuguese ruled South America and Britain ruled the waves, and war was ever present as the Brits, under swashbuckling privateers such as Henry Morgan and Sir Francis Drake stalked the trade routes between the New World and Europe, harassing and being harassed by the French, Spanish, Dutch and Danish. All these at one time or another coveted the sheltered waters of the Virgin Islands as a useful trading port and base of operations from which to carry out their various activities far from their home countries.

The BVI on the other hand still gets quite a lot out of this relationship. There are grants for education, health services and infrastructure. Tourism is the second most important source of income for the BVI, and links with Britain and Europe no doubt help that trade. Finally, and to some surprisingly, there is the British Virgin Islands' prime source of foreign income; financial services, and close ties with the centre of international commerce that is London are an obvious asset to all concerned.

For the past few decades the BVI has carved out a niche as a haven for trusts and corporations wishing to minimise tax and legally hide their business affairs from the roving eye of authorities and governments. In 1994 when these events which I am retelling took place, the population of the Virgin Islands was less than twenty five thousand, and at the time there were over one hundred thousand foreign companies which had their head offices based on Tortola alone.

A moment's contemplation of those numbers makes you realise what a staggering figure that is.

Does this mean that Road Town had thousands of staffed offices, with millions of employees and huge skyscrapers bursting through the few wispy clouds in the skies above Tortola? Not a bit of it. These corporations are there in name only, existing on the spreadsheets and ledgers of lawyers and trust companies, who administer their limited roles from nondescript buildings lining the main thoroughfares of the sleepy capital. Amazing what goes on, behind closed doors.

Returning to our story, early in the New Year not long after the last of the champagne corks had fallen to the ground,

Heather asked if I would like to accompany her on a little sailing expedition in the coming days. This was peak yachting season, when the clear skies and warm consistent breezes of the hot Caribbean winter virtually guarantee a successful excursion for any lover of the waves on any given day. Heather was a keen sailor, which had been one of her and her unfortunate late husband's main hobbies before his untimely demise, but she rarely got a chance to sail any more. She could probably afford any yacht she took a fancy to, but possessing a boat is a big responsibility at the best of times. They require almost constant maintenance, and are a permanent drain on finances to anyone lucky enough to own one. There are mooring fees, off-season lay-ups to arrange and pay for, seaworthiness checks, boat surveys, engine overhauls, sail repairs, and insurance. And should you ever find the time to actually go sailing, you have port fees, provisions, fuel for the inboard engine, and then the inevitable and tiresome clean-up after the guests have gone home, scrubbing the vessel from top to bottom and stowing everything neatly away for the next time you take it out whenever that may be.

Considering all this it wasn't surprising that Heather chose not to own or keep a boat. But she did still love to sail, and when a friend of hers, a retired German doctor who worked part-time in Virgin Gorda's one general practice surgery up a small rise at the back of Spanish Town, offered her the chance of a jaunt around the Islands on his sloop, she happily accepted.

There was a tiny fly in the ointment, which was that our landlady although fit for her age, would admit herself that she wasn't as sprightly as she used to be, and as for the old doctor he was significantly less animated than Heather. This meant that they required one other crew person to come along and help out, and Heather suggested me for the role. I knew I was being taken along mainly as dogsbody but I didn't mind. I could sail a little bit and always enjoyed the water, and a day out is a day out.

The day arrived and before we left the house at the crack of dawn, Heather handed me some Dramamine tablets for seasickness. I had suffered most terribly from this as a child, and if I ever had cause to cross anything wider than a river was often violently ill as soon as we left sight of the shore. But a lot of years had passed and I had sailed with no ill effects on many occasions since, so I declined to take the preventative medication on offer.

I would come to regret that decision most severely in the following hours.

We drove north through the pass to Leverick Bay where the good doctor lived and kept his small but capable craft moored to a buoy in the spectacular natural harbour of North Sound, floating in the water amongst hundreds of other similar vessels. A quick stop at the chandlers for some boating bits and the supermarket for provisions, we then took a small tender out to his yacht, and tying it to the stern to buffet along behind us during the day's sailing, Heather, the doctor, and I climbed aboard.

Our intended destination was the Soggy Dollar bar on the Island of Jost Van Dyke some twenty five nautical miles away. Named the Soggy Dollar because in the days before the jetty was built, the only way to get to and from the beachfront saloon was to sail into White Bay, drop anchor and jump over the side for the short swim to the shore. 'Informal' was probably the best way to describe this crazy place, and the name soggy dollar doesn't need much explaining. On the blue plywood wall above the counter hung a glassed picture frame containing an array of obscure bank notes from around the globe, which customers had either unsuccessfully tried to buy a drink with and then left behind, or else just handed over hoping it would be added to the collage and become part of the history of this famous watering hole.

Unhappily for our skipper the winds were fairly strong today, and not in our favour to reach Jost Van Dyke and return home again before nightfall. After a quick discussion the plan was scaled down to head for a smaller island closer by, where we would stop for a bite to eat and then return to Leverick Bay hopefully around dusk.

Had we carried out the original voyage it could quite easily have turned into a six hour trip each way, and I thank heaven above that we didn't throw caution to the wind and decide to chance it, because as soon as we had weighed anchor and turned to face the breeze for our first tack, I felt a terrible queasiness swell in my belly and in a few short minutes I was totally incapacitated with the worst nausea I had experienced in a decade or more.

Too late for Dramamine now, the small bucket reserved for such purposes attached to the railings on the side of the boat was soon being filled by the contents of my stomach, dropped into the ocean rushing past underneath my forlorn head, emptied, rinsed out with seawater only to be filled again within seconds. Soon I had nothing more to heave and was reduced to that awful state of being gripped by acidic retches and accompanying stomach spasms that just refuse to stop until you are back on dry land.

I tried to take some medicine but it didn't stay down long enough to work, and to the consternating smiles of my elderly crewmates I suffered, and suffered. And here I was thinking that I was going to be the hero of the hour, nimbly climbing up the rigging, guiding the tiller, winding the windlass and generally entertaining the others with my derring-do. What a sad case I must have looked, as the two fogies taught this young whippersnapper a thing or two about what preparation and experience can do to combat the exuberance of youth.

For three full hours I sat with my head in that bucket, oblivious to the sights whizzing by as the sharp breeze made our boat go faster and faster, bouncing harder and harder on the white-crested blue ocean, each thud exaggerated in the pit of my stomach like the call to arms for first vomit then just groans to issue from my listless jaw, involuntary tears streaming down my face and mingling salt with the bitter taste of bile in my mouth.

When the boat at last began to slow and we prepared ourselves to pull in to our half-way point, I virtually leapt out of the yacht and into the tender in my almost hysterical desire to get to shore as fast as humanly possible, and if it wasn't for the fact that the beach was sandy, would have kissed the ground gleefully the second we arrived and I stepped onto the mercifully stable land.

My companions looked at me with sympathy and more than a touch of concern as we sat under a palm-leaf canopy adjacent to the makeshift but deceptively well-stocked beach bar. We were on one of the small islands that dot the ocean around the BVI, but I cannot even remember which one, racked and dishevelled and consumed even in my moment of joy at arriving on solid ground with dread thinking of the unavoidable homeward journey. This was sure to be another three hours - or more depending on the winds - of pure unadulterated hell to come.

I toyed with the idea of jumping ship and staying there under that rustling umbrella, maybe getting a job at the bar and forgetting about my wife and life back on Virgin Gorda and living out the rest of my days as a bone fide beach bum. Anything to prevent me getting back on that carriage of Hades.

But like the trooper that I wanted so much to be in the eyes of my crewmates, I clung to the delusional thought that they needed me, and I couldn't let them down. Mooring the yacht at the very end of the excursion was the most difficult of the tasks that we had to fulfill, and though I'd been worse than useless so far I was determined to show my true mettle before the day was out.

Who was I kidding?

And so, under the amazed gaze of my fellow crew of two, I manfully ordered a burger, fries and coke, and put all thoughts of remaining there forever in that idyllic spot firmly out of my mind. This was now a matter of pride.

After forty minutes or so that passed achingly fast, it was time to leave. We climbed into the tender which had been dragged up near to where we sat in the shade, and returning to our yacht, set the sails once again for the journey to Leverick Bay.

The winds are known to be changeable in the Leeward Islands of which the BVI are part, which is a major reason why sailors love it as this makes it a constant challenge to keep the sails correctly trimmed. As the sun had risen in the sky and heated up the cauldron of ocean, so the eddying air currents had swung around half-circle during lunch and the flurries that had been in our faces all morning were once again stinging our eyes as we turned for home.

Tacking is the art of sailing into the wind, and actually works contrary to what most people believe, on the principle of suction rather than blowing. No comments please.

Similar to air moving over the wing of an aeroplane providing lift, once forward motion is established by an initial gust, the shape of the now arched sail forces air to move faster over the leading side than the rear, which creates a vacuum ahead of the vessel, and the boat is in effect sucked along rather than blown. It then gathers speed and momentum, and can sail virtually straight into an onrushing wind with skilful use of the rigging and rudder. Efficient tacking uses an angle of forty five degrees, where a yacht sails diagonally into the approaching weather, then at a certain designated point the crew tacks and quickly switches the sail to the other side of the boat whilst swivelling the tiller in the opposite direction, and most importantly watching your head as the boom below the sail swings around incredibly fast and can knock you over the side if you are not careful. Speed is then built up again advancing at forty five degrees into the oncoming wind but now from the other side. This zigzag course means that even if your destination point has a gale blowing directly at you, it is still possible to sail there allowing for the extra time it will take in relation to distance covered. And of course if you have a strong stomach.

In this way and facing a reasonably strong headwind we slowly made our way back to Leverick Bay, tacking again and again and getting a little closer to home each time. I was fractionally less deathly ill than before, perhaps due to the adrenaline coursing through my veins as I knew that every turn we made brought us a few metres closer to the end of that day of beautiful hell.

As late afternoon approached, we at last rounded a point and sailed into the bowl of North Sound, catching sight of the white-painted villas scattered high up on the amphitheatre of the tree-covered hillsides surrounding three sides of the bay. Seeing many of the yachts already returned and moored from their own expeditions, their occupants heading ashore, raised my spirits and gave me the strength to continue for one final push.

The ability to sail like a pro is a point of pride for many of those who venture out onto the water, pitting human and machine against nature, and our skipper had more than his fair share of hubris in this regard. During the day I had become a little tired of his order-giving and manner, and when he got up as we approached our mooring and bent over to tie a knot in a rope lying on the deck in front of me, and one of his testicles accidentally lolloped out of a leg of his shorts, I couldn't raise a smile at what would normally be an incredibly funny event. Why he had chosen to go commando that day I will never know, and if he was aware of what had happened he certainly didn't let on. I was too scared to look at Heather to see if she had seen, but I think she had judging by how quickly she looked away and busied herself unwinding and recoiling another nearby rope which was already perfectly neatly stowed on the deck.

Together we pulled in the sails and our captain started up the inboard engine. We slowly eased between the lines of boats facing the breeze which was now fading to a light hush along with the dissipating light. As our designated buoy came into view, Heather took a long pole with a hook attached to the end built for the purpose and leant precariously over the bow in order to snag the line beneath the floating buoy, so allowing us to attach the yacht securely to it, pack everything away, do whatever cleaning was necessary, and then mercifully go home.

It is a further point of pride with many sailors that the buoy line should be hooked on the first attempt, the down-revving engine bringing the craft to a gentle stop exactly at the point where the buoy is anchored to the ocean floor, the vessel perfectly under control at all times, and all will be well with the world. There is a practical side to this display of machismo, which is that if you miss the buoy and have to turn between tightly packed rows of yachts in overcrowded harbours like the North Sound, it can get quite tricky for a cumbersome sailing craft to do this without encountering some problems. The inboard engines and rudders are not really designed for accurate manoeuvring backwards and forwards jockeying for position in a small space - for example when trying to snare a buoy rope at the end of a hard day's sailing.

Heather's enthusiastic efforts leaning through the railings with a pole twice the length of her body at full stretch while trying to introduce the hook and rope proved fruitless, as did our driver's questionable navigation and throttle-control of the engine. We missed the target again and again, and it has to be said the margin of error got worse with each failed bid.

The skipper tried his best to look like it wasn't his fault. He knew he couldn't blame Heather, even though I could see that he really wanted to, and as they had both perfectly understandably declined my offer to help due to my awful performance throughout the day, he could blame me even less.

Try as we might we could not catch that wet slimy line. Back and forth we went, my German friend peering at the darkening water ahead, trying not to stare at Heather's backside as she leaned over the bow repeatedly launching the pole forward, slapping as it hit the surface of the water, and pulling back to reveal fresh air and a dripping hook once again, but no rope.

On another day it would have been funny but I was far too glum to see any humour in the situation.

The final coup de grace was performed when the doctor nudged the accelerator just a little too hard, and we ran straight over the rope which proceeded to become entangled in the spinning propeller. Now any true sailor will tell you that at this point the last thing you should do is try to disentangle a rope so bound by using the engine to spin the propeller the other way, a few revolutions at a time, in the hope that somehow the knot will miraculously untie itself. All you are likely to achieve is to tighten the knot and make the predicament worse. Having been in this situation myself I can admit with some humility that I have done exactly that, and just as our captain did next. After all, who really wants to go down into the water and struggle to untie a rope stuck fast around a propeller shaft? Much easier to try and release it using the comfortable power of the engine from a warm and dry deck just in case it works. On occasion (very rarely) it does, which gives all in such situations a vague hope to cling to and encourages them to at least try.

Nevertheless mostly it doesn't help. In fact usually it just makes matters a whole lot worse.

With a mix of frustration and blind optimism he kept on going. Easing the throttle forwards, then slowly dropping it into reverse for a few seconds, sometimes jamming it backwards and forwards fast and furiously to see if that would do the trick, until eventually he accepted what Heather and I had been quietly trying to tell him for the past fifteen minutes, that this simply was not working.

The solution was now clear; someone had to go down and try to release the twisted rope by hand.

Perhaps this was the reason that fate in all its intricacies brought me there that day, and now it was my time to shine and attempt to recoup a modicum of dignity after my pathetic show so far. I was desperate to get home to a warm soft bed, shut the curtains and sleep, and if this was the only way for me to get to this tantalising end, then a man has got to do what a man has got to do.

I prepared myself for the task by first taking off my shirt and deck shoes and leaning over various parts of the stern to try to get a good look at the problem and determine a plan of action. I endeavoured to see where the rope was lying under the boat, how much slack there was on the line, and any other knowledge I could glean that might help me whilst submerged. I knew that once in, the water would be cold, dusk was falling and the sea was blackening by the minute. I would also have the considerable shadow of the boat to contend with restricting what little light still penetrated the water.

We conducted a quick search of the boat for a snorkel and flippers to help me in my task but there were none to be found, and so after fixing some reference points in my mind to get my bearings under the water, I was just about to take the plunge when I noticed the engine was still running.

I asked our skipper if he would switch off the motor whilst I dived down and tried to loosen us from our twine predicament, but he refused.

I thought for a moment that he was distracted by something and didn't understand what I was getting at, so I explained in simple terms that I was about to descend underwater and wrestle with a propeller attached to a forty horsepower engine, which if it were to jump into life even for a split second could rip my arms out of their sockets. Mind-bogglingly he still refused. He mumbled something about the starter-motor being problematic, and that if he switched it off he might not be able to start it again in a hurry should he need to. He was concerned that we might be left drifting momentarily and risk our boat bumping up against and scratching other nearby moored vessels. The risk to my arms was apparently a gamble he was willing to take.

I had to bite my lip to prevent me from saying what I thought about that, but in deference to his position as captain I held my tongue. Discipline and the chain of command must be maintained while at sea, but I couldn't help thinking that his priorities were ever so slightly out of whack. Maybe he reasoned that as he was a doctor, should my arms become severed he could sew them back on again.

Heather tried to fight my corner, but to no avail. The captain would not budge. Instead he stood resolutely at the helm, both hands on the wheel, staring forward, commando style and briefless as he was.

There is that word pride again.

It was me who blinked first. I was so desperate to get this day over and done with that I agreed to go in with the engine still ticking over. Shaking my head and shivering from head to toe, but not with the cold, more with the fear of knowing what might happen in the next few minutes, I took a few deep breaths, swallowed hard and dived over the side and into the murky water.

Disconcertingly I could hear the throbbing of the motor as I felt my way along under the keel. Reaching the propeller I trod water whilst examining the puzzle for the first time close up. Sound travels well through water, and I made a mental note to listen for any sharp changes in the tone of the engine, so that should it spring to life I could try to release my hands from the propeller as quickly as possible, no matter how futile this would probably have been.

I found the slack end of the rope, and began feeding it back into the knot, twisting the line as I did so, easing gently back and forth until I could just make out the tangled mess starting to loosen. My lungs were still okay, so I carried on without resurfacing and moved to the next part of the knot, repeating the action, until in just one long breath of perhaps a minute, the rope mercifully came away from the propeller and began dropping in slow motion down into the dark depths. Quickly grabbing it with one hand before it was lost from my view, I swam back to the surface victorious.

Heather was delighted, sweet person that she always was, and exclaimed that after I went in both she and the doctor had chastised themselves for not reminding me to keep a hold of the rope once it was untangled - assuming that I was successful.

As I hauled myself back up the side of the boat and stood dripping triumphantly on the deck, the skipper turned to say something to me, as he did so clumsily knocking the vertical handles of the still-humming throttle, roaring the engine instantly to life. The propeller span and the yacht lurched forward several metres nearly wrenching the hard-won rope right out of my hand before he panickingly regained control.

Heather and I stood in silence glaring at the doctor, as should he have carelessly knocked that same lever a minute earlier, he could quite possibly have ended my life.

Chapter 6 - On finding a flat and proceeding to fill it with the necessities of life

Having survived my day of seaborne tribulation, a bit of luck soon followed to balance out the karma of life on the island.

In our search for somewhere to rent, through a contact of Heather we were directed one day to an address in the Valley.

The first thing I noticed as we drove into the quiet residential street was that fortuitously the house lay about half-way as the crow flies between Spanish Town and the two Trunk Bays, meaning that it was within easy walking distance of everywhere that really mattered to me at the time.

The building was new and looked freshly painted, and as if to prove the point an overalled man out front with a brush in hand stopped what he was doing and turned to look at us as our jeep pulled up.

The guy with dark forearms and paint on his fingers turned out to be a laid back local Islander by the name of Joshua, and impressively the two storey house which we now stood admiring had been self-built by him and his wife Mary.

In the pragmatic way of many BVI residents, once having secured appropriate land upon which to raise their dream home and family, they rolled up their sleeves and set to work, and then simply kept going until the money ran out, restarting only when finances allowed. It's perhaps easier to do this in a climate where central heating and protection from harsh winters are not required, so house design can be more streamlined than in regions with more changeable weather. As long as you have running water, a generator for some light and power, a fan to cool you on a particularly hot day, and the roof doesn't leak when an occasional tropical storm hits, life can be pretty decent in the Caribbean with the barest of essentials, and mod cons can wait for another day when the purse strings hopefully loosen up.

The boxlike structure of Joshua's house had thus been erected bit by gradual bit, and consisted of smooth white cement walls and deep-set windows to keep out the worst excesses of the sun. The roof was a flat slab of concrete, which became the ceiling of the second storey, and would one day be the floor of the third. There were several half-height concrete pillars with steel reinforcing bars poking unevenly out of the top dotted about its upper surface. These would eventually provide the bases for the supporting columns of the next planned level, and if it were not for the regulations in the Valley restricting developments to three storeys, I imagine that it would not have stopped there and Joshua would have kept going until his house broke through the treeline or he went broke, whichever came first.

I could see straight away that the work was of a very high standard, made even more remarkable as Joshua himself claimed to be not a true 'mason' but merely 'handy'. My time on Virgin Gorda had taught me two things on this subject; that the term 'mason' meant anyone professionally employed in construction, and also that the British Virgin Islanders were an extremely versatile and dexterous people, being able to turn their hand to just about anything practical if they had a mind to.

I had previously only come across such natural skill when travelling through Australia and New Zealand as a teenager with Jenny, and discovering the way of life down under.

On one occasion in Auckland we had been invited to a barbeque, and during the afternoon the Kiwi homeowner showed us around what Antipodeans refer to as the back yard.

For a European this conjures up images of a small, usually concreted area at the back of your house where you keep a rusty lawnmower, a couple of kids' bikes and a wet bag of charcoal briquettes, but to Kiwis and Ozzies this means something entirely different. To them the bare minimum plot of land required for a home to be civilised is a quarter acre (about 0.1 hectare), and as we walked around what to me as a Brit seemed an enormous rear garden, he took us down through some trees at the back to a small stream running along the perimeter of his land.

Built over this stream was a beautiful arched wooden bridge with carved handrails and delicate balustrades, wide enough for one person to walk comfortably across and spanning perhaps two metres. It was a construction of some skill, and I asked if he had bought the bridge pre-made from a joinery workshop.

'No, I knocked it up myself', was his casual reply.

I was impressed and said so, which he shrugged off in the endearing nonchalant way Antipodeans do, and just said that his countrymen and women are bred that way; to be hands-on.

It seemed on Virgin Gorda that the Kiwis had met their match. First there were jovial George Tyson's mechanical ma-

rvels at his home-made gymnasium, and now I saw this beautiful home that Joshua had built with his own two hands.

Joshua was it has to be said an incredibly relaxed man, pausing just short of being actually comatose, but not by very
much. He spoke almost as slowly as he walked, and far more
slowly than he thought, and yet he managed to achieve a lot
by virtue of the fact that he never stopped moving, albeit at
his own leisurely pace. He was in his thirties, a short cropped
beard and moustache adorned his face, and he had an easy
carefree way about him which I was not entirely certain was
genuine or merely engineered as a buffer to the world. Lean
and solidly built with a lazy handshake that belied his true strength, he greeted us without making eye contact, and expecting us he took Jenny and me around to the side of the house
where some bare concrete steps led up to a side door into the
interior of the second floor.

I took a guess that when the building was finally finished
the steps would be enclosed to make it a more standard design for a single dwelling, but for now this exterior staircase was
the sole access to the upper level. We had to watch our step as
there was no handrail, and the three of us made our way up
and into the open doorway.

This floor had been arranged as a self-contained apartment, but there were telltale signs everywhere of future alterat-
ions and adjustments to come. In some places the doorways,
lights, bathroom fixtures and a few fittings were still awaiting
installation in the upcoming final phase of construction, when
presumably the whole house would all be joined, perhaps once the anticipated third floor was completed, into one large family home.

In the meantime it served Joshua and Mary's purposes to rent the current top floor out to bring in a little extra income in order to help fund the next stage of building, which was still probably a year or two down the line.

The apartment hadn't been advertised anywhere yet and we were viewing it before anyone else could get a look, so giving us the jump on other prospective tenants.

Inside we met Mary, who was standing dressed in a bright orange frock at the kitchen sink rinsing out some cloths and wiping down the adjacent sparkling new food preparation sufaces. She was shy and friendly, with a pale freckled face unusual for an Islander. There was obviously some mixing of the races not too far back in her genes, and she had a suggestion of European features, together with long rich brown Afro-Caribbean locks which she kept tied in a flared ponytail falling halfway down her back.

The unfinished parts of the apartment, as in the odd taped-up light switch, a few blocked-off drains and a doorway to one of the rooms which still had no door didn't faze me in the slightest. I couldn't read Jenny's face as she was playing just as shrewd as I was, but to me the place seemed perfect. There were three bedrooms notwithstanding the doorless one, a large bathroom, two toilets, an open-plan kitchen and living area, and three, yes three balconies! It was fantastic. And the fact that there was still a little construction left to do meant that we could indulge in a little good-natured bargaining.

As a boy in one of my first forays into the world of commerce I had bought an unwanted tent from a neighbour for ten pounds, and promptly advertised it the next week in the local newspaper for twenty five. It was snapped up immediately and as the lucky buyer left my parents' house with his newly-acquired camping equipment under his arm, soon to be utilised at a music festival with his girlfriend, the man turned to my mother and said; 'I'm a car salesman. When he gets older, call me. I'll give him a job.' I always did love to haggle.

Joshua's house including the flat upstairs had running water and electricity, and aside from the few odds and ends still to finish, I could see that he would not be bothering us too much with building work as the ground floor where he lived with Mary and their two precocious young daughters was already a home complete enough for their needs. The work that remained to do in 'our' flat (we already saw it as ours) was of the long-term variety, as it pertained to the house being made into a three storey residence at some far off future date. If we could put up with an eighty percent completed apartment, but which was clean, freshly painted, with a brand new kitchen, white marbled floors, and balconies on three sides to watch the sunrise/sunset/world go by on a lazy day, then as far as I was concerned there was a deal there to be done.

The only real drawback was that it was to be let unfurnished, and of course we had no furniture and what's more had no desire to acquire any. The last thing we wanted to do was buy bulky household items, only to have the hassle of selling or otherwise disposing of them at the end of our tenancy.

After being shown around to our satisfaction Jenny and I asked to have some time to ourselves to chat about it, and we followed Joshua down the exterior concrete steps with its little vegetable garden to the side, past the shrubs and newly-planted miniature trees in the dusty soil to the front, and up to the entrance gate.

As we passed through it Joshua, still looking, up, down, around, anything but directly at us, mentioned in his peculiarly lethargic way what a lovely place it was and how there would probably be lots of interest once it was officially advertised...

He trailed off and if there was an end to that sentence he showed no sign of sharing it with us as he picked up his brush and went back to painting the wall. So we smiled politely, said thank you, and walked off up the road.

We guessed that this was Joshua attempting a little hardball, in his own inimitable style.

As soon as we were out of earshot, we tried not to give too much away with our body language in case we were being watched and it might queer negotiations on the price, as we both looked at each other and excitedly agreed that it was a keeper. A good location, perhaps not as close to the centre of town as we would have liked, but easy parking for Jenny's jeep, lots of living space for us, and the three balconies were a dream come true. After all, why live in the Caribbean if you can't actually see it?

The only question was the aforementioned lack of household equipment as well as many of the usual necessities required for day to day living such as plates, saucepans, cutlery etc. which the flat also didn't come with.

More importantly while there was a cooker the kitchen had no fridge, and no washing machine nor dryer. Mary had let it be known that hanging wet laundry out on the balconies would be unacceptable so lack of the latter may become an issue.

The flat did however have a wonderfully large and low king-sized bed with two equally low bedside cabinets in what we called the master bedroom, although Joshua and Mary hadn't named it as such.

After a quick discussion we saw the furniture issue as resolvable with a little thought and spending as few dollars as possible, and realising that these were much easier problems to overcome than starting our search all over again for the perfect apartment in just the right location with all mod-cons present, we decided to call off the hunt and immediately returned to the home of Joshua and Mary to secure our new accommodation.

Coming back to the house we found Joshua now at the rear continuing with his paintwork.

He looked up and half-smiled before dropping his head and returning his attention to the brush.

'You're back so soon?'

He smiled at his speckled hands and continued to stroke the walls with white.

'And what do you think you'll be doin' then?'

It was difficult to be hardnosed in the face of this cheerful pecuniary assassin, and so we simply said we would like to take the apartment subject to a few conditions.

First there was the price; it was a little above what we were hoping to pay and we had plenty of other places to look at that day if we could not strike a bargain. Okay this wasn't completely true, but when bartering you have to start with the basics.

We gave a good enough show to persuade him to drop the rent by a modest five dollars per week.

Round one to us.

Next came the question of furniture, and it was plain that Joshua and Mary initially had no intention of supplying this. The only reason that a bed was there at all was because it had come their way recently and they had nowhere to put it, and so in the apartment it went. Joshua was not best pleased at the thought of spending his precious time scouring the island to aid us in sourcing what we needed, and who could blame him?

Nevertheless he was a nice chap, and he couldn't escape the fact that good tenants are as hard to find for landlords as good properties are for tenants, so agreeing to help us as much as he reasonably could, he proffered a limp hand and we immediately went home to tell Heather the news and start packing our things.

With an admirable attitude of 'if you decide to do something, then you might as well do it with a smile on your face', over the coming days Joshua took me in his yellow pick-up truck and we tracked down a dining table set, a sofa, a couple of armchairs, and a solid looking fridge-freezer which we found lying outdoors in a scrap yard cum bric-a-brac shop, as well as several other things that seemed as though they might come in handy.

Heather kindly stepped in and lent us a few bits, and a trip to a hardware store secured us the rest of what we needed including some kitchen utensils, one sharp filleting knife (which I still have to this day) and importantly some wine glasses and a corkscrew.

On unloading the yellow refrigerator from his matching truck, Joshua and I discovered mercifully before we carried it up the outside staircase that despite being assured by the owner of the emporium to the contrary, it didn't actually work.

Not only that, in our exertions during transportation the larger and lower of the two doors had become dislodged, and now hung precariously by its top hinge alone, the bottom swinging slowly back and forth like a flat rectangular pendulum.

Joshua displayed his usual calm acceptance to fate and resolved to fix the defect rather than return the item. It had been fairly cheap to buy and we split the cost, and was the only example we had come across which had a freezer and fridge combined which was my preference. Also although a little the worse for wear on the outside, it was robust in construction and clean inside which was the most important thing. The styling was Art Deco with chromed door handles and smooth rounded corners and was quite an attractive piece, and we reasoned that if we put our heads together it shouldn't be beyond the two of us to figure out what was wrong with the motor and also fix the door, and thereby give it a new lease of life.

First came the motor, which turned out to be nothing more than a frayed wire just inside the electrical panel on the rear of the unit. A new mains cable of adequate length being found amongst Joshua's spare parts, we connected it to the appropriate place on the machine and attached a plug to the other end. After testing to make sure that the motor engaged - it did - the rear panel was replaced and we turned our attention to the drooping door.

This was a slightly trickier conundrum.

On closer inspection we saw that the lower hinge had completely sheared, and looked as though it been teetering on the brink of failure for quite some time. There were bubbles of rust in places on the yellow casing and a faint smell of mould in the otherwise pristine white interior, indicating that it had probably laid in the scrapyard exposed to the elements for quite some time. It wasn't surprising therefore that metal parts which were not designed to take such treatment didn't react too kindly to those conditions.

Rooting around in toolboxes stuffed with an assortment of engineering leftovers, we found an old door hinge, and then another which was of a similar size and shape. They were not identical, and neither matched the ones already on the fridge, but Joshua hit upon the idea of removing the top hinge on the damaged fridge door and replacing both originals with the newly-found ironmongery.

I wasn't convinced of this as drilling into a fridge to attach new brackets risked releasing CFCs into the environment, and also as the hinges didn't precisely match meant that the rubber door seal might not line up and close properly. This would result in the motor working overtime to constantly re-cool the interior air, and introduced the unwholesome prospect of various creepies and crawlies finding their way into our food-stuffs if the door wasn't shut tight.

In 1994 the CFC debate was already effectively over and common sense had prevailed, reducing the reliance on chlorofluorocarbons in refrigeration equipment. I had lived in Australia where this had been a constant news item in the early 1990's, and so it had been fairly drummed into me that when disposing of or working on a fridge it must be done very carefully to avoid the inadvertent release of invisible but dangerous gases. The thought of me breaking this cardinal rule just to save myself a few dollars trying to repair an old fridge door made me stop and think about what we were potentially about to do, and I mentioned my concerns to Joshua who was a lot less bothered about holes in the ozone than I was.

We agreed a compromise and armed with a silicone gun and a tube of sealant, I took charge of the drilling while my erstwhile colleague stood by ready to immediately plug the holes I created with some wet silicone. This would be of dubious benefit in stopping any wayward emissions if we punctured something we oughtn't, but after all we were piercing the door not the cooling unit so I was satisfied we were okay. Using this method we marked and drilled the sixteen screw holes required - eight on the door and eight on the fridge - lined up the hinges, and attached the door.

Covering all the screw heads with an extra thick smudge of liquid rubber for good measure, I looked on with my fingers crossed as Joshua swung the door shut for the first time. To my pleasant surprise it worked perfectly. It closed securely and opened freely, the heavy chrome latch on the door engaging exactly as it should in its keep on the side of the casing. We then inspected the rubber seals and found that they fitted snugly together when the door was shut, thus adequately reassuring me that once stocked with food everything would be cool, fresh, and insect free.

Everything we needed to live in relative comfort having now been acquired, we said our grateful goodbyes to Heather with promises of mutual visits, and eagerly moved into our new home.

It was a little difficult to get used to at first. Although bright and new our apartment didn't have the character of Heather's older house, not to mention other more tangible assets like a television set, bookshelves stacked with endless reading material, and of course Heather's kindly presence.

The lack of a washing machine and dryer also meant that our main living area soon more often than not became bedecked with damp laundry, strung out along two makeshift inddoor clothes lines that I tied diagonally across the room at head height. The lounge did have two balconies on adjacent corners, bringing in a constant through-draft of warm air and so aiding the speedy drying of anything we hung up.

The actual washing of clothes took place in the bathtub, and was one of my regular daily chores as I was starting to feel a little guilty about my lack of effort and general application in life in comparison to Jenny. She was working a flexible schedule which meant that her forty hour week usually gave her at least a couple of hours with clients every day, and it must have irked somewhat to have to go and massage someone's back or pluck someone's eyebrows, while I had a full day of nothing ahead of me and was still not doing much of anything constructive with my time. Some money was coming in from our investment property in England, and we had savings, but it was obvious that I needed to get my act together and do some real work, and soon.

Bit by bit we settled into our home. It was clean and spacious, and everywhere had cool shiny marble under our feet. The all-pervasive Caribbean atmosphere gently wafted in through the shutters day and night, constantly reminding us of how lucky we were to be here.

Three things of note caught our attention during those first days in our new apartment, which I will relate.

The first was experiencing a minor earthquake as Jenny and I sat talking together on the sofa one afternoon. No more than a tremor really, it lasted some ten or fifteen seconds, and the low rumbling murmur which came out of nowhere and seemed to jostle the very molecules of the air coupled with the chinking of vibrating glasses on the draining board by the kitchen sink, made us immediately stop what we were doing and look about us in wonder and some trepidation. We thought at first that it might be an extremely heavy vehicle passing by, but the only large lorries on the island were the garbage trucks which invariably rattled past at around 6am, which was as cool as it gets in the Caribbean and was the hour that was least unpleasant for the refuse collectors to clear away festering household waste. It was also the time that the rubbish so disturbed and releasing what could sometimes be a putrid smell - unavoidable, it was the tropics - would be of least offence to any inhabitants nearby. Only this was not 6am, it was a lazy four in the afternoon, and the garbage trucks along with their drivers were sleeping.

We soon comprehended the cause of the disturbance and took it for what it was. We smiled nervously at each other pretending not to be overly concerned as the rumbling went on and then rapidly faded away leaving us silent and a little tense.

Over the following days I mentioned this tremor to Joshua and some other local people and was told off-handedly that it happens two or three times a year and never seems to do much harm.

About a year later in July 1995, a previously dormant volcano on the nearby island of Montserrat, also a British protectorate, exploded into life, causing massive damage and two thirds of the population to flee. Many of these subjects of Her

Majesty the Queen were offered safe haven in the United Kingdom, and a large number chose to remain after the initial danger had subsided. Partly this was because the land was now irretrievably altered due to the massive destruction caused by flowing lava and settling toxic ash, devastating the tourist and farming industries. Some though simply wanted to take the opportunity to have a stab at life in the Old Country and see what may come their way, which they had every right to do.

The second and third noteworthy things were more observations than events, but memorable to us all the same. Both involved the eccentric owners who shared the building and lived directly below us in our concrete palace.

Joshua and Mary had two daughters, one aged four and the other six, and they were the most charming, mischievous devils in disguise imaginable. Both parents were devout Christians, and schools in the British Virgin Islands as in much of the Caribbean follow this strong religious leaning. These adorable girls were usually dressed even at play in their school uniforms of red pleated skirts and bleached white blouses which Mary never allowed to be left untucked. As the two of them walked off down the street each morning hand in hand to meet their classmates they looked like butter wouldn't melt in their mouths.

But to listen to these girls talk and play in the yard below, as Jenny and I could not help but overhear sometimes from our balcony, was an ever present source of joy for us. These two rascals were absolutely hilarious and cheekily rude when they thought that no-one was listening to their chatter.

In their thick Calypso accent and exaggerated vowels, they would giggle and loudly whisper furtive children's swear-words (nothing too unwholesome, fear not) daring each other to say them ever louder, and talk about boys they liked or didn't like as the case may be while they played jump-rope or hopscotch, and had us in stitches time and again if only they knew it! (Four and six and already discussing boys!)

I will never forget those cheerful happy-go-lucky girls, nor their equally memorable parents.

Joshua and Mary were both pastors of a local church which had a small but dedicated following of Islanders. This we were not aware of until on our first Sunday we were awoken to the I'm sorry to say worst singing I have ever heard outside of a TV talent show. In the absence of an actual church building, this little independent sect of Christians were using, perhaps temporarily, perhaps permanently, we never did find out, the apartment below us and the abode of our landlord and landlady, as their regular place of worship.

Joshua would keep time with his robotic guitar strumming, also taking the lead in the vocal cacophony with his amazingly out of tune religious renditions, possibly self-penned.

Periodically the singing would stop, and various members of the congregation male and female would take it in turns to presumably (for we never actually saw) stand and give praise to the Lord, loudly and with deep passion and conviction in their voices. Then the hymns would start again, and so on for two full hours every Sunday morning from eight until ten, and the occasional evening too.

I don't seek to mock religion nor the spiritual beliefs of anyone, less still our helpful and happy hosts, but the excrutiating sounds that filtered up to us filling our ears every Christian Sabbath will stay with me forever.

I can still hear now one of Joshua's most common adulatory refrains, where he ended each verse of a particular song with a few solo words of his own; as the crowd finished singing their part and fell silent he would continue alone in a sincere droning voice; '...and, y-e-s, He pro-ba-bly will!'

The 'He' no doubt referred to God, and was I expect referring to a certain deed that the singer thought was about to come to pass.

I don't know if it was the vagueness of the word 'probably' inserted into the lyrics, or the manner in which it was sung, but if the Lord is joy, then we certainly had our share of that on those warm Sunday mornings, lying in bed sipping tea and smiling at the sounds echoing up from below through our marbled floors and half-open shutters.

Chapter 7 - Paradise lost (or 'w t f?')

Seven weeks and a day after arriving in the Caribbean, Jenny came home from work and we fell into a silly episode of bickering.

I expect it appeared to the world at the time that we had a solid marriage, but the reality was a little different. Tensions had been rising between us and we were moving, although we couldn't articulate it at the time, inexorably towards a crisis point in our long relationship.

We had been together almost since childhood, first dating when Jenny was fourteen and I sixteen, and our union had run its course, only both of us were too scared to admit it. We still loved each other very deeply, but that just wasn't enough anymore, and the events which had caused us to marry on a whim a year earlier may have seemed at first glamorous and carefree, but were actually on reflection being exposed as the opposite.

In fact six months prior to marrying we had tentatively decided to call it a day and it had been a painful break-up for both of us, but I guess through weakness and a fear of the unknown as well as clinging to the thought that the love that had originally been so strong might possibly be rekindled, we remade contact and jumped straight back into a relationship with both feet, and our eyes firmly shut. Without thinking it through we married virtually immediately upon getting back together, and now that we were no longer distracted by all the planning surrounding coming to Virgin Gorda which had kept our minds occupied for most of 1993, life was settling down and the cracks were starting to show.

Forget trial separation, this was a new and novel twist - a trial marriage. Perhaps we should have accepted fate, celebrated the good times, hugged each other and moved on with our separate lives. We had both been through very difficult family upheavals as kids and helped each other through those tough times, and we had travelled the world together as bright-eyed teenagers, and you simply can't share the history that we had and never look back without at least some pain, only we didn't have the strength to face those fears and make that break permanent.

We'd really had an amazing life up to that point, and I am immensely proud to have been part of that young couple who took on the world. But times change, and sometimes people do too.

I left Jenny at home alone that evening after our argument over nothing at all, and in a fit of pique took the jeep and drove through the Valley to the yacht harbour and the municipal square, parking behind the Bath and Turtle pub in search of a beer and some company.

It was a Wednesday evening, and being one of the regular twice-weekly live music nights a loud modern reggae band with a female vocalist was playing on the edge of the dance floor by the satellite bar, entertaining the partygoers and patrons with their fast Calypso beats and smooth vocals. Around fifty people were strutting their stuff on the square between the band and the verandah, perhaps another hundred or so were gathered in the restaurant and bar. I went in through one of the side entrances to the main saloon and stood queuing to buy a drink, looking around to see if there was anyone I knew in the throng.

The place was packed and reverberated with a typical Caribbean party atmosphere which tourists yearn for and locals accept with a slight air of superiority, knowing that they reside in this dream and that a high proportion of the envious tourists wish that they did too. In paradise or purgatory it's the people and emotional connections that make life worth living and not so much your environment. But still, it does help to be warm, tanned and relaxed, surrounded twenty four hours a day by tropical air, inviting seas and crystal sand beaches. Yep, notwithstanding our current life issues, being here was still a pretty solid plus.

Through the tight mass of people I spotted a couple I recognised who had recently become an item, and in the way of Virgin Gorda where everyone knows everyone else and often their private business too, I knew well enough to chat with and pass a part of the evening in their company.

My acquaintances were sat on tall stools at a table just inside one of the two doorways that led out through the canopy-covered restaurant to the dance floor beyond.

I was happy to stand next to their table and exchange some gossip above the noise, feeling the humidity from the night air condense on the cold surface of my bottle of Heineken and form into droplets, gradually increasing in size until they reached critical mass and slowly trickled over my fingers and down the side of the green glass. As we talked I swigged from the bottle, quietly surveying the social scene around me.

The music outside rose to a small crescendo, and then to enthusiastic cheers from the crowd the band took a few bows prior to leaving for a short break, a DJ ready to take over the helm for a while so as not to lose the atmosphere for the partygoers, and those who wanted to continue to get their groove on during the band's absence wouldn't have to miss a step.

As the band played its final chord and the applause had not yet completely faded away, the first notes from the DJ's turntables already rising to take over, I heard a commotion outside on the dance floor, and casually looked out through the open doorway to see what was going on.

I couldn't tell at first if it was an argument or just horseplay, and to be truthful I wasn't all that concerned either way. In the short time that I had been on Virgin Gorda I hadn't seen anyone seriously misbehaving, despite the copious amounts of alcohol consumed by many visitors and locals alike.

It sounded like some small fireworks were being set off in the crowd, and being from England where kids were and certainly I was in my time quite mischievous, I imagined that some boisterous boys (probably) were harassing some of the dancers by throwing a few harmless firecrackers around to get a bit of attention.

On reflection this didn't actually make a lot of sense. I'm sure that kids behave similarly everywhere, but youngsters just seemed generally nicer and more polite in the BVI, and it would have been extremely out of character for any to be throwing fireworks about, even more so this late at night when they were all usually tucked up in bed.

I took another sip of beer.

Then something unexpected happened.

All the revellers outside on the square suddenly began screaming and running around in an immediate state of terrible panic, scattering wildly in every direction tripping over tables and chairs in their haste and desire to leave the area as fast as possible.

I looked to my left and saw most bizarrely my two drinking companions dive under their table and huddle together on the floor, then stare wide-eyed up at me with a look of terror on their faces. Seeing them do this without any warning was almost comical, but however strange and vaguely funny they looked, kneeling down there in a tight embrace like a couple of children hiding under a bed afraid of the bogeyman, it was obvious that they thought something bad was happening, and perhaps they knew more about it than I did or they wouldn't be acting this way. But I had absolutely no idea what on Earth it could be.

What was going on?

I had just decided that discretion was the better part of valour and whatever the problem was, if everyone else was ducking for cover or scrambling for the exits then perhaps I should do the same, when as I turned back inside the doorway to seek my own shelter from this unknown threat, I felt a huge thud in the centre of my back.

The force of the impact caused me to lurch forward a couple of paces until I stood alone in the middle of the pub. I became suddenly dizzy, and realised with a sense of detachment that my lungs had stopped working. Try as I might I simply couldn't draw breath. This was even more confusing than the events of the previous few seconds; it just felt as if my lungs weren't there any more, and my entire chest was a solid leaden mass of flesh with no moving parts in it at all.

While I was trying to make sense of this, to my further surprise my legs buckled and I crumpled to the floor and cracked the side of my head sharply on the hard ceramic tiles. The co-ordination in my arms apparently no longer worked either as I had failed to gather my senses quickly enough to put my hands out in front of me and even attempt to break my fall.

Everything began to feel as if it was happening to someone else's body, and my mind was now looking on with interest at this wasted man, suddenly and inexplicably lying where a few seconds earlier I had been upright talking with friends and contemplating taking another swig of refreshing amber nectar.

My jaw jerked open and I began gasping for air.

From the instant I'd felt the impact in my back to hitting the ground had been no less than two seconds, no more than three, and in those last brief standing moments the only thought that I could articulate before falling was; 'That was uncalled for.'

None of it simply made any kind of sense.

I noticed that I was choking now as my throat seemed to be blocking up with something, and my left cheek pressed heavily with the full unsupported weight of my head into a warm sticky substance on the floor. As I watched, the ground in front of my face and upper body changed colour as a fast-growing circle of black centred at my chest began spreading out across the tiles. A sweet salty sensation filled the air, like the smell of a fresh slab of meat being sliced open at a butcher's, as the circle of liquid at first fully encompassed, and then quickly surpassed my entire stretched-out frame.

I had fallen fortunately more or less into the recovery position on my left side, and with my head tilted sideways and resting on the cold tiles I looked directly across the smooth floor to the vertical wooden bar panels a couple of metres in front of me. I was transfixed by this rapidly moving pool of black as it raced towards and then touched and bounced back off the kicker boards like a wave hitting a sea wall.

It reminded me of hot black treacle, and I began to think rather worryingly that this dark crimson moving mass looked a lot like blood. I put the facts together and with horror grasped that it was mine.

There was yet more twisting and turning of screws inside my mind, finding what would normally be the simplest of things almost impossibly difficult to fathom.

Isn't blood supposed to be red?

Of course. That's what the smell is.

There was now so much blood all around me that it permeated the air, which was something I had only ever once previously encountered on a visit to an abattoir, and that experience like this was not a pleasant one. It appeared very much as though more of this precious liquid was now outside of my veins than in them, where instead it ought to be, giving me life and vitality, and nothing good could come of that.

Disquietingly I also noted that it showed no signs of stopping as more and more claret relentlessly poured from me. It was coming from my mouth, my nose, possibly my head where it had slammed onto the tiles, and from some brand new uninvited holes elsewhere which I knew should not exist. It felt as though a violation had taken place upon me that I had been powerless to control or stop. In fact for the first time in my life I really understood the word violation and what it meant, and all the horrible connotations it holds, and I have never quite managed to completely shake that awful feeling that started in those first helpless seconds.

I realised then in my first true moment of lucidity what may seem obvious to anyone reading this, but what when it is actually happening takes a brief period to dawn on you and be able to put the thoughts together succinctly and in a coherent way, backed by logic and therefore capable of analysis; that I was in a very bad situation of which I'd had no warning, and was now suddenly in very serious trouble indeed and fighting for my life.

Sometimes you have to make something complex at the beginning in order to simplify and understand later. It's a process, and my cognisance was evolving and unfolding as each new snippet of information came to my attention and I was able to consider it and try to fit it into the puzzle, revealing the truth to me piece by gradual piece.

Yet with this realisation that I might be about to die, I was still deeply confused and desperately wanted to know why I was in this condition, what had happened, and what was happening right now to my crumbling body. In the separation of mind and body, this vexing question and my yearning to understand and make sense of it all seemed incredibly at the time of equal importance to the act of physical survival that I was currently in the midst of, convulsing and retching, choking and vomiting blood onto the floor, my head exploding in pain and my heart threatening to tear open my chest and fly across the room it was beating so fast and so loudly in my ears.

Noticing this incredible pounding for the first time I turned my attention to the source of it. Until now I had barely registered the thundering of my heart, masked as it was by the unreality of the situation. I heard it now - it was becoming so loud it was impossible to ignore. It built incessantly to a petrifying roar making my head spin and concussively pulsate with each superfast contraction of my heart muscles, forcing blood at immense pressure up through the arteries and into my skull. Each sledgehammer heartbeat almost knocked me unconscious like being smashed about the inside of my head with a padded cosh, and I began to wonder how much more of this my heart and the blood vessels in my brain could take, and along with everything else that was happening to me I became extremely concerned that one of these two most vital organs might give out and I would either go into cardiac arrest or suffer a stroke.

It felt like a pneumatic drill was being hammered into my chest, with the full weight of the burly jack-booted user standing on my torso and bearing down on me along with his machine, and I was unsure what would make me pass out first; the lack of oxygen as I couldn't breathe, or a heart attack, and either seemed not only likely but imminent.

All the while my mind was going round and round in growing frustration verging on almost anger at my ongoing state of confusion, thinking; 'What the hell just happened to me?'

When I'd first been struck it had felt like a punch between my shoulder blades from Mike Tyson, instantly knocking every cubic millimetre of air from my lungs.

I had been in a few fist-fights in my life, and knew what a punch felt like, and deep down inside I knew that whatever it was, it hadn't been that. It couldn't possibly be; no-one is capable of inflicting that much carnage from a single strike, and anyway that couldn't account for the sheer volume of blood escaping me right now.

So what was it then?

Time for theory number two.

Had one of the boisterous boys that I assumed were there on the nearby dance floor aimed a lit firework into my back?

In the absence of other information this outlandish conclusion began to seem reasonable, so I decided to run with it until something better came along.

Okay, extrapolating, if I have been hit by a firework, then why? Didn't my unknown would-be assailants know or care how dangerous that could be? And why had it affected me so badly? It was only a firework after all, and a firework can't do this much damage, can it? Besides, I hadn't actually seen any troublemaking teens... so who then?

I didn't know any of the answers to these questions, and this infuriated me as my body separately dealt with its own problems below.

My left eyeball was now immersed in a lake of blood but I found on trying that I couldn't close the eyelid. I didn't seem to be able to do anything except lie there and convulse. As I stared across the floor at the rapidly cooling blood, I gave careful consideration to the thought that there was a good chance I had just seen my last day. And I was at a total loss as to what I could do about it.

It was also soberingly clear that due to the obvious severity of my injuries, which although I didn't know exactly what they consisted of but sure as hell my condition was far from good, should I somehow manage to survive then in all probability nothing in my life was ever going to be the same again. This wouldn't be a pleasant concept to be presented with at the best of times, much less the nightmare I was buried in.

Like a schoolchild caught doing something naughty and wishing that the clock would miraculously turn back, I longed for the exit, the pause and rewind or game reset buttons, but they were nowhere to be found. There was no way out, no winding back the clock. No - 'What if I had ducked sooner?', or 'What if this unexplained thing had missed me?' or 'Maybe if I hadn't gone out tonight or had an argument with Jenny, or moved to the Caribbean...'

No choices were left to remake, no decisions to reconsider and change or possibly re-arrange. No ifs, no buts, no options. No saying 'sorry' and burying my head in the pillow and hoping that it will all go away. Just this. Blood coming from everywhere, pain like hell, total confusion and possibly rude untimely death. And, should I survive, my brain was still functioning enough to know that my body would from this day forward probably be completely screwed up and never work correctly again. There was simply too much damage that I could see and perceive for it to be any other way, and you didn't have to be a doctor to diagnose that.

From the age of twenty four until the day I died with any luck as a very old man, even if I managed to live through this terrible night I might now be disabled for the rest of my life. I didn't see any other possible outcome. It was a horrible thought and it sank like lead through my consciousness, overriding all the noise from my heart, the wet sticky lake of blood, and the pandemonium which was still going on all around me as the other patrons of the bar wrestled with their own fears and confusion and thoughts of escape, and their own mortality in the face of this shocking turn of events that no-one had expected when they went out for a drink that night.

It was 10.30pm, Wednesday the 2nd of February 1994.

Great. I wish I'd stayed in bed.

PART II - The Dissection of the Consequences of a Crime

Chapter 8 - Comprehension is not always at first easy

I hadn't heard the fourth shot, as this was the bullet that hit me.

As I lay on the floor looking up at the people running helter-skelter around me, apparently still oblivious or at least uninterested at the present moment as to my predicament, somewhere in the back of my mind the truth started to signal me, waiting for an opportunity to reveal itself and let my conscious mind into the secret.

Despite the deafening noise of my heart and a disconcerting gurgling coming from my chest, I became aware that the bar had suddenly gone very quiet.

The people nearby froze in mid-motion as if they had all been playing an extreme version of musical chairs and the music had stopped.

I marked a slow stalking movement in the doorway behind me and a felt a presence materialise and grow in the peripheral vision of my uppermost right eye. Without turning I could just discern a West Indian man in a Hawaiian-style shirt and dark trousers standing over me at my back, his arms hanging loosely at his sides, in one hand a silver metallic object which reflected the light on its many angles and curves.

The shape of the man, merely the shadowy essence of a human being as I perceived him, looked down at me. The slight nuances of his body movement and stance, the forward-tilt of his head on his shoulders, the limp arms, and the object in his hand that seemed to repel his fingers, almost dropping it, but not quite, to the floor. It did not fall, but remained unwelcome in his grasp as he stood considering and said nothing.

I sensed that he was detached, and wondered if he would finish the job and end me right there and then, but that would not be logical. Then again none of this had so far been logical, so how could I predict what he would or would not do or what would happen next? This was all crazy, and predictability had gone right out of the window and circumstance was just winging it from now on and would let me and everyone else know when it found out and not before.

After a few seconds he lifted his head and then following with his body as if in a trance slowly walked towards one of the side entrances of the bar and stepped out, leaving the building.

There was a brief lull, and then the frenetic rush of bodies began again in earnest, alongside ear-piercing screams and the occasional coherent shout of 'Is everyone okay?'

The crowd began to thin and slow to an aimless shock of wandering figures, milling around trying to assimilate what had just happened, as I was too but probably with more interest in the result.

No-one at first seemed to notice me; I guess they just blocked it out, self-preservation foremost in their minds. In the earlier panic some had literally stepped or jumped over me without even stopping to look down in their zeal to leave the pub and just get the hell away from there.

As the shrieking became less of a continuous cacophony and died down to intermittent yelling and the odd random scream, I turned my attention to the now perceptible gurgling sound coming from the middle of my chest. Twisting my head ever so slightly I could see redder blood this time, bubbling out of a penny-sized hole in my sternum like the contents of a kettle boiling over and spitting out liquid in fits and starts.

Confusion again. Had that been a gun in that man's hand? No, can't be. Couldn't be. Not possible.

Back to my current hypothesis.

If I had been hit in the back with a firework, and if all this blood was indeed mine as I was sure that it was, then why is blood now spilling out from my chest as well as my back? What is that other hole doing there?

And who was that man? How was he connected to all this?

My brain was protecting me from something, but wouldn't tell me what.

My t-shirted left arm when I had fallen had jammed awkwardly with the elbow trapped under my waist, the forearm standing vertically in the air half-wedged against my belt-line. This had kept it clear of the blood on the floor and aside from a few red-splatters was still mostly the colour of skin. I lifted this forearm now and moved it up my torso, lightly touching my left hand to my chest for half a second, at the point where the gurgling noise was emanating from my sternum.

I pulled my hand away and looked at it. In that brief contact it was now completely gloved from the tips of my fingers to my elbow in bright red blood.

I thought up until that point that the hole in my chest was not leaking too much in comparison to whatever was pouring from the location of the sinking pain in my back, but I could see now this wasn't necessarily true.

Two holes? Why two holes? And what was the level of damage to my back?

I imagined that there was a hole between my shoulder blades the size of a fist, judging by the severe blood loss, and I didn't see any way that I was going to live through this. I think if I could have cried right then, I probably would have.

More confusion.

Question:

If I have blood coming from my chest, could a firework have somehow entered my back, pierced my body, perhaps severing my spinal cord (I didn't even want to try to move my legs or think about the consequences of that horrible thought just yet), through all those bones and organs and flesh, and was now lodged right the way through the middle of my body, the tip of the rocket pressing against the underside of my sternum? Was this the cause of all this bleeding from my front as well as my back?

This just didn't seem plausible.

It couldn't be a firework, could it?

It can't be anything else.

Is the rocket still on its launching stick, and the whole thing currently inside me? Can the people behind me see the base of a firework sticking out of my back? How will I get that out? How will they get that out? How could anyone get it out without killing me?

How could I possibly survive that?

I had seen a man. He had come and stood over me.

He'd had something in his hand.

What? A gun?

But we don't have guns in England?

You're not in England.

No, it's a firework.

Must be.

Has to be.

English people don't get shot.

Yep, it's a firework, definitely.

Now I really knew if I didn't already, that I was in mortal danger. Blood can in theory be made to stop, if lucky, and with transfusions etc. replaced, so if this was the only issue there might still be a chance that I could pull through. But if I had been pierced by an object like a firework, still on a dirty wooden spike, full of gunpowder and bacteria and God knows what poisons and pollutants, in these tiny islands of the BVI, miles from any high-tech medical facilities, then the chances that I would come out of this alive even if I didn't bleed to death there on the floor or my vital organs give out were seriously remote. Infection, blood poisoning, blood loss; the odds against my survival were just getting longer and longer.

Fight.

I realised with a growing sadness that my chances were now almost zero. I was going to leave now, life over, the end, goodnight. A few minutes more at best. Shit, was that all I had? My one chance, finished, over?

Fight.

Strangely, bizarrely, like a bolt of lightening, my mind became clear. I knew what I must do, in fact all that I must do.

FIGHT DAMMIT!

I can't explain where that thought came from, so loud and so clear and so lucid, so pure and filled with undeniable and unshakeable purpose, except to say that I went completely into survival mode, focussing totally one hundred percent on living, and nothing else - nothing else mattered. Of course there was the issue of the confusion still distracting me, but that was wrapped up and inextricably linked with my survival because if you understand something, you might be able to start to find a way to combat and even defeat it.

My mind began to race and turned into the final furlong, as the fog that clouded my brain, preventing me from seeing the obvious simple truth of the situation for whatever reason, slowly began to lift and clear.

A firework?

That just doesn't make sense.

What has happened to me? Tell me!

It was then that I noticed a different man, just an innocent bystander like I had been. He had stopped and was looking down at me. In his mid-twenties, English I guessed but I didn't know why, dressed in improbably white trousers, standing in front of my body about half a metre from my chest. So close in fact that he must literally have been standing in the thick pool of blood that surrounded me.

White-trousered man was staring transfixed at my chest, open-mouthed as if not really comprehending what he saw, the angle of his head suggesting to me that he was focussing on my torso and the holes that were now there. I couldn't see his eyes very clearly but I remember his short brown coiffured hair, a wealthy tourist no doubt, and the dumbfounded expression on his face was palpable even with my deteriorating vision as my sight drifted in and out of focus.

'Are you all right mate?'

He asked in the way one might ask someone who has just had both legs sliced off in a horrific road accident if they thought they would be okay to walk the dog later.

I could not quite believe my ears.

Was this guy for real?

I think it was fairly clear looking at the state of my broken body that I was not 'all right' and that a glass of water and a little lie down probably wouldn't do the trick.

I supposed that he must be in some kind of shock.

But if he was in shock, how did he think I was feeling?

I turned my head as much as I could, and looking up at him I tried to draw breath to speak and failed. Summoning a miniscule amount of air from somewhere in my blocked throat I haltingly choked out my first words since the incident, coughing red droplets into the air and onto the floor as I tried to speak.

'No, I've been shot, get me a doctor.' I dropped my head back into the blood exhausted with that short effort.

He didn't move a muscle.

He just stood there staring down at me, his mouth shutting then opening again.

'Are you all right mate?'

What? The same shocked slow monotonous tone. The same dumb question.

I was beginning to get a little annoyed with this bloke.

Was this going to be the last person I am to converse with before I die?

Was this going to be my testimony, my final words here on Earth? Bantering here with this man when he could be trying to get me some medical attention however hopeless that might be?

I lifted my head again, more slowly and deliberately this time, as I really wanted him to be left in no doubt of what I was trying to explain what his eyes must have been confirming, but which he was obviously blocking out in an effort to protect himself from the horror of the situation.

As indeed I was, so I suppose I can't blame him.

I cleared my throat as best I could, swallowed a mouthful of blood and squeezed the very last molecules of oxygen that my throat held in the direction of my vocal cords. Looking up in the approximate direction of his head because by this time I was too far gone to even try to focus anymore and seek out his eyes I managed to croak out and enunciate in a faltering voice;

'No, I've been shot. Get me a doctor.'

One last effort. Let's hope he gets it this time.

I dropped my head back into the blood finally and stared across the floor. I really could not do or say anything else and was struggling now to maintain consciousness. I knew innately however that if I passed out, that would be that. I would not wake up again. I was nearly at the end, close to the point where you stop caring, and then you really do know that it's all over.

As I had said it out loud for the second time, my subconscious and conscious minds connected and put the final piece of the jigsaw into place. The huge burden of confusion suddenly lifted and I could now concentrate all my efforts on trying to survive instead of also attempting to uncover what all this had meant and what exactly had just happened, using up valuable brain power and calories which I urgently needed elsewhere. My voice had spoken the words before the rest of me could put it all together in a neat thought package, and smiling, proudly present it as conscious analytical data at last.

Ah, that is what my mind has been trying to tell me all this time.

I've been shot.

Obvious really, when you come to think about it.

Chapter 9 - Shark tales and crocodile teeth

I didn't know what proportion of my lungs were still functioning, but at last through forcing myself to speak those few words I was managing to force a tiny amount of air into them with a monumental effort of each breath.

It's hard to convey how much noise my heart was making; it was almost deafening, which if I describe as 'roaring like a freight train' or 'pounding like a jackhammer', they are not just flowery descriptions, they were actual tangible feelings in my eardrums and chest.

My heart felt like it was exploding.

It was so loud in my ears it had drowned out the noise of one hundred and fifty people yelling all at once only a few paces from me.

It was beating so fast that I could not begin to count the contractions and I could not believe then and still marvel now that it did not give out that night.

Either my heart is as strong as an ox's and can take any punishment life could ever possibly throw at it and will outlast every other organ in my body, or else the amazing effort it made in keeping going that night has weakened it to the extent that I should be very careful what I do from now on, as the slightest knock might cause it to finally say enough is enough and stop beating. I don't know what the truth of that little conundrum is, and honestly I don't really want to know either.

I am inclined to think the former, but then again I've always been a glass half-full person.

In any case my heart was pounding like a jackhammer and roaring like a freight train, and you will just have to take my word for it.

I was dressed that night in a pair of khaki shorts (typical ex-pat uniform), sneakers, and a snazzy turquoise blue t-shirt with an ocean-scene motif, emblazoned with a picture of a great white shark surfing purposefully through foaming waves from the back and around one side to the front. The fabric had a thick texture and the design was screen printed on with bright oil based paints, and although it might sound like the fashion police should immediately have been called and arrested me on sight, actually at the time I thought looked quite good.

Lastly I wore two pieces of jewellery; my wedding ring made of two concentric bands of differing shades of white gold, and a single crocodile tooth held by its root in a little silver cup, which hung on a thin silver rope-chain around my neck.

I had bought this tooth from a trinket store in Adelaide whilst backpacking around Australia, and had travelled with it through virtually every continent on Earth and had so many adventures wearing it that I'd come to think of it as my lucky charm, and it was my pride and joy.

Quite small, at about four centimetres in length, it was slightly browned with rough ridges running down its length. When I wore it and my leather Ozzy bushman's hat and spoke with the slight Australian twang that I had involuntarily kept after a year spent down under, I liked to think that I might even have been mistaken for a true blue Jackaroo from out back o' Dubbo. But maybe not.

Either way, the first of my items of clothing I was to lose that night was my blue shark t-shirt, as it was cut off with a very large butcher's knife at the hands of the next (German) sea captain to enter my life; the amazing Harry Schoenauer.

When mister white-trousers had finally grasped the situation and gone to fetch help, he returned with a tall man in his late twenties or early thirties, speaking perfect English but with a heavy European accent, and a strong flat voice which instantly took charge. I say the voice took charge, because I couldn't focus my eyes too well nor really move them much in their sockets, so my only real connection now with the bar and the world in general was through what I heard above the machinations of my body.

As soon as he saw me lying there Harry took action where others just stood and stared. I think he had originally been dining outside in the open-air restaurant just on the other side of the doorway where I had been standing, and had probably been one of the voices I had heard moments ago asking if everyone was okay. He had evidently met white-trousered man going out as he was coming in, following the growing commotion of people gathering around me.

The voice calmly but firmly gave instructions, mustering the leaderless people into a cohesive group of first-aiders.

He asked for and got clean towels brought in from the kitchens as well as a large sharp knife. He then leant down, and supporting my torso gently rolled me forwards and then back, seeking the entry hole - single or multiple, nobody knew at the time - and possible exit holes and ascertaining to the best of his ability what my condition was.

Taking the enormous razor-sharp blade which someone hurriedly handed to him, Harry then carefully and quickly cut away my t-shirt and placing one finger over the centre of the pain in my back and another over the hole in my chest, said clearly so that everyone around heard and were now duly informed, four words that I can still hear in my mind today;

'Clean entry, clean exit.'

I realised that in his opinion at least, and he seemed to know what he was talking about, the bullet or bullets that struck me had passed right through, which was far better than being lodged somewhere inside me I guessed, and infinitely better than being skewered by a large wood and paper firework, which up until moments before had been my best flawed guess of my predicament.

So things were looking up. However small a piece of positive news this was, a plus is still a plus. I probably didn't look all that positive to my helpers, but what did they know? None of them could see inside my head and know that I was still very much up for the fight.

I felt my body being pushed and pulled in every direction as I was at last rendered first-aid. It was all hands to the pump and seemed as if most of everyone who was there at some point gave assistance, and those who were closest trying desperately to stop the bleeding must soon have been wearing and sharing a fair amount of it themselves. But however terrible and totally hopeless it must have seemed to anyone looking on, inside myself crazily I was still okay, and my mind was functioning at a pretty good level. While my body was now beyond my control and completely in the hands of others and fate, I kept myself going with constructive thoughts.

Glass half-full.

Think positive.

I knew this much so far and numbered these facts aloud in my mind:

1. I'm alive.

2. I'm probably dying.

3. Where there is life there is hope.

4. Where there is hope there is life.

I kept it simple and clung to these last two, and repeated them over and over in my head.

I let my body go limp, and just let my helpers do what they must. I could do nothing to help them, and I needed to conserve my energy. And so I dove deeply into my mind and swam around in there, searching for something, anything to cling to which could conceivably help me.

Captain Schoenauer, in Spanish Town with a few guests of his large charter yacht to chaperone them on a night out in Virgin Gorda, turned out to be the fulcrum of everything that came next and the key to my survival. He was an intelligent, quick to analyse and make a decision, efficient German, and an unflappable man. Although he must have been in some state of shock himself - who wouldn't be? - he still had the presence of thought and co-ordination to rise above the chaos and take charge while everyone else just scratched their heads.

And he did save my life, because it was Harry and no-one else who was responsible there for that little insignificant piece of history. People live and die every day, it's the way of the world. But that day, that man saved my life.

Back inside my head I was continuing my search for hope. Okay, I thought, the odds look bad. So what can I do to try to restack them even ever so slightly in my favour? After all, if this skipper had faith that I could be saved, and judging by his efforts he did, then that would make two of us and that gave me a fighting chance.

I began to formulate a plan of action. Fanciful in the extreme I knew, but I had to do something to keep my brain active and this seemed as good a way as any.

First I decided to work out exactly how close to death I was, mathematically speaking, and then try to work with those numbers to see what extra tiny amount of life I could squeeze out of them.

Captain Schoenauer was meanwhile beavering away in the cause of extending my life. He frantically rolled up white towels and applied them to my body which then instantly became red towels. Instructing one man to jam his knee into my back with one of the rolls between his knee and the rear bullet hole in an attempt to stop the bleeding from that side, Harry himself simultaneously pressed others to my chest with the force of both of his arms and the full weight of his body turning me into a human anvil.

As this went on, I could hear some of the locals saying in their West Indian lilt;

'He's dead. He is dead.'

I perceived these unknown shapes shaking their heads as they spoke, while I listened on, thinking;

'Well I may look dead mate, but I'm not ready to give up just yet.'

I began the exercise of calculating the odds of my pulling through.

I had and have a strong interest in history and specifically World War II, and several years earlier had visited the Bridge on the River Kwai, near to Chiang Mai in northern Thailand. This is an infamous part of the Burma Railroad, where Japanese soldiers tortured* and worked to death over one hundred thousand Allied prisoners of war in the early 1940's. Most of these were brave Asians and Indians, but also tens of thousands of British and Australian, American, New Zealanders and other nationalities imprisoned and enslaved by the Japanese, were transported there and forced into building a railway across the jungles of South East Asia in order to service the Axis military machine.

(*I have worked with and known many Japanese people over the years, and respect and like every one I have ever met, I'm just relating historical fact. War is hell and every country has tortured at some time or other.)

A famous film was made based on these events starring the wonderful late actor Sir Alec Guinness, and the end of the film, one of the most well-known finales in movie history and having no basis in fact whatsoever, sees Sir Alec mortally wounded by a mortar blast. Staggering and falling in the very act of his death he collapses onto a plunger which sets off an array of explosives, thus destroying the bridge that he has ironically worked so hard to build as a Colonel of forced labour, and so disrupting the Japanese war effort at the last.

It is a great piece of movie history, if not actual history, as it was in truth American bombers which did most of the damage to not one but eventually three Bridges on the river near Kanchanaburi during that time. However I had stood on the current Bridge where there was and I presume still is, a plaque which commemorates those who died so awfully in that pit of hell. I had chosen this spot to stop and have a sombre moment of contemplation, when a Japanese tour bus pulled up at the end of the bridge, and fifty cheerful people disgorged and started snapping away with their cameras all around me.

This little event came to my mind at that moment on the floor of the Bath and Turtle. My experience on the Bridge on the River Kwai, and the film which immortalised that World War II story, became curiously relevant to my plight.

That enduring celluloid image of Sir Alec Guinness, knowing that he is dying, and knowing that he has only so much energy left, managing to stagger forward a few last paces before collapsing and dying, played out in my mind.

I wondered how much energy I had left in my broken body, and what reserves I could summon if I had to.

It didn't matter to me that it was only a movie; he did it, he staggered on. I reasoned that there must be some element of truth in that people can keep going in the face of imminent death if they are motivated enough to do so. I made up my mind at that moment that I would stagger on, metaphorically speaking, and keep staggering on and delaying my demise for as long as was humanly possible. I would stretch out my life to my glorious end, only mine would not be sabotaging a bridge with high explosives and helping to stop a war, it would be plainly and simply the survival of one human being - me.

If there was a way for me to live through this night, I was going to find it.

I was still choking and retching, but less so now, and as my body stalled my mind began working overtime.

I imagined that should I be absolutely required to, I would have just enough energy to roll over onto my hands and knees, crawl perhaps three metres, then collapse and die. I could think of no reason why I might want to even attempt this, but I was Alec Guinness, and this was my bridge.

How many calories would that tiny physical challenge use up? The act of climbing onto all fours and crawling a few feet? If I could work that out, I could work out how much energy I had left and ration it accordingly.

I thought back to my biology lessons at school and calculated that if a grown man uses approximately 2500 calories per day, that would break down to one hundred calories per hour give or take. A person uses almost as many calories while sleeping as they do when awake - I had obviously been paying attention in that lesson - unless they are heavily exercising or engaged in energetic mental activity. So if my goal was to survive for one hour, I would need at least one hundred calories to achieve this. If I relaxed and conserved energy, I could maybe stretch that out a bit further. I was losing massive amounts of blood, so that would not be helping, but it was a start; I had something to go on and some numbers to work with and that was all I needed to save me from despair.

Next I thought of a chocolate bar, and the calorific value that contains. I guessed at three hundred. How many bites would it take to consume? Five? Right, so each bite of a chocolate bar is sixty calories.

So how many calories would it take to roll and crawl as previously described?

Five? Ten?

Knowing this would give me an idea of how much longer I had to live.

I chose to think positively and call it fifteen.

Okay so I had fifteen calories of energy left in my body, or about a quarter of a bite of a Mars Bar.

Shit. That didn't seem very much.

Totally unscientific, but that wasn't the point. I needed to regain some sort of control over my destiny, and knowledge is power, the power to think what I should or could do next.

I decided to go Zen, and from now on I should stop doing anything other than that which was not directly related to my survival, which in truth I was already pretty much doing anyway, and see if I can make these meagre fifteen calories see me through.

Then another thought occurred to me.

What if I stop thinking so much that I forget to fight?

Sounds silly maybe, but there was a chance that if I relaxed too much, I might slip away, mentally as well as physically, and so I determined that I should not let this happen. It was a fine balance to strike - expending just enough energy to live, but not so much that I hastened my death.

So I let my mind wander just a little, bringing it back and reigning in my thoughts every now and then when I felt that I was losing track of the real task at hand, in case that led to blessed sleep, and that most tantalising termination to the deafening noise in my ears, the blood, the smell, the taste and the horror.

To lead me away from temptation and the danger of letting go and succumbing to the inevitable, I began to think of surreal ways that I might survive this night, and of possible scenarios that might develop that could either help or hinder me in this goal.

My thoughts, probably prompted by the close proximity of my current Teutonic saviour went to the original German sea captain, the one who had nearly killed me on his yacht due to his lack of empathy and seamanship and a large overdose of pride.

This old doctor had retired many years earlier in Germany, and in the way that many Caribbean nations operate, he had been offered a part-time position as a GP on Virgin Gorda with a supplemental income and help towards the rental of a villa, and some other enticing perks. This can be a lot cheaper in the long run for Caribbean governments' wage bills as opposed to paying a full-time local doctor, and is a method of cutting expenses that many small countries use in employing white-collar staff in medicine, the police service, auditors, town planners and the like.

Caribbean civil services are peppered with British, French, German, Filipinos, American, Dutch and other nationalities -

you name it, they are probably there - often newly-retired government workers, supplying services at a cut-price rate to the local taxpayer. This also gives the retiree a slice of life in paradise in which to enjoy their early old age, as well as still keeping a hand in with their career, which many people miss terribly and are only too glad to be given an opportunity to do. Some such as police officers only require twenty years' service in their home nation to qualify for pension rights, and so can conceivably retire in their mid-forties. These people therefore still have a lot of work left in them and have a lot to contribute, and this second career abroad can on occasion prove to be more than a sojourn and becomes a whole new lease of life, where they bring their families and start anew somewhere fresh and unexpected.

The particular elderly German doctor with whom Heather and I had been sailing, was just such a European retiree and lived alone in Leverick Bay. He was at the time the only serving physician on Virgin Gorda, and held twice-weekly surgeries in a small two-roomed clinic on a hill at the back of Spanish Town, helped by two local nurses.

He had a questionable reputation with the people I knew on Virgin Gorda, amongst other things for carrying out superfluous to requirement 'TUBE's, or Totally Unnecessary Breast Examinations whenever a young woman went to the clinic for something as innocuous as an earache. Whatever the problem, if the patient was female and vaguely attractive, he would apparently find a way to get their blouse off. And I had heard this from more than one trusted source with first-hand experience of the precise situation just described.

I'd already formed the opinion after meeting him that this man was incompetent, and the thought of him being potentially summoned all the way from Leverick Bay that night to treat me, was almost enough to send shivers up and down my spine at what this might do to detrimentally affect my chances of survival.

I reasoned though quite rightly that as it must be now approaching eleven o'clock at night, and bearing in mind the twenty or thirty minute drive for him to get here should he even be asked to attend, no-one would seriously consider calling him for help, and thankfully they didn't.

Chalk another one up on the scoreboard for my survival odds; things were looking up again.

Of the two German sea captains that I'd come across in the BVI, I definitely had the right one in my corner tonight.

I next let my mind wander to Sir Richard Branson and his private island of Necker just to the north of Virgin Gorda.

I had not been there at that point, but my wife had many times, to give treatments to some of the incredibly wealthy people who were lucky enough to vacation there. I also by a strange set of coincidences knew three of the managers of Necker, having gone to school with the general manager Peter Wynne, scuba dived with the male assistant manager Chris, and my wife had become friends with Ginny Hawksley, the female ex-assistant manager who eventually married a local guy and remained in the BVI after her employment ended.

Having spent time with all three and spoken about their jobs and lives, I understood that, to my surprise, Richard did not own a helicopter that specifically serviced the island. He did however have access to one or more for his and his guests' use whilst there, kept at one of the other nearby islands but I was unsure which. I then began to wonder if maybe one of these aircraft could be brought into play, and some enterprising person may think to 'call Richard' and this flamboyant billionaire could ride to my rescue!

This was nonsense of course, as firstly Richard Branson was not staying there at the time, and secondly who in that bar at that moment would in all honesty think to call Necker Island and ask to borrow a helicopter?

But still, this occupied my mind for a few more precious seconds, as my life stumbled on and my energetic saviours led by the honourable Captain Schoenauer discussed what to do with me next.

As I lay listening to my thundering heart, drowning out the loud conversations of people all around me, contemplating several virgins - Virgin Island, Virgin Gorda, Virgin Helicopter - my life began to fade.

I'm old enough to remember cathode ray tube television sets, which had thick convex glass screens and huge bulky plastic rears which hissed and whistled and hummed when in use, and more so during the periods of warming up and cooling down long after being switched off.

It was the switching off of these old CRT television sets that came to my mind next.

When a television was turned off in those days, prior to the advent of plasma, LCD and LED, there would be a delayed reaction to the process of closing down. On pressing the off button the picture would remain fully intact for a moment, then slowly it would distort at the edges and start to shrink, the frozen image twisting slightly and pulling away from the perimeter, gradually getting smaller and smaller, until it became a mini version of the image that had previously spread right across the glass, eventually becoming no more discernible than a bright dot in the middle of the screen.

The sound in contrast would continue on for several seconds as if nothing had happened. Although no longer bearing any relation to the picture, it would slowly lower in volume, as if the people speaking were moving farther away. The volume would gradually fade, the voices still perceptible, ever fainter until they would still be talking but far off in the distance. Finally the tiny white dot in the middle of the screen containing the now unrecognisable image would get suddenly brighter, then disappear with a slight popping noise. The sound from the broadcast would stop, and the television set would be at rest at last.

I describe this because that is very close to what I experienced next.

I could see Captain Harry and hear his voice rallying my helpers. It seemed like they were losing the battle and some were giving up. I could make out others, still rolling up white towels and unrolling red ones, pressing them to my body then releasing them and studying my bullet holes to see if the bleeding was slowing down. Other people were talking, milling around, looking down at me and sharing premature prophecies of my doom.

I noticed the voices of those nearest me starting to drift, becoming quieter, more soft and gentle, and the crowded image of human forms began shrinking. The edges of my vision pulled away, leaving an indistinct perimeter of darkness which gradually thickened and became more solid. Yes, I have to say it did look a lot like a tunnel, with everything that had previously been in my line of sight still in perfect proportion, but in miniature as if looking at the world through a rolled up newspaper.

It all felt quite pleasant and nothing to be afraid of. I was happy, and it was a good place that I was going to - that I think we all go to. I just felt it. It was nice. It was okay.

I watched the images of heads and shoulders leaning over me gently fall away, their expressions merging, their voices quiet, the darker edge of my awareness getting thicker and closing in until almost all was now in shadow. In the middle of the blackness a tiny picture of people in motion, my helpers, living in another existence, in another world, a world that I was no longer a part of. I was leaving this one now. It was a release, an acceptance to fate, a realisation that my time was at an end. Young? Sure. Too young to die? Maybe, but them's the breaks.

Then a part of my mind began questioning the inevitability of all this; of my 'fate'. Quietly at first, gaining confidence and getting louder with every silently spoken line until it was virtually yelling inside my head from I don't know where;

'Hold on a minute...'

'Wait...'

'I haven't finished!'

'There is more I have to do.'

'Whatever it is I am supposed to do in my life I want the chance to fulfill it. Give me that chance! I want that chance!'

'Don't you realise that I am a fighter?'

'Do you think I am going to give up?'

'There is so much I have not done. I am not ready!'

Nobody heard these exclamations except me, and with the last rousing refrain I forced my eyes wide open and they slowly swung back into focus. First Harry, and then my helpers, one by one growing and filling up my vision, the shadow around the edge almost - but not entirely - disappearing. Their voices were now as close as ever, and even the noise from my heart was back, thundering away and shouting down all else. But I could hear the people again and see them, that was the main thing.

I was alive, and I was happy about that.

I think now and have always believed that I brought myself back from death at that moment. I feel absolutely certain that was indeed death I saw, and though it was far from an unhappy destination, and certainly nothing to be scared of, I was not ready to go there, not yet. I chose to live.

There is no doubt in my mind that had I decided not to fight, death would have wrapped me in its comfortable arms and taken me. But I had willpower, and I survived, and I always remind myself of that today whenever the chips are down.

Perhaps this is what people mean when they say that a person just 'gives up' and dies.

For myself, twenty minutes had now passed since the shooting.

My imaginary fifteen calories had still not been completely spent, and gratifyingly for the moment I was still in the fight.

Chapter 10 - Sex and death and David Copperfield

I can break down my initial battle for survival after the shooting into two twenty-minute periods.

I had survived the first round, by virtue of a mix of good fortune and sheer determination, and now I was back and ready for round two and the decider.

I tried to listen in to what was being said around me and hear what decisions were being made by others regarding my fate - not that I could have altered any conclusions drawn by my helpers in any way. Perhaps if I had heard something that I really didn't like I could have made my feelings of dissatisfaction known by a grunt or some other attempt to get their attention, but I wasn't even sure that I was able do that. And would they have listened anyway seeing the condition I was in?

In truth by now I don't think I would have raised an objection even if they had chosen to call my old shipmate the German doctor from Leverick Bay and put my life in his incapable hands, so disconnected I now felt between my mind and my body.

Well, maybe I would have made an exception and objected to that...

Actually I was only half-aware of what was being discussed, and half that again of what was meant by it, as I slipped ever deeper into myself. However I was still here, still fighting, and my mind still fairly clear, although it has to be said it was getting a little fuzzy at the edges at this point.

I later found out that during massive blood loss - the term is ischemia - blood stops pumping around the extremities of the body in order to conserve blood supplies and therefore maintain a flow of oxygen to the three most vital areas; the head, heart and lungs. Blood supply to the legs and arms is restricted quite quickly through the body's natural and subconscious ability to constrict certain blood vessels, so ensuring that as much of the vital nutrient content as possible goes to where it is needed most. If a leg or arm loses blood supply for a short time, it will likely do little long-term damage, whereas a brief restriction of oxygen to the brain can be catastrophic. The brain is the most important thing, as that carries everything that you are; all that you have ever been and ever will be or may become is stored in that mass of neurons and nerve fibres, and if that breaks, even if you live, what are you?

Once blood supply has been reduced to the extremities, should your body determine that this is still not enough to guarantee survival, then blood is further restricted to the digestive system, kidneys, and finally liver, leaving a much shorter route around the body. Instead of an arduous journey circulating around every blood vessel that you possess down to the tiniest capillaries at the tips of your toes, blood is now simply required to go from the heart, to the lungs, back to the heart for a quick burst to the brain, and repeating the cycle until either you get better through your body regenerating lost blood, which it can do amazingly fast, or through a blood transfusion - assuming that the places in your body where you are losing it from have been stemmed - or you die.

I had lost so much blood at this point - somewhere around half of all I had - that my legs, arms and digestive system were now being severely starved of oxygen, and there was barely enough to go around even the restricted circuit of brain and lungs.

By now the blood had mercifully stopped pouring from my body though, as the entry and exit wounds had been plugged temporarily with both towel fabric and the external pressure applied by strong men, and at last was beginning to coagulate which was my body's small contribution to my first-aid. My lungs however continued to bleed internally and I struggled for every incomplete breath.

I then heard the amazing (anyone who saves your life is always amazing) Captain Schoenauer make a decision. After exchanging some words with several Islanders to help with local knowledge, it was decided to take me to the clinic up the hill at the back of Spanish Town, hopefully not to await Harry's compatriot doctor, but to bring some proper medical supplies into play and provide me with some more professional treatment. I required stabilising before my clearly necessary evacuation to somewhere with better medical facilities and into the care of people with proper training, incredible though my first-aiders' efforts had so far been. As there were no hospitals on this tiny island, a journey of some sort would have to be undertaken and by a method as yet undetermined, and it was judged that in my present condition I would not survive the physical stress that this would entail. Something more needed to be done with my severely injured body before risking leaving Virgin Gorda and setting off to wherever.

Once this had been decided, a vehicle was quickly sought, and with four people carefully lifting me I was carried through the Bath and Turtle pub and out of the side door which I (and later my attacker) had used a little over an hour earlier, and into the partially lit rear car park.

There I was lain along the back seat of a waiting taxi - sorry to the owner for the blood I must have left there - whereupon I was driven across town to the clinic, one person holding my head up to stop me choking and another supporting my torso in more or less the same position in which I had been lying on the floor. This meant that the bullet holes, just to the right of my spine, were slightly raised and so helped just a little to stem the flow of blood.

We slowly negotiated the roads of Spanish Town, the driver taking great care not to make me feel too uncomfortable, although in truth I was too out of it to care much what he did, and we soon turned into the narrow dedicated rise up to the little surgery. I could see the main entrance doors open wide, the lights in the building blazing. Lots of bodies were milling around in the contrastingly dark car park. They gave the appearance of being tense and were obviously awaiting my arrival.

I was carried out from the back of the taxi and lifted onto a medical trolley, a red blanket laid over my lower half, and wheeled inside. Instructions were being given by two West Indian nurses who miraculously were not only there, but were dressed in their white nurses' uniforms - bizarre, this was eleven o'clock at night; did they actually sleep in these clothes? No, they had just immediately donned their uniforms and rushed to open the clinic on being telephoned and told of this emergency. That's true dedication, and I was glad of it.

It was here in this bright buzzing waiting room that I met Jenny.

Someone had thought to go and tell her in person the horrible news (we had no phone in our apartment and this was long before the days of mobile communications) and then brought her to the clinic where they expected I would be delivered once people had applied a bit of common sense and worked out what do with me.

Jenny was blank faced. She was sat on the edge of one of a row of plastic chairs and stood as my trolley was brought to a halt next to her. We were left alone for a few brief seconds while the nurses and other helpers rushed forward into the surgery-proper to carry out whatever preparations were necessary before taking me through.

I don't think Jenny said anything, and I didn't speak as I was now swiftly approaching the second of my near-death moments and was fading rapidly.

Before we could connect I was grabbed and hurriedly wheeled into the rear surgery, my wife remaining in the outer waiting room. I saw a woman and another person I knew stay with her to offer comfort, and then my view was obscured as someone pressed an oxygen mask hard to my face, securing it in position with elastic cords behind each ear. I saw a wooden doorframe quickly pass, and then shiny yellow clinic walls and dazzling fluorescent lights filled my stinging eyes.

Looking down the bed I could see a supplies cupboard open and a nurse stretching up on tiptoe searching for something, and I became aware of a deep soothing female voice so close to my face I could feel the moisture from the woman's breath. Through my blurred eyesight I made out a female form, and smelt a sweet heavenly perfume - my first olfactory sensation since the all-pervading blood smell that had filled my nostrils since the pub.

I then heard an Italian-accented voice speak.

'Greg, Greg. You are going to be all right, Greg.'

A gentle hand stroked my hair in time with each melodic word, each syllable individually carefully pronounced in the way that a non-native speaker enunciates when they want to make sure that they are understood. And it was beautiful. A wonderful ray of anticipation in that dark night.

At that moment my life ebbed away. My eyes shut on the world and my too-short life closed its final chapter.

Unlike my previous deathly experience a few minutes earlier, this really was the end now. Whatever magical energy my imaginary fifteen calories had imparted to me and however improbably long I had managed to string out those meagre morsels of hope, every single last one was now completely spent.

I did not even have the cohesiveness to articulate the thought that I was dying, I simply had no choice but to let my eyelids drop and my awareness fade to nothing and that was all there was. No time for goodbyes, no tunnel, not even the microscopic calorific value that it would have required to pass even a single thought from one neuron in my brain to another. How little energy is that? What tiny, tiny fraction of measurable energy must that be, to fire-up one or two brain cells and send an electrical spark of consciousness from one to the other to register a single solitary thought?

Whatever miniscule amount that could conceivably be, I no longer had it to give.

I was spent, gone, finished, and my futile fight for life was over, and I had lost.

At that exact, precise, amazingly fortuitous moment in that night of fortuity - apart from the troublesome aspect of being shot - the nurse who had been painstakingly searching for something in the cupboard that was way too tall for her evidently found what she was looking for, and an adrenaline shot went sharply into the bicep of my right arm. My eyes flew open like Uma Thurman in Pulp Fiction, only with less of the body spasms and jumping around in a basque.

I was awake, and boy was I awake.

My senses returned, my thoughts gathered, and my vision began to refocus.

And what did I see, the first thing that my eyes gloriously beheld when I came back from death that second and final time?

A pair of beautiful, incredible, voluptuous breasts.

Quite the most wonderful thing I had ever seen in all my life. They were virtually bursting out of a low-cut grey pinafore dress, heaving with every breath that their lucky owner took, the silky skin of their cleavage not fifteen centimetres in front of my face and framed with long golden hair tumbling down over this mystery woman's chest as she leant forward over my bed.

And who did they belong to?

The sweet Italian voice, the one that had been getting my name wrong moments before, the owner of the soft hand I felt stroking my hair, and from now on my very own Agnes, and that is what I shall call her.

They say that sex and death are the two strongest emotions, and are often combined, and I can see that now first-hand. I had always liked women, but now I loved them. This was my saviour, not physically medically but just as real nonetheless. My light, my sweet perfumed angel bringing me back from the brink and delivering me from death. And my goodness did I desire her right there and then. Whatever awful condition my body may have been in, I wanted her, more than I had ever wanted any woman before in all my life.

I think if the blood supply to my extremities hadn't been so severely restricted then I possibly would have demonstrated how I felt about her at that moment; I was instantly smitten.

I know it's terrible, thinking of my wife nearby in the other room being comforted by friends, presented with a situation that I would not wish on my worst enemy, but the fact is that in my heart Jenny and I had long since passed the point of no return.

I simply felt what I felt at that moment in the clinic as I saw this vision of beauty before me. It was not there to be analysed, it just 'was'. Forget sensibilities, forget manners and honour and pledges and loyalty. I was dying, and then I was brought back to life by the timely injection of some chemicals to kick-start my body and bring me around just enough to hopefully survive the next part of my night of trials, and now I was back, temporarily maybe, but back all the same, and nothing is more precious than life when you can see it ebbing away. I can no more apologise for my raw emotion at the instant of my expiration and then rebirth than I could have changed it, and that is the plain and simple truth of it. My old life was over; my new life was beginning, and Jenny was a part of my old life, which in truth she had been for a long while, only both of us had been pretending that it was not so.

The time for pretence was over. I should not have been wasting my energy and having these thoughts about my marriage here on this trolley, but I had them all the same. Perhaps I am a bad person. I still didn't know if I would survive this night, although the odds were definitely improving, and when you are in that situation of life hanging in the balance, then trust me, emotions are magnified, and life in all its raw glory becomes infinitely magnified, and there are no apologies deserved or required for that. It is simply life, and the deep, deep desire to live it, and according to your rules and following your dreams. For hurting people's feelings, sorries come at another time, but in the moment of death, there is only life, no vindication necessary.

When you are suddenly, shockingly, jolted and shaken to your very core, you instantly (if you are lucky enough to have a moment to do so before your death) examine who you are, the path of your life that has led you to that moment, and who you yearn to be. I knew that however much Jenny and I had loved each other, and to a great extent still did, this part of my life was over and we could never go back. And as the night wore on that realisation began to grow and develop, becoming clearer with every passing minute. I had not thought of Jenny at all in my time of greatest need, and that tells the whole story in itself.

So now I struggled to open my eyes wider and to look upon my Agnes, and see the face that belonged to the shining light that had been my first sensation after my return from the nothingness of death.

But there was something bugging me.

With a Herculean effort I gathered and directed whatever amount of oxygen I could summon to my lungs, and lifting my right arm (I was still lying on my left) jerking and twitching like I was remotely controlling a robot crane at a fair-ground kiosk, I grasped my oxygen mask in one hand, and pulling it to one side I looked my Italian angel directly in her eyes for the first time.

'It's not Greg. It's Craig. C-R-A-I-G. Craig.'

Having fulfilled my mission and made my point I let the mask snap back into place and my arm fall over the side of the trolley and it hung swinging there until a nurse lifted it and placed it back on the blanket at my side.

The look of shock on this young woman's face was priceless. She obviously until that moment thought that I was just about dead despite her words of comfort assuring me (and maybe herself) to the contrary, either that or I was too far gone to have any hope of returning, and had resigned herself to selflessly easing my passing.

I didn't know who she was, or how she came to be there, or why it was her and not my wife that stroked my head as I lay on that trolley, but that is exactly the way it happened, and if I am to be damned, then I will be damned for telling the truth, and that is that.

Chapter 11 - It never rains..

As I lay on that trolley, basking in my new infatuation for this enigmatic presence that had been there at my rebirth, a cannula was pressed into each of my forearms by one of the nurses. A clear fluid bag was connected to each one, the liquids inside soon dripping down long twisting tubes and into my veins.

I guessed that one contained saline and the other plasma, but I'm not entirely certain.

Now the question was raised once again of what to do with me.

I heard but played no part in the discussions, which took place in the doorway of the surgery. I think that everyone but Agnes and possibly the nurse who had injected me thought that I was pretty out of it, but they were wrong; I was sentient and my fighting spirit had returned with a vengeance.

Captain Harry was still evidently in charge, along with my new friend and saviour the mysterious Italian woman, who I could tell by her tone and manner was used to giving orders, and who also had a flair for organisation that at least matched Harry's.

Ideas were bounced to and fro as to whether or not to order a medevac, what insurance I had (Jenny helped with that) and the best place to take me for treatment.

To answer these in order, a medevac was impossible as the dirt airstrip on Virgin Gorda was too short for a jet aeroplane, and could not carry out night-time take offs and landings even if it were long enough as it had no navigation lights or radar.

Second, yes I did have insurance, but not on me as it is hardly the sort of thing you bring to the pub when out for a pint, especially as I was effectively living on Virgin Gorda now anyway and not on vacation. Besides, there were reciprocal health agreements between Great Britain and the BVI, so local treatment wasn't issue, just exactly where it would take place and the extent of it.

Puerto Rico was mentioned as a possible alternative by Agnes. This Americanized 'almost' State was the largest of the nearby islands and apparently had the best medical facilities in the region.

Also considered was St Thomas, the capital of the United States Virgin Islands, just over the horizon beyond Tortola and where my wife and I had been married a year earlier. The USVI are, although of a similar size to the British Virgin Islands, far more populous, and the huge number of wealthy American retirees who chose to make the USVI either their winter vacation or permanent home meant that the medical facilities on those islands were all purportedly excellent.

Again there was the question of how to get there as the only option appeared to be by boat. Although I had perked up a bit my situation was still precarious, so would I survive the journey?

Finally the decision was made; we were to head to the small local Peebles Hospital on Tortola, the least well equipped but closest of the facilities being only a forty minute boat ride away, and to hope for the best.

This being agreed (no-one asked me) the hospital was contacted and told to expect my arrival. Someone having acquired a pick-up truck in the meantime, I was loaded much more comfortably this time onto the open rear of the waiting utility vehicle. I was stretched out upon several thick blankets and surrounded on all sides by nurses, helpers and generally good people who wanted to do their part and together we drove back down the little hill, past the Bath and Turtle to the ferry dock. Here a Speedy Boat fast ferry was chuntering noisily and rocking up and down in the slightly choppy black sea, in the process of being made ready for our departure as soon as I had been brought on board. The ferries didn't normally run at night, so this vessel had been commandeered and hastily made ready for our sole use by a few of the nearby crew who had been contacted to staff the boat for the journey to Road Town. Everybody really was pulling together in my cause.

The oxygen being delivered through my mask had helped to clear my head and breathe ever so slightly more easily. Now that I could draw a few short sharp breaths I found that it was actually extraordinarily painful to do so, but this was a small price to pay for being able to at last provide my body with some life-sustaining air. I reckoned I was able to draw about a quarter of my normal breath with great effort, but I was content with that for the time being and readied myself for the fight ahead. I had survived my two wobbles teetering on the brink of the abyss and had so far pulled through, and if I had anything to do with it I was here to stay.

The reality however was that despite my bravado I still might not make it. I had lost half of my blood, my lungs had collapsed, my heart, even though I have not mentioned it for a while, had not stopped its thundering for even an instant (what a heart, I still can't believe what it did for me that night) and I was still nowhere near any comprehensive medical facilities. It was the middle of the night, I had no doctors attending me, and I was stuck on an island in the middle of nowhere about to get onto a boat and head off into the inky unknown. Things can hardly be said to have been good, and though I was feeling a bit more optimistic, there was a way to go if I was to live through this night and I knew it.

No lights were on inside the main passenger cabin, and in the bowels of the ferry it was darker than the night outside. The Speedy Boat skipper had been raised from his bed along with a couple of nearby crewmembers, and as we crossed the gangplank and they made ready to depart I could tell that they were all slightly disoriented.

The cabin could normally seat around forty people, with room for perhaps twenty more outside on the decks and benched roof area. 'Speedy' of Speedy Boats fame was the nickname of one of the three best known businessmen on Virgin Gorda, and so named as he had made his fortune first as a taxi driver, developing into a car rental firm, and finally grew to have the largest garage on the island as well as one of the two major ferry companies in the BVI. I had met Speedy several times since arriving on Virgin Gorda, hiring a car from him once when Jenny and I had wanted a vehicle to explore the island, and for some reason her jeep was not available - come to think of it, it was in one of Speedy's garages getting some mechanical work done. I think that's called a monopoly.

Speedy was definitely a character. He wore a grease-stained Hawaiian shirt at all times above overalls with the fabric arms tied permanently around his waist. His shirt was invariably open to the navel showing off a huge gold medallion hung around his neck. He seemed a nice guy to us, and spoke with a deep manufactured Mississippi drawl uniquely blended with his strong Caribbean accent, and strode around looking confident and happy with his lot in life, and I don't blame him.

The final preparations having been made to the satisfaction of the crew (Speedy no longer worked the boats himself) and after Harry and my helpers had carefully laid me out on the floor of the passenger aisle on a bed of thick blankets, checking that I was ready the signal to cast off was given. The mooring ropes were slipped from the dockside, and our night-time journey across the bumpy ocean to Road Town began.

It was now around an hour since the shooting, and as I stared up at the dark ceiling of the charcoal cabin listening to the crew as they berated their bleary-eyed skipper for going too fast and causing me to bounce across the deck every time we struck a particularly large wave, I began to refocus on relaxing and tried to rediscover my Zen.

A couple of my helpers suggested that they sing a song to keep my spirits up, but in truth this was not necessary. I was quite capable of pepping myself up, and needed no motivation for that. At one point a guy asked if anyone knew 'Kum-Ba-Yah', which he proceeded to sing and hum alternately when he forgot the words, which was all too often. Mercifully no-one saw fit to join in and he trailed off and stopped pretty quickly. Joshua came to my mind then and I wondered how many more times in the Virgin Islands I would be forced to endure singing that was only marginally worse than mine.

Others who had come along for whatever reason and were sat elsewhere in the cabin, ignored me completely and quietly discussed the shooting amongst themselves in a sort of early group therapy session, which was probably repeated by a lot of people in the coming years who were in the bar that night.

I assessed my situation.

I was alive.

I had received very competent first-aid - certainly more competent than I could have given should the situation have been reversed - and I was at last on my way, albeit unconventionally, to a hospital.

I concluded therefore that things could be worse.

It seems though that the powers that be had one or two jokes left to play that night, as around fifteen minutes into the journey I noticed the engines start to splutter and then actually stop altogether, as the boat quickly pulled up in the water and was suddenly being buffeted by sideswiping waves.

Heated hushed discussions followed. Apparently something was being said that they did not want me to hear, but I moved my mask to one side and whispered to my nearest helper asking what the problem was. Reticent at first to tell me, eventually I was let in on the secret. In their haste to leave port and get me to Road Town the crew had forgotten to check the fuel levels in the boat, and it was now almost empty and we were adrift at the mercy of the ocean's currents.

For several awkward minutes we floated there in the dark, half-way to Tortola, half-way from Virgin Gorda, the chopping of the ocean diminishing just a touch perhaps to help me in my time of need. Everyone sat not knowing what to say and thinking about what was going to happen next, me most of all.

I was still endeavouring to remain in my Zen, just concentrating on relaxing and conserving my energy, but I admit I was starting to get a little worried by this latest turn of events. Was someone trying to tell me something? Should I have expired an hour earlier; was that the Great Plan? Had I ruined some destiny of the Earth by fighting so hard to cling to life? Was Fate making one last grab for me before it gave up and admitted defeat?

And how much more bad luck could one person put up with anyway? I asked myself this question a few times, then realised the futility of it and started to force myself to be a bit more optimistic. I wondered why someone hadn't thought to radio ahead to Tortola or one of the intermediate ports, to maybe ask for a speedboat to come and meet us on the ocean between the islands. Just as I was pondering this I heard a crewmember suggest that very thing to the Speedy Boat skipper.

This was actually not as great an idea as it at first sounded, as we had no power, so no lights, were floating far out at sea, and would be almost impossible to find unless they tracked down a rescue boat with radar, fuelled and crewed ready to leave from some nearby port immediately, which all things considered was fairly unlikely.

Not to mention that I didn't fancy being bounced at high speed across the water on the deck of a speedboat; not just at that moment anyway.

Then a solution was hit upon. The reserve fuel levels were measured, distances calculated, and decisions made. The skipper informed us that we might just have enough in the reserve supply to get to the ferry terminal at Beef Island, approximately half-way between Tortola and Virgin Gorda and just to the north of where we lay.

Beef Island was joined to Tortola via a causeway, and this would now mean that to get me to Peebles Hospital in Road Town would involve a trip by road across the causeway and over the mountain that further divided those two islands, as opposed to the more direct route of the ferry. It was a long shot but we had no choice. The motors were gingerly restarted, and with careful revving and no excess throttle, the boat was pointed north, and we headed for the looming shadow of Beef Island with several sets of fingers crossed, including mine.

Chapter 12 - Planes, trains and automobiles

I don't know how much fuel remained in the boat's tanks when we drew up to the quayside at Beef Island's ferry dock, but it couldn't have been much.

Whether the extra fuel the crew conjured up was from an inline reserve supply which many marine engines hold for emergencies or it came from good old-fashioned jerry cans remains unanswered. From whatever source the result was that about thirty minutes after leaving the jetty at Spanish Town's yacht harbour, we arrived safe and sound although with nerves slightly frazzled at our new mid-point destination on the way to Road Town and Peebles Hospital.

Once the decision had been made to head for Beef Island the skipper had radioed the hospital to ask for an ambulance to divert and intercept us at the airport dock, and the ambulance drivers must have really motored because they were there waiting for us when we arrived. The journey over Ridge Road which was the more direct route rather than skirting the lowland bays, was normally a fast twenty minute drive from the capital to the airport but could easily take forty if there were hold-ups en route.

In the same way as there had been many concerned people milling around in the car park of the little Spanish Town clinic, the concrete landing was already busy with a small crowd, presumably present solely to await my arrival as there would be no other logical reason for them to be there at this hour. The British Virgin Islands are a small community and news travels fast - in this case extremely fast - and the good part of my soul imagined that these people now assembled on the quayside were well-wishers and would-be helpers, coming to meet the ferry in order to offer assistance to anyone who required it, as opposed to the merely overcurious.

Parked haphazardly amongst the crowd were several vehicles, signifying perhaps that firstly as one, then another arrived on the scene, there had been few people present and so they just parked wherever was convenient and as close to the water's edge as possible, the crowd then building and filling the space between the automobiles as it grew. For the most part they appeared to be pick-ups and people carriers, and perhaps in the main were therefore taxis normally stationed at the nearby airport.

One stood out immediately however as a medium-sized white box-van, which looked like an ice-cream truck except it had large spinning orange lights above the cabin where the oversized novelty ice cream figurines should be. There were no markings on the side to signify its purpose but it was undoubtedly the centre of the shoreside activity.

I could see all this through the bank of ferry windows, as I was lifted through the cabin and onto the deck of the Speedy Boat then carried across the gangplank to dry land. I noticed as we made our way over the rough ground and passed through the crowd that the two rear doors of the white van were fully ajar, revealing a brightly lit interior, two blanketed trolleys and some medical paraphernalia lining the walls and front bulkhead.

It was clear that this was an ambulance, but in comparison to the paramedic units I had seen previously in my life it appeared worryingly makeshift.

As we approached, a uniformed man and woman unbuckled the left gurney and lifted it out of the ambulance. I was laid upon it and my fluid drips connected to a raised stainless steel frame at the head of the bed. The whole lot with me on it was placed back into the rear compartment, and I then secured to the trolley and the trolley secured to the van. I was left alone with the doors still ajar, looking up at the fluorescent lights on the ceiling and listening to the voices of the crowd talking outside.

I heard my wife among them and tilted my head to look, and could make out Agnes and Harry presumably speaking with the ambulance crew about their assessment of my condition and what they had done for me so far.

The ambulance staff turned out not to be medics at all but merely drivers, and consisted of a West Indian man and a West Indian woman, both quite young and not too concerned with any complicated medical information. They had been sent from the hospital to collect the patient and their job was simply to get me back there as quickly as possible and that's all they knew or wanted to know.

Neither of the drivers accompanied me in the back of the ambulance, and I neither saw nor heard anyone else enter, as the doors were then shut and the engine started up. This was a little concerning as I had hoped that this part of my journey would signify the start of more intensive medical treatment. It seemed though that this would have to wait a little longer.

There is a certain haziness in my memory as to what happened next, or more accurately a small part of it. In general I have almost total recall of that night, with only one unclear detail.

We pulled out of the car park and onto the main road to Tortola. Rounding a long corner I felt the ambulance drop slightly and the road surface change, thereafter continuing in a straight line for a short while which I deduced was us traversing the causeway.

Completing the crossing we climbed again steeply, my tethered body bouncing in time with the juddering axles as we hit seemingly every bump and dip on the road from Beef Island to Road Town. As my head tried to stay on the pillow I began to get the feeling that someone else was there in the cabin with me.

Throughout the journey this figure was sometimes laying, sometimes sat upright at the foot of the other bed, leaning forward, elbows resting on crossed knees, indistinct eyes boring into me.

I never tried to identify who it was, or even confirm or deny their existence. Instead I kept my eyes totally focussed on the strip lights directly above me.

This unsettling presence reminded me of the feeling I'd had when the gunman had stood over me in the bar. I can't say that I ever saw him (my attacker) clearly, and yet through my peripheral vision my brain had filled in the blanks and locked his features away in my subconscious. This 'person' here in the ambulance, and I still was unsure if they were really there, projected a different less oppressive aura. Here what I perceived was inquisitiveness and a desire to comprehend.

There were three possibilities:

Either I was alone, and I had imagined the other presence.

Or it was my wife silently watching over me.

Or it could be another person, someone who I had not as yet understood their part in this story, and which would unfold and become clear in time.

At some point during the journey it dawned on me that while my thoughts had been diverted elsewhere contemplating the existence or otherwise of my mysterious fellow passenger, I had lost sight of something vaguely disturbing.

Why hadn't the hospital sent a medic with the ambulance, and why were there no medical staff attending me now?

I twisted my head to look up at the bulkhead dividing me from the driver's compartment, and could see a small open inspection hatch at arm's length behind and above me in the centre of the white panel.

Through the small black rectangle I could hear periodic gear changes and the noise of a straining engine. In amongst these artificial sounds were voices, and with a little effort I filtered out the background clutter and could just make what was being said.

And this is what I heard.

Female voice: '...yeah I think I will. My sister is going to be there, if she can get a babysitter.'

Male voice: 'You mean Shanice? Damn, she has her baby already? I didn't even know she was pregnant!'

Female: 'Yeah, she is fast like shit!'

Both now laughing.

Female: 'But I have nothing to wear to the party on Saturday. I wanted to wear my new yellow dress, but I am not sure... I don't think it looks right on me.'

Male: 'Girl, 'you kiddn' me? I have seen you in that yellow dress and you look fiiiiine!'

More laughing. He was obviously trying to pull her, and perhaps she had a boyfriend, perhaps she didn't, but she was enjoying his attention all the same. Neither was giving a single solitary thought to their patient a couple of feet away.

I looked up at this rectangular hole in the bulkhead, and wondered if tonight could get any more surreal.

At half past midnight we entered a sleeping Road Town and I felt the vehicle slow, and turning draw to a stop. The back doors opened to reveal a dusty car park and a short flight of concrete steps leading up to the main entrance of Peebles Hospital.

Chapter 13 - Memories are made of this

As I was lifted from the back of the ambulance several other vehicles drove in through the gates and parked randomly around the hospital car park. I saw people who had been with me on the ferry getting out of various cars mingling and talking with each other, the atmosphere now changed from one of tension to more subdued; the beginnings of the calm after the storm.

Jenny was there and she walked alongside holding my hand as my ambulance crew wheeled me across the car park and carried me up the wide stone stairs to the colonnaded verandah at the top. We passed through the main hospital doors and into the foyer. Jenny and I still had not exchanged a word since the shooting and notwithstanding the nagging question of who if anyone had spent the journey with me in the back of the ambulance, there seemed to be an emotional distance between us if not manifestly physical. Perhaps this was shock on Jenny's part and dulled senses on mine and nothing more.

My heart had slowed to just a Gatling gun at full pelt inside my chest, and the fight for every breath had settled into a rhythm of short painful gasps which was fast becoming normal. It felt like breathing through razor blades, and again, this too was becoming normal and I braced myself accordingly with each new inhalation. I was buoyed however by the fact that I had arrived at last at a proper medical facility.

We stopped briefly in the entrance hall, some paperwork exchanging hands between the ambulance drivers and hospital staff. I looked around at the bare walls and noticed a man sitting alone on a row of chairs. He was totally oblivious to my presence, his afroed head bowed engrossed in a dog-eared paperback novel held in both hands on his lap.

I studied him for a moment as he seemed out of place and was the only person in the foyer not in hospital uniform apart from Jenny and me. I deduced two things from looking at him; firstly that he gave the appearance of a man who had gotten dressed in a hurry. Second that it was impossible to tell this man's social status, as his proud unkempt bearing could have made him anything from a caretaker to a prime minister, and each just as likely.

He appeared to be in his late forties or early fifties, with huge semi-wild hair greying at the fringes and smudged over-sized steel rimmed glasses pressed tightly to his face. He had an angular frame and even from his seated position I could see that he was unusually tall.

My reverie over I was wheeled onwards now, continuing down the main hallway, coming to a stop in front of two heavy white doors with blackened windows at head height and a radiation symbol on the adjacent wall.

The doors opened and a technician held one ajar on its springs while I was pushed inside. Jenny let go of my hand at the doorway and said something to me quietly as my notes were handed over, the door swung shut and I was left in the company of the radiologist.

There didn't seem to be any great imperative to rush by any of the staff which I had thus far encountered, rather bearing in mind the late hour everyone conducted themselves with a cool efficiency and just quietly went about their business without paying me much attention at all.

I imagine there was not a huge call in this small provincial hospital for night-time X-ray services, however it must be required from time to time for road accidents and suchlike, and so a system was fortunately in place to get someone out of bed and the X-ray machine up and running for emergency admissions. Although the technician was wide awake the same could not be said for the equipment which was still warming up as I waited.

When everything was finally up to speed the radiologist opened the door to the corridor and called to some staff for assistance, and with their help I was lifted onto the X-ray bench and laid in such a way as to get the images he required. They tried very hard to ease my obvious pain as they moved me several times, leaving the room on each occasion and returning to move me a fraction this way or that. Eventually the radiologist was satisfied and I was lifted back onto a new wheeled bed and taken down a long corridor and into what appeared to be a pre-op room. I could see lots of medical equipment, some I recognised, some I did not. A long white counter lined one of the walls, and there was a pair of double swing doors at either end of the room. Through them medics dressed head to toe in green theatre scrubs were coming and going. My bed was brought to a stop lengthways in the middle of the room, the foot-lever brakes applied and the porters left me surrounded in a sea of green overalls.

Several of the medics were hunched over some paperwork on the counter by the doors I had just come through. I noticed a conspicuously tall man amongst them leaning over pointing to something and speaking while the rest looked on.

Others quietly moved around me, reading and noting the fluid levels in the drips in my arms, taking my blood pressure and attaching various wires and tubes to different parts of my body.

It seemed like I was here to stay so I guessed that this wasn't the pre-op room after all but the actual operating theatre.

The tall man then turned and walked over to me and I immediately recognised the oversized steel-rimmed glasses and wild hair poking out from the sides and back of his green bonnet as the man I had seen buried in some pulp fiction in the hospital foyer. Having ignored me completely as my trolley had been brought to a stop by him earlier, now his demeanour completely changed. He pulled his fabric mask down revealing a reassuring professional smile and introduced himself.

'Hello, I am Doctor Smith, the consulting physician, and you are Craig, is that right?'

I made to open my mouth inside my oxygen mask but he lifted a hand to halt my efforts.

'We are going to attend to you now and fix your injuries as best we can. First we are going to take a look at you and give you some local anaesthetic, if that's okay.'

He turned away and went back to the counter. Taking one last look at the notes and giving further instructions to some of the other attending staff, he returned to begin his work.

There are some hours that you are quite happy to remember every detail of to bring out and savour in years to come, and others that you would rather forget.

The next hour that I lay fully conscious in that operating theatre easily falls into the second category. If I could forget it I would, but I can't, and after twenty years it is still uncomfortably fresh in my mind.

At first Doctor Smith, helped by his attending staff who had divested me of the remainder of my clothes, gently rolled me back and forth investigating the nature of my injuries, in much the same way as Captain Schoenauer had done earlier on the floor of the Bath and Turtle. It was now around 1 am, and two and a half hours had passed since then.

He next compared what he had seen from his physical examination with the X-ray images, holding each one in rapid succession up to the bright circular operating light in the ceiling above me, quietly passing comments to his colleagues when he saw something relevant to the task at hand.

I had been externally cleaned up periodically throughout the evening and the dried or drying blood on my body crudely wiped away, but now this cleaning was done much more thoroughly. I could smell the strong odour of hospital disinfectant through my oxygen mask and feel the cold cotton and gauze swabs doused liberally in iodine brush firmly all over my upper torso. A lot of attention was given to disinfecting my right arm, armpit and ribcage, but as yet I didn't understand why.

Once I had been washed and prepped to his satisfaction, Doctor Smith tapped the now bleeding hole in my sternum with his finger and then pushed his fingertip inside the bullet hole up to the first knuckle, feeling around the walls of the wound. The scab had been rubbed off with an iodine gauze and now blood overflowed and streamed out of the hole and down the side of my body. He withdrew the gloved finger which emerged bloodied and with bits of flesh and bone stuck to the sides, which he then wiped away with a disinfectant cloth before moving on to the entry wound in my back.

A syringe of local anaesthetic was then prepared and injected into the skin around the bullet wounds, and also into the holes themselves. Then rather strangely my right arm was lifted up and more local anaesthetic was injected liberally into my ribcage just below the right armpit.

Two nurses held the arm aloft while Doctor Smith moved to my right side and bent his head very close to my body, meticulously feeling with his fingertips as he located and plotted in his mind the courses of the upper ribs. Finding the correct spot he kept one finger pressed there, and then produced a scalpel which I had not previously seen and cut hard and deeply between two ribs, penetrating my chest. I could feel the flesh between my ribs snagging and being forced apart with every short scalpel stroke, as the hole was scoured out and further deepened and widened. Despite the local anaesthetic I felt a sharp pain with every slice, and was desperate to flinch but somehow didn't.

My heart redoubled its almost deafening pounding. Or had it been like this all along, and I had simply tuned it out as the night wore on? I don't know but it was here again now, roaring in my ears and echoing around my head, and I wondered again for the hundredth time how much more of this my heart could take.

Doctor Smith turned and handed his scalpel to an attendant which he swapped for a long shiny silver tube about the thickness of a pencil and with a curve at one end.

A nurse hurriedly applied more swabs to my side smearing away floods of new bright red blood, and while I was still wondering what Doctor Smith would do with this four hundred millimetre long metal instrument, he placed one end into the hole he had just created in my armpit and in one swift movement pushed the whole thing right down inside my ribcage until just the short curve remained above the surface of the skin. The shock drew me rigid and I involuntarily clenched both fists, one in the air in a kind of Black Power salute and the other lying alongside me on the bed.

Immediately blood shot out of the free end of the tube and began spraying the wall opposite and Doctor Smith himself before a transparent plastic hose was hurriedly attached by a nurse, thereafter red liquid gurgled out of the metal tube and wound its way down the long flexible hose. There was an incredible release of pressure, and I felt my diaphragm go rigid and my stomach muscles tense and lock, temporarily making my chest spasm and for a few scary moments I could not breathe at all.

I could smell blood in the air once more, and as my body bent retching I saw the other end of the flexible pipe being placed into a large glass demijohn which was then sat on the floor at the far end of the room. The long convoluted tube quickly changed from transparent to a constant stream of dirty red, moving along almost too fast for my eyes to keep up with until the entire length was opaque with semi-congealed blood. From then on blood continuously moved down the tube and drained into the glass bottle for the entire time that I was in the operating theatre.

A medic in the ubiquitous green overalls came to stand at the top of the bed and placed her hands down on the mattress either side of my head. Through her mask she asked me to relax and concentrate on my breathing as this was 'really important'. I wanted to yell at her in frustration; 'I'm bloody trying!'

This was the last straw and I finally decided that I'd had enough.

From the moment I had first been hit with the mystery blow to my back, seeing the floods of blood, all through the confusion and pain and horror, the realisation of what had happened to me, my comprehension of mortality, I had been calm.

I had teetered on the brink twice and once even brought myself back from certain death through willpower alone. My spirit had been strong and my resolve unwavering. But now this really was becoming too much.

I felt fingers inside my ribcage once again, digging out shrapnel and bits of bone, from bullet holes that should not be there. Did I invite this horror? Did I ask for any of this to happen? Why then? Why me?

This was not welcome. None of this was.

And now my chest had been opened up in front of my eyes, and my blood, more of my precious blood I'd seen shoot across the room and decorate at least one of the walls and several of my helpers in floods of red. Not clean blood like before, but dirty and half-clotted and spurting now in fits and starts down a long winding plastic tube to the other side of the room, bits of black and pink and flesh and God knows what amongst it. Again the disgusting smell of blood filling my nostrils, this time inextricably linked with a sickening emptiness in my chest as the buildup of pressure inside me over the past two and a half hours was released.

I wanted to escape, to run away, but there was nowhere to run, and no way to make my legs move even if I could detach myself from all the tubes and machines and get past my green-coated captors.

I tilted my head upwards and set my eyes on the female medic with her hands on the trolley, who I eventually was to learn was a doctor and not the theatre nurse I took her for.

Her gloved thumbs were just touching my hairline above each ear ready to prevent my head from flinching during the operation, her palms spread on the mattress.

She saw and felt my head move and looked down at me. Above her mask she had kind exotic eyes which seemed to ask what I wanted.

I lifted my hand, and before she could work out what I was doing and try to stop me, for the third and final time I moved my mask to one side, cleared my throat and said; 'I don't want to see this anymore. Can you cover up my face?'

She seemed a little confused for a second; perhaps my words hadn't come out very clearly, and then understood as my plastic oxygen mask snapped back into place. She looked around the room and then reached down to a low shelf and retrieved a small green folded sheet which could have been a large pillow case. She let it out to an appropriate size and then held it aloft by two outstretched arms so that the lower longer edge gently rested across my neck, so shielding my eyes from what was happening to my body.

All I could see now was this woman's eyes above her medical veil, and for the next half an hour or so her eyes locked on mine and mine hers, and I listened to the thundering in my chest, and worried incessantly about a heart attack that never came, vaguely being aware but trying to block out the feeling of the surgeons working below.

But that didn't matter anymore, because all I knew were those eyes, and that was enough to calm me down and keep me going for as long as it took to get me through to the end of this awful experience.

I had nearly lost my nerve at the final fence, but this nameless woman helped me through emotionally which at the time felt just as important as the technical procedures being carried out to fix my physical being.

I hadn't been given a general anaesthetic and so was forced to remain awake for the whole procedure because the anaesthesia would have killed me, so poor were my vital signs when I was brought in. No-one could ever really explain how I had managed to survive any and every stage of the events of the previous evening, much less arrive at the hospital conscious. I don't know either, except to say I thought of it as a trial which I was determined to see through to the end. At no stage had any of the medical staff let on to me just how concerned they were when I was wheeled into the operating theatre, and how surprised they were that I was wheeled out again alive after.

At last Doctor Smith required my sheet-holding angel's presence for something, and she had to reluctantly put the cotton shield to one side to assist in the closing stages of the operation.

I looked down and saw Doctor Smith sewing up the hole in my chest, then place some similar stitches around the protruding end of the steel tube, pulling it tight and locking it in position. I could feel the cold of the metal against my skin every time I moved, and it was evident that Doctor Smith intended for it to stay in me and would not be removed now that the operation was over, nearly a foot of steel remaining deep inside my body for the time being at least.

Finally I was rolled forwards so that the hole in my back could be stitched, and a last clean-up of my torso carried out with yet more brown iodine and ice-cold swabs.

Operation over, the sheets under me were changed as they were saturated with blood which had already crusted and stiffened most of the fabric. I can't imagine that they were ever fit to use again. My naked body was covered with a fresh blanket, disconnected from some of the electronic gizmos chaining me to this white and green antiseptic prison, and other smaller machines placed on mobile trolleys and wheeled devices to allow them to come along for the ride. I was then pushed out of the far set of doors this time, and down some hazy corridors and past rows of beds, finally coming to a stop in a small brightly lit private room.

I saw my wife standing by the window, curtains drawn shut, looking tired and drained. After the various pieces of equipment which had been brought along with me had been set up by the attending nurses, we were left alone.

I tried to move my mask to speak but Jenny seeing what I was doing stopped me. I motioned that I wanted to say something and made a sign with my hands simulating writing on paper. Having located some supplies outside at the nurses' station on the ward to which my room was attached, Jenny handed me a notepad and pen and supported the paper as I shakily wrote;

'I'm scared.'

'Don't worry', she said.

'I don't want to sleep. I might die.'

'You won't.'

'Have you told my family?'

'No.'

'Please don't.'

'You must rest, you must sleep. You'll be fine.'

I laid my pen down and let my head rest on the mattress, half-heartedly fighting off the wave of exhaustion that suddenly engulfed me.

My final thought as I drifted off to sleep was that I hoped Jenny had not telephoned my parents. The last thing I wanted was to involve them in all this.

I remember my heart thundering away, still beating as fast and as hard as ever, and although I was still very concerned that it might give out while I slept, or for that matter die during the night for any one of a dozen other reasons, I let sleep take me. I was petrified that I would never wake up, and if I could have remained awake the whole night I would have, but it was just not possible. The energy to fight as well as the will was simply not there any longer.

It was now a little before 3am in the Caribbean, and as I finally shut my eyes the last thing I saw was my wife leave the room to go and telephone my parents, about to go to bed on a cold February night four thousand miles away.

PART III - Trial and Tribulation (The sun is always shining somewhere in the world)

Chapter 14 - Murder in mind

The sun streamed in through the open curtains stoking up the atmosphere of the hospital room. The intensely dry air had parched my throat as the oxygen mask loosened and slipped during the night, turning my first swallow of the day into a sticky rasping action as I awoke.

I was awake!

The world past the window was warm, bright, and welcoming; another day in paradise. Jenny was sunk deep into an armchair adjacent to the window. She looked up.

Slowly I pieced together my last memories of the night before, then worked backwards to the shooting, and finally to the argument with Jenny that had led to me going out alone to the Bath and Turtle in the first place.

I looked across at Jenny now, the same person I had always known, and wondered just what the hell to do next.

On the one hand I knew it was over between us, but fighting back in the other corner and giving a good account of itself was the natural reticence that anyone has when deciding whether or not to end a relationship of many years, coupled with the blindingly obvious statement that this was neither the time nor the place to even be thinking about it. But if not now then when? What if I only had a short time left, do you continue to live out a lie for the benefit of others, or say what you think and be damned? Okay I had woken up, but that can hardly be a definitive statement of fact that everything would be fine from now on and I would just continue inexorably getting better. I didn't believe for a moment it could be that simple.

What it came down to basically was trust.

The issues between us were personal, but the reason the shooting had brought our relationship into sharp focus was because trivialities immediately ceased mattering to me upon the impact of the bullet. What I wanted more than anything now was total security, which is impossible, but I wanted it nevertheless. During our break-up the previous year trust issues had surfaced which had never been truly resolved, and as of yesterday for me these suddenly became paramount. Realisation of mortality can do that to you.

Would I be having these feelings if it wasn't for the shooting? Eventually, yes I think I would, and on that basis I can't blame this event for having these thoughts on ending our marriage. It was more like the catalyst for wanting to end it sooner rather than later.

If I was to die from my wounds, which I guessed was still possible, then I wanted to die with people around me who I believed in, or no-one at all. And if I were to live, I wanted to recover in a similar fashion, surrounded by loved ones in whom I could put my total faith and trust and build a future with, or again no-one at all.

Crucially I had to be honest with Jenny. Despite all of our issues we had got married, albeit unconventionally, and at the time meant the vows we took. We had embarked on this latest adventure together, and although it hadn't exactly turned out the way either of us could ever have expected, we had to see it through as a unit. I resolved to tell Jenny of my feelings therefore as soon as I was well enough, and to discuss everything as best we could to see what if anything could be done to salvage the situation. This was a huge decision to make and would have far reaching consequences for both Jenny and me, and most of what transpired in those conversations over the coming days and weeks will remain private. I can say though that the subject of our relationship was raised and no conclusions were drawn for now.

I turned my attention to my physical condition, and consciously assessed the state of my body the morning after the night before.

First I listened for my heart, and that in itself was a good sign; I had to strain to hear it.

The beating was quite erratic and a little too fast - but much, much better. Almost normal.

Second, my breathing. How is this?

Short; painful; laboured; requiring effort to maintain, but I was alive and thinking, so oxygen was obviously getting into my body in significant enough quantities to support my basic life functions. The hissing coming from my mask was the reassuring noise of a continuous stream of low velocity oxygen being fed into to me, enhancing my natural breathing, and whatever the statistics of it the mix of artificial and regular air was apparently working.

I took a moment to consider the possibility of brain damage due to oxygen starvation. I decided everything was fine. Others may disagree.

Gingerly pushing away the blanket covering my top half I peered down at the wounds in my chest.

Frankly it was a bit of a mess.

There were three ugly black stitches in the middle of my sternum pinching up a small mound of skin in the centre of an indented area of bone. This was the exit wound, now sealing off my insides from the outside world. The skin all around was smeared with trails of dried brown iodine and masses of caked blood. More bunched black nylon secured a few centimetres of protruding steel in position under my armpit, a long plastic tube connecting it to a large sealed glass jar now semi-full of blood sitting on the floor past the foot of the bed.

I touched one of the straggling ends of thread and lightly pushed the knot inwards.

Wow. It really did happen.

The door to my room opened and a nurse entered, smiled that I was awake, and left again returning with a blood pressure monitor and some other bits. After checking my vital signs she told me that the doctor would be in to see me shortly, and before leaving for the final time she returned once more with a jug of water and a plastic urinal bottle. I decided to keep hold of all of my bodily fluids for the time being, considering how much of them I had lost last night.

I looked now and saw that one of the clear fluid bags on the raised frame above my bed had been replaced with a sachet of blood. Human I hoped.

So now I'd had a blood transfusion too.

Add that to the list of new life experiences this past day had brought me. They were really starting to add up.

Through the open window I could hear the morning sounds of a waking Road Town; traffic moving along the street outside, people walking on the sidewalks calling to each other, aeroplanes coming in to land or take off from Beef Island just over the hills to the north.

All these people, happily going about their business; to work, to school, living their regular lives. A normal Caribbean Thursday, just like a thousand Thursdays before and a thousand more to come. Many would already be aware of the big news story of the day. Some would have heard it on the radio over their morning cornflakes or breakfast roti, shrugging and asking someone to pass the coffee, giving it no more thought than the latest cricket scores and probably a whole lot less before moving on to something more relevant to the day at hand.

Life goes on.

The pen and paper were still on the table by my bed, so I picked them up and in this way Jenny and I communicated for the first few days, until I could comfortably get out a decent set of words without making my throat any more raw than necessary. At first that morning we 'talked' about the mundane things which needed to be done, such as what Jenny was doing about work, where she was staying on Tortola, had the police been to see her and did we need to do anything regarding insurance just yet.

After we had exhausted the dull, we moved on to the ignorant. I was probably the only person relevant to the shooting that still didn't know what really happened, and what caused this chain of horrible events to unfold.

Jenny then filled in the blanks with what she'd found out so far, which was a lot.

(This is the full story, in part from what Jenny told me that day, in part from what I learned later.)

Firstly Jenny gratifyingly told me that the suspect had already been caught and was safely being held in police custody.

Second, she shocked me by saying that the gunman was himself a serving officer of the Royal Virgin Islands Police Force.

I will not say his name anywhere in this story, as it does not deserve to be spoken, but apparently he was quite well-known in the local community on Virgin Gorda, and not just for his job.

The gossip was that this guy had been having some marital difficulties, and this had boiled over last night and resulted in the shooting that I had unwittingly been a victim of. The couple had come originally from Dominica, another one of the nearby Caribbean islands, and settled in the BVI the year before. Here he had trained and recently qualified as a police officer.

The BVI police are not routinely armed, a throwback to and indicative of the close ties to Great Britain where police seldom carry guns. But like the United Kingdom, there are firearms available should the need arise. In the BVI these are kept inside secure storage cabinets in police stations, the keys to which are placed in the care of the senior duty officer in charge at each station at any given time.

There were several police stations in the BVI, the main one being Police Headquarters in Road Town, as well as several other sub-stations on Tortola, one on Virgin Gorda and one on Jost Van Dyke. This last island lay off the western coast of Tortola, and was a favourite haunt for sailors and tourists visiting these islands and the home of the famous Soggy Dollar bar on White Bay, which had been the original planned destination on my day of sailing hell.

The gunman's common-law wife Lucianne had a part-time job in the Bath and Turtle where she worked as a barmaid on Wednesday and Sunday live-band nights, usually serving customers at the outer satellite bar by the dance floor. I knew her by sight, but we had never spoken apart from to order drinks, and she didn't know me amongst the crowds of people who frequented that most popular of establishments. There had lately been accusations of an affair between her and one of the doormen at the Bath and Turtle, and the policeman husband had apparently found out.

He and Lucianne had two children together, although they did not take his surname, and they all lived together in the Valley on Virgin Gorda. Usually he was based at the police station in Spanish Town, but periodically he was sent to work on one of the other islands as part of a regular shift rotation.

Unfortunately the accusations of her infidelity had reached the point where he had made deadly threats to his wife, and also to her lover, once involving a knife and another the verbal threat to use a gun. This was all reported to the authorities, and in an attempt to keep a lid on it the officer was sent to cool off for a three day tour of duty on Jost Van Dyke, where he was on occasion, specifically on night duty after the day staff went home, left in sole charge of the station and therefore everything in it. This included the keys to both the police launch tied up to the jetty outside, and the gun locker containing the station's only weapon, a silver .38 Smith and Wesson Special service revolver and eleven rounds of hard-tipped ammunition.

Quite properly given his recent threats to kill as well as other multiple reports of domestic violence, he was ordered by his superior officers not to touch the weapon.

Apparently trusting that this order alone would be sufficient to curb his growing violent tendencies and assuage his anger at his wife's alleged infidelities, he was then left to his own devices on Jost Van Dyke, approximately one hour's speedboat ride from Virgin Gorda where his wife was only too pleased to be separated from her increasingly unstable husband.

On the first night of this particular three day shift, the husband was seen drunk on White Bay near to the Soggy Dollar bar, with the service revolver in his belt, a bottle of rum in his hand, wandering up and down the beach for most of the night bewailing his poor fortune and shouting curses into the air. He was supposed to be on duty and had therefore abandoned his post as well as being drunk and illegally carrying the Jost Van Dyke police firearm, not to mention swearing at random members of the public that got too close, and on any measure this was totally unacceptable behaviour.

The events of that night were first reported to Jost Van Dyke police station where no-one was found to be home, because of course the officer who was supposed to be there on sole duty that night and taking such calls was the very same person who was the cause of all the distress. Getting no response, the incident was then reported further up the chain to Tortola and to the Police Headquarters in Road Town.

The next morning, Wednesday 2nd February, a team of senior officers took a police boat from Road Town to Jost Van Dyke and confronted the hung-over officer and once again impressed upon him the seriousness of the situation, and was told once more on no account to remove the gun from the armoury without specific permission from a senior officer.

Incredibly in the face of this mounting evidence as to his erratic behaviour the armoury key was not taken from him, as according to police statute the sole officer on Jost Van Dyke had to have a key to the gun locker, in case an emergency arose requiring its use. They could have suspended him from duty, removed him elsewhere to a busier station, or at the very least sent another officer to work with and watch over him until his tour on Jost Van Dyke was finished and they could reassess the situation, but none of this was thought to be worth the trouble.

The senior officers satisfied that they had done their duty, at around mid-day on the 2nd February then left the officer once again in charge of the police station and all of its accompanying equipment, including the aforesaid .38 Smith and Wesson revolver and all the various modes of police transport assigned to that island.

At around 9pm, on the very same day, the officer took the key to the armoury, opened it, removed the gun and all eleven bullets, leaving a note inside the box for the next person to discover before locking it up again.

He switched off the lights in the Jost Van Dyke police station, left through the front door which he also locked behind him, and climbing aboard the police speedboat set off across the dark ocean to Virgin Gorda and the Bath and Turtle Bar and Restaurant with murder on his mind.

Arriving just after 10pm at the Spanish Town yacht harbour and tying up alongside an empty Speedy Boat ferry, he then walked the short distance across to the municipal square, entered the north section where a local reggae band was just leaving for a short break, and made his way up to the small satellite bar near to the dance floor where he knew his wife Lucianne would be working. He then pulled out his now loaded gun, and took aim at his wife's head as she served beer to a Canadian tourist who happened to be standing there at the time.

Now whether by great fortune, or perhaps due to the trembling hand of an uncertain killer, or, what I actually believe, that he just couldn't bring himself to put that bullet into her skull from point blank range, he aimed away at the last second and the first bullet merely grazed the side of her head, ricocheting off into the night.

Recovering herself remarkably quickly Lucianne ran out from behind the counter, diving through the crowd on the dance floor and heading for the main bar and hoped-for sanctuary. Probably from there she intended to make for one of the rear exit doors and escape through the car park to wherever.

Perhaps thinking that a moving target was an easier sell to his conscience than a stationary one, he also gathered his senses quickly and returned to the terrible purpose of his visit to Virgin Gorda. He fired three further shots in quick succession through the crowd of revellers in the direction of the main pub where his wife had just run, and where an Englishman happened to be standing in a doorway, sipping from a bottle of Heineken, wearing a snazzy blue and white shark motif t-shirt and chatting with a couple of friends.

The gunman probably hadn't seen me fall, with so many people running and true pandemonium having immediately set in, and just for good measure he fired a fifth shot, at no-one in particular as his wife actually had sprinted right past the side exit of the pub and already left the municipal square far behind. The fifth and last bullet spun harmlessly off into the air landing nobody knew where. Then as the people scattered he must have seen a person lying on the floor just inside the pub doorway covered in blood. This was obviously not his wife, and also not her lover.

And so the rogue policeman followed his fourth bullet inside to inspect his handiwork. Having stood and stared down at me for a few seconds, he then calmly walked through the bar, and leaving through a side exit, departed the scene of carnage of his creation. After walking the short distance back to the nearby harbour, he dumped his gun over the concrete quayside into the black water, and went to find a quiet bar to sit and have a contemplative beer, which was where his policemen colleagues found him half an hour later sitting on his own, a drink in front of him and appearing relaxed and unconcerned.

The Bath and Turtle was almost empty by this time, the remaining crowd having left in a convoy of vehicles headed by a taxi going in the direction of the little clinic at the back of Spanish Town, the patrons of that night left to unravel and make sense of the events of the evening as best they could.

Chapter 15 - Soggy Dollars and night nurses

It could quite reasonably be asked why the authorities had not seen fit to take action when this obviously unstable man went AWOL on White Bay and threatened patrons of the Soggy Dollar bar.

In any case once the shooting happened the police belatedly swung into action, and immediately dispatched officers to search the local area, finding the gunman dressed in civilian clothing in a little bar off the main drag hiding out amongst the other mainly local customers. Escape it seemed was not something that he had given much thought to, and when the officers entered the bar and spotted him, he gave himself up immediately.

Another set of officers searched the ground around the Bath and Turtle and from there down to the ferry dock where witnesses said they had seen him throw something into the water, and where Jost Van Dyke's police launch had been found moored and unoccupied.

Acting on this information a police diver was summoned, and the water around the boat searched, a shiny Smith and Wesson revolver and several bullets quickly recovered from the shallow sea bed. To give them credit where it is due, after the debacle of allowing this event to occur the Royal Virgin Islands Police pulled out all the stops to wrap up the case in short order. Also unbeknownst to me during the night a male police officer and a WPC came to Peebles Hospital following up leads, and while there they selflessly each gave up a pint of their own blood for immediate transfusion into me, which while I slept I gratefully received. I asked but never found out who these two mystery benefactors were.

As for the gunman's wife and the other tourist who had been shot, they both got off comparatively lightly. The Canadian man who had been standing at the bar ordering drinks from Lucianne had caught one of the stray bullets and sustained a deep graze to his neck. After receiving first-aid at the scene, he had departed the Bath and Turtle and Virgin Gorda, and no-one had seen or heard anything of him since.

Lucianne had also sustained a minor injury; a cut to the side of her head as the first bullet glanced off her skull. Apparently she had been with me on the Speedy Boat over to Beef Island, where she sat quietly in a corner with chaperones of her own. Although she was walking wounded, she did not appear to be in shock according to those who saw her. She had half-suspected what her deranged husband might do, and was prepared for it as much as anyone can be which explained her lightening quick reactions upon being faced with a loaded gun. Having met her since, and witnessing first-hand her refusal to give evidence against her husband, I am ambivalent towards this woman. On the one hand I feel very sorry for her situation and facing down death from someone who at one point she must have loved. On the other she then refused to help put this obviously violent and dangerous man away when he did what he did. But I guess she had her reasons.

Knowing that Lucianne had come over on the ferry with me did raise an intriguing possibility in my mind; was this the mysterious female presence I had sensed in the back of the ambulance on the journey to Road Town? Had it been her looking at me from the other trolley?

Back on that sunny Thursday, Doctor Smith paid me a visit late on accompanied by two Danish student doctors. One was tall, the other short, both men, on a working holiday to the BVI. They were very new and very green (or was it white?) and played no part in my examination, just stood around looking slightly disoriented as if they had come straight from the plane to the hospital and were still jet lagged, which they may well have been.

'You are a very lucky man', was the only thing one said to me as the three of them left to continue their rounds.

The next couple of days passed without much incident except that I picked up a fever on the second night, for which the Dickensian treatment was a bowl half-filled with hot water and a splash of spirit vinegar, into which a wet flannel was dipped and draped around my forehead periodically by the nursing staff.

On the third morning after two very uncomfortable nights my fever reduced, and I was told that I was now well enough to go into the main ward. There were only a very limited number of private rooms available in the small hospital and these were in great demand, and not wishing to cause a fuss I agreed and soon found myself being wheeled out of my lovely sunny sanctuary and into a slot along one of the walls of the large ward next door.

The ward routine went something like this; during the day it was a free-for-all. Relatives, friends, pets, well-wishers, school children, the postman, travelling salesmen and window cleaners all passed through as the days went by.

Families brought in food, as well as all the necessaries required for preparing and eating it. Laundry was done, games were played, merriment was made and beds were left unmade. Children ran up and down the aisles shouting and singing and generally having fun, while patients had to use commodes and undertake intimate examinations, or had medicine administered either swallowed or inserted, with the ever present risk of the curtains being whisked away by a curious toddler causing embarrassment to all but the oblivious child.

It was crazy. Some of the patients were elderly, and even those who were used to this sort of care looked bewildered by the constant hubbub and goings on.

The nights were worse. Late in the evening when the last of the relatives and well-wishers had all finally gone home, the stragglers usually leaving at around 10pm, the night staff would take over and begin their shift.

Thereupon a seldom seen - by me at any rate - version of nursing unfolded, as seemingly most of the staff, who plainly didn't see the point in paying for babysitters or child minders, brought their children and occasionally very young babies to work to share their shift. The older children being eternally curious and with boundless energy, would play 'war' between the hospital beds until the early hours of the morning, screaming and yelling and shouting 'Rat-a-tat-tat' as they ducked behind pillows and bedside cabinets pretending to shoot one another, sometimes diving under and crawling the entire length of the ward beneath all the beds, only to reappear grinning from ear to ear at the far end and call out gleefully to their friends announcing that they have just discovered a new game. From then on it was a race, and all of the kids present took it in turns to run and jump and crawl under and over the beds, back and forth again and again, while their mothers the nurses completely ignored them unless they played around the nurses' station, which was forbidden. This desk at the far end of the ward the staff sat at catching up on paperwork and various other nursing duties, helpfully keeping the entire set of dazzling fluorescent lights on all night long, never once being dimmed until the even brighter sun came up and poured daylight in through the open curtains at 7am.

Oh yes, and let's not forget about the music.

Now, I like reggae.

Love it actually.

Blues?

Wonderful.

Otis Redding, yes. Bob Marley, yes. Etta James, yes. But not all at once, at three o'clock in the morning. Please!

Apparently it is very important for patients in Caribbean hospitals to have a permanent nocturnal cacophony of reggae, soul and blues music blasting in distorted volumes throughout the entire night from a large portable cassette deck plugged into the wall by one of the very unfortunate patient's beds. (Not mine, thank God.) This no doubt helps digestion of medicines and the relaxation centres of the brain thus aiding sleep and the speedy recovery of the sick people contained therein.

The first night on the main ward I actually had no sleep whatsoever. I seemed to be the only one which it affected enough to want to do something about it though, and heaven forbid even have the nerve to complain. In truth I could see by the tired strained eyes and zombie-like state of the dishevelled patients as they paced around the ward the next day, that they were all having as hard a time as I was. Guantanamo could learn some lessons here, pay attention CIA.

But why did no-one seem to want to complain? Were they simply too scared? The night nurses were indeed formidable to behold and looked like they could hold their own in any potential rebellion of the sickly patients.

On the second night I could take it no more. My vocal chords were starting to work again, the oxygen mask being reduced already to part-time usage. I had been given strict instructions by Doctor Smith to try to speak at every opportunity, and to breathe as naturally as possible to expand my lungs and so help push the fluids and blood collected in my chest cavity down the long plastic tube to the disgusting glass jar now standing on the floor next to the head of my bed.

I decided to take his advice to heart in a little tete-a-tete with one of the nurses.

My concerns were twofold; I wondered if we could possibly have the lights dimmed for what was left of the rest of the night, which wasn't much, and also if we could drop the volume of the music a couple of decibels from jet engine to electric lawnmower.

I didn't yet know that sarcasm doesn't go down well in the Caribbean. It was a quick lesson.

I'm not sure I would go so far as to say 'if looks could kill', but the response was not a positive one and to be honest a little scary. Reading people's faces is always a bit hit and miss, but if I could put her expression into words it would be something like; 'Are you nuts? Who the hell do you think you are telling me how to run my ward?'

I decided not to challenge her authority any further in my delicate condition and to wait until morning to recruit some allies or at least await reinforcements, before attempting to resolve this unacceptable situation with strength in numbers.

No-one else seemed up for the fight so when Jenny arrived I implored her to do anything - beg, borrow, steal, yell - anything to get my insurance company to underwrite the cost of returning to a private room so that I could get some blessed sleep and at last try to recover. With the help of the local insurance company representative who was a very helpful chap - more of him later - this was quickly arranged, with the promise of a further ten nights' private treatment covered and more should it be required after that.

It was with great relief then that later that day and before the night staff arrived, I was returned to my little private room off the end of the ward. At night I made sure that the thick wooden fire door was always firmly shut, leaving the children's night-time simulated D-Day landings safely the other side of two inches of mahogany; Omaha outside, Utah within.

Chapter 16 - Journalistic licence

After a couple of early wobbles I made a very fast initial recovery.

Daily visits from the hospital physio garnered better and better results, and within a week I could walk cautiously around my room and sit in the armchair for a while, and soon raise myself unaided to wash, clean my teeth and generally feel less of an appendage to society. The omnipresent glass jar in the corner of the room filled once to the top with blood and then after being emptied and cleaned, filled half-way again, as the fluid slowly drained from my chest.

Being attached to this reminder of the events of February 2nd, feeling the cold metal move inside me with every twist of my torso or each time I breathed was like serving a community prison sentence; never able to stray farther than the maximum the plastic tube stretched as the terms of my house arrest. The rigid steel rod acted like a lever, pivoting at the top when the bottom moved and vice versa, making virtually every adjustment of my body a tense and apprehensive exercise as I waited for the inevitable scraping sensation of metal against my diaphragm or the inside of my ribcage. The only respite I got was lying completely still and slowing my breathing down to a whisper.

From time to time the physio or Jenny if she was around would carry the glass bottle for me, and I would excitedly escape the confines of my room for a few minutes and walk to the nurses' station on the adjacent ward and back. This was a welcome change of scenery and began the process of getting my frozen joints active again. I was still far too weak to even consider lifting the jar myself.

I took to covering the bottle with a pillow case, as in the heat of the room the blood started to go rancid and frankly it stank, making me feel sick and was none too welcoming for any guests who came to visit. The medical staff didn't like this one bit, and would tut their disapproval and remove the offending cloth whenever they saw it.

Trying to breathe properly was still incredibly painful, but it was all relative. Compared to the night of the shooting I would describe it as easy, compared to normal breathing it was not. The problem was that I could not afford to rest on my laurels, as if I wanted to get well then I would have to keep pushing the envelope and expanding my lungs until they were fully re-inflated. This meant constantly straining and disturbing the scar tissue inside my lungs and chest wall, which would have been quite happy to be left alone to heal.

The doctors would visit daily, and if Doctor Smith judged that the circumstances warranted it he would loosen the cleverly designed knots holding the curved steel end of my chest tube in place, and breaking the scabs at the surface ease the metal out a few centimetres. This was to stop new tissue forming around the base of the rod which would make it very hard to finally remove when the time was right.

My right lung had collapsed completely immediately the bullet entered, passing right through one of the upper lobes, and the massive blood loss that followed then put the left lung under enormous pressure partially collapsing that one too. Talking with the Danish doctors one day I got answers to one of my unresolved questions about that night; why was the blood on the floor of the bar black in appearance, and why then was it bright red later? The answer was oxygenated/deoxygenated.

Blood is naturally blue in colour and can appear quite dark, only when it's packed with oxygen from the lungs does it become red. The entry wound had released massive amounts of dark deoxygenated blood indicating that a major vein had been severed in my back. The blood from my chest however had been bright red and there was generally less of it, so the vessels damaged at the exit wound must have been smaller arteries carrying oxygenated blood.

This was actually a bit of good fortune, as arterial blood is under higher pressure so if it had been reversed and a major artery had been severed, it would have been far more difficult to stop the bleeding.

Unfortunately I had still continued to bleed internally even after the visible wounds were sealed, and the purpose of the steel tube was to allow all that blood to escape so that my lungs could reinflate.

The main danger now was that this blood filling up my chest was extremely nutrient rich, and my chest nice and warm, and if any bacteria had found their way into my ribcage during the shooting or subsequent surgery then this would provide a haven for infection.

And so I breathed, and it hurt, and the blood gradually drained, and after about a week I judged that I could eventually draw around half of my usual breath.

I became quite friendly with those two Danish doctors, who had more time to spare than their superiors. One day they came in - together as always - and informed me that the jar was to be disconnected and the drainage tube removed.

They detached the winding plastic pipe and placed a rubber stopper over it, and another over the protruding end of the steel rod in my armpit.

Free at last!

I was taken to get another X-ray just to make sure they were not taking the tube out prematurely, and excited at my first taste of freedom I pushed away all offers of help and walked myself hesitantly down the corridor. I arrived at the X-ray department pretty spent and had to be wheeled back to my room after, but it was great to be walking again.

A short time later Doctor Smith joined us and they set about prepping me for the tube removal which was to take place in my room. Jenny had just arrived for her daily visit so the privacy curtain was drawn around my bed, and she sat in the armchair by the window. The door was wedged ajar for any quick assistance that might be required of the nearby nurses while the tube was being withdrawn, and we began.

I was asked to sit upright, which I could now easily manage, and then gently twisted left and right by the doctors as the bullet holes were examined. My heart was listened to, and generally my body given a thorough check-up to further confirm that nothing was amiss.

There are several types of pain, some slow-burning and relentless, some quick and excruciating. I had been through the whole range since being shot, and I was beginning to get quite confident that I could take just about anything life threw at me.

As I sat on the edge of the bed the doctors twisted my body beyond the farthest point so far attempted, and the dried blood and scar tissue inside my ribcage adhering the lungs to the chest wall all tore at once.

This was probably the most painful single event of the whole shooting experience. It was so unexpected and so unbelievably excruciating that I forgot to breathe, temporarily preventing me from screaming. The fledgeling repairs to my lungs opened up forcing fresh blood to seep out of the skin around the rim of the steel tube, and then the scream came.

I can count the number of times I have actually viscerally screamed in my life on the fingers of one hand, and this was one of them.

Lungs normally move freely inside the chest wall as you breathe, slipping up and down inside the ribcage as the lungs expand and contract. After internal bleeding the lungs sometimes stick to the chest wall as the blood dries, which is what had happened in my case. If some of these scars tear a little at a time it can be incredibly painful, but here they sheared en mass.

It was like having a huge plaster ripped from the inside of my lungs.

The two young doctors looked extremely concerned, even the normally unflappable Doctor Smith dropping his guard momentarily and appearing worried, as the three of them rushed to support my wilting body in sudden danger of slipping off the edge of the bed.

Hearing the yell a nurse rushed in from the ward outside and as she entered the curtained-off section around the bed, the corner of the yellow fabric swished away in the speed of her passing. As it quickly flapped up before gently wafting down again I saw Jenny for the merest instant with a terrified look on her face leaning down and peering through the briefly open corner at the foot of the bed.

I was in the process of passing out, my brain started to fizz and my eyes rolled, and then I saw my wife, and knew that I could not do that to her. Seeing me fall to the floor, assuming that the doctors didn't catch me, after that scream, would have been terrible for her to witness. So I dug deep, and used this as an incentive to stay conscious. The initial spasm lasted perhaps fifteen seconds, with waves of aftershocks continuing for a lot longer after that. The first chance I got I caught my wife's eyes again and smiled to reassure her, I don't imagine all that believably.

This was the first of lots of similar experiences over the next few months, as the blood and other internal fluids dried and formed scabs on the surface of the lungs, which then stuck to my chest wall, and ripped when the scars decided that it was one movement too far. This in turn caused more bleeding, and more scabbing, and more sticking and more tearing. It was like a war of attrition.

On occasion it became so bad that I began to fear any kind of movement, and it was a sheer effort of will to not just lie still all the time, mortally afraid of the next assault. As time would go on and I hadn't had a scar tear inside me for a while, my confidence would build and I would wonder if the previous one that I had felt was the 'last one'.

I don't actually remember the moment I had the last attack, but it was many months later back in England. One day I just thought to myself; 'That hasn't happened in a while', and it never bothered me again.

In the BVI after this first event, the attacks continued. Daily at first, then once every two days, twice a week and so on. It was not linear though and sometimes weeks would go by without incident boosting my confidence, then I would have three rips in a day and be back to square one.

The funny thing about it was, it occurred most often when I laughed. There was something about the jogging of my body when chuckling and the sharp intake of breath that always set it off. It was fatal, but funny. I would find myself thinking about something amusing and start to laugh then catch it and instantly freeze, which would then make me laugh even more until I just had to go with it and wait for the ticking time bomb inside my chest to explode.

I saw this as quite karmic though. Almost nothing is all bad, and the shooting had certainly developed my philosophising. If the price of laughter was some discomfort, that was okay with me, and eventually, the smiles outlasted the pain, proving that happiness usually wins through in the end. The sun is always shining somewhere if you take the time to find it.

Having given up on the plan to remove the drainage tube for the moment, the plastic pipe being hastily reattached to allow for a new batch of fresh blood to escape me, on the eleventh and last day that I spent in Peebles Hospital, Doctor Smith returned and finally removed the metal from my body. It had already been detached from the jar and sealed off, but left inside me for a day or two longer in case I suffered another relapse. But now I was going home, and it was time to relieve me of the last of my shackles.

Alone this time, an obviously confident Doctor Smith after swabbing the area with iodine and loosening the retaining stitches, looked me in the eye and asked me to relax, and on the count of 'three', to breathe out slowly as he withdrew the rod.

I was fairly nervous, but overriding this I was anxious to have it out, so I braced myself and gripping the edge of the bed, counted along with Doctor Smith with my nodding head.

One, two... and... deeply exhale...

It was out! No drama at all. I can't say that it wasn't an interesting sensation having a foot of metal pulled from my body, but all things considered it was absolutely fine.

No scars ripping, no blood apart from a little oozing from the fairly substantial aperture under my armpit, and with a nifty little tweak of the sutures that had previously held the tube in place, the cleverly designed knot was pulled tight by Doctor Smith and the hole was sealed for good.

Another tick in the positive column, I was almost home free!

Home however was a subjective term, and where exactly that would be was still up for debate.

We had our apartment back on Virgin Gorda, but that was at the top of a flight of stairs, and not practical at all for me. It was decided therefore that we should decant to a hotel in Road Town for a week as a stop-gap measure and to gather our thoughts. This would be close enough to the hospital for me to receive my daily physio, and in case of any sudden medical issues help would be within easy reach. Once I had built up confidence in my recovery which hopefully this week would achieve, we could return to Virgin Gorda or head back to England or whatever else we decided to do. Jenny by now had returned to work part-time, and so we chose a hotel not far from the ferry dock to allow her easy transfer between Tortola and Virgin Gorda, and once my drainage tube had been removed signifying the end of my medical incarceration, we packed up my few possessions and made ready to depart.

Just before leaving Peebles Hospital, as Jenny was off buying a few provisions for our stay at the hotel, I received a phone call from England.

My little room did not have its own telephone, the hospital instead utilising the 1990's version of mobile technology, being a regular telephone with a very long cable pushed around on a trolley. A nurse wheeled this through into my room for me, I picked up the receiver and opened with a cheery hello.

A male voice on the other end of the line spoke;

'Hi, is this Craig Hantwell?'

'No, it's Hartwell.'

'Ah, sorry about that. I'm from the Sun Newspaper in England. I hear you've had a spot of bother over there?'

My hackles went up but I wasn't sure why.

'You could put it like that.'

Straight to business;

'You see we want to do a story about you. We've heard that you have had an adventurous life, living in Australia, travelling the world, and we heard also that you wear a crocodile tooth necklace...'

What the hell was this man talking about? How on Earth did he know that?

'Well it's a single tooth, not a necklace as such. But what do you have in mind?'

I have to admit, this was kind of intriguing.

He went on; 'Well, we want to do a story, you see; a kind of feature. We understand that you have a wife and that she travelled with you around the world. And - can I ask what you are doing in the Caribbean? Anyway, we want to do a feature, a big story, we are thinking front cover, and we want to say that you got shot in the chest, and that the bullet bounced off your crocodile tooth, which diverted the bullet saving your life. Kind of a real-life Crocodile Dundee thing. It'll be great.'

What?

'...Er... I'm not sure about that. First of all I didn't get shot in the chest, I got shot in the back, and the bullet exited my chest not the other way around, and anyway it just isn't true!'

'Ah I see. There may be some money in it for you. We do pay for these kinds of human interest stories, and so some sort of remuneration may be possible to arrange... if you sign off on the story we want to write of course.'

So it's true; journalists do make things up.

I was feeling a little uneasy about all this.

'Look, Mr. _____, it just did not happen that way, and I'm not going to sign up to something that isn't true. I'm sorry but the story is the story, and I don't see why it needs to be changed at all...'

'Okay Mr. Hartwell, Craig, sure sure, I understand. I see, yes... Look, have a think about it okay? This is how things are done, it's only a bit of fun, a good story, you know? Anyway, see how you feel and let me know what you decide. But we need your say-so if we are to go ahead, okay?'

I said I understood and asked what would happen if I didn't tell the story as he wanted to hear it.

'Ah, well, I don't know,' he said, scratching around, 'we will probably still do it the way you say it happened, but with a couple of column inches somewhere there is space in the paper I expect, if that is all you want.'

I said goodbye and repeated the story to Jenny when she returned a short while later.

The story of the shooting never appeared in the Sun at all to my knowledge, although it did make a few newspapers back in the UK and abroad, but for the most part it fizzled out before it ever got going.

After the phone rang off, I absentmindedly reached up to the silver rope-chain around my neck, feeding it through my fingers to find the crocodile tooth hanging in its little silver cup.

It wasn't there.

I got up and went to the mirror, and ran the chain a full three hundred and sixty degrees one way and then the other.

The clasp was there, the silver cup was there, but no tooth.

I took the tiny silver cup which had held the tooth by its root and tilted it up to the mirror. I could just make out a couple of chips of white enamel still stuck inside, and that was all.

How? When? Where was my good-luck charm?

I retraced the events of the past days, and realised that I couldn't recall actually seeing or feeling the tusk since the night of the shooting. Judging by the pieces of splintered root still remaining in the cup, it looked as if it had been forcibly broken off or wrenched out. But when? How would I not have noticed that? It was possible that it had come away of its own accord, but that seemed very unlikely. It had been around my neck for years, surviving everything life could throw at it. So why would it give up the ghost now?

I let the silver cup fall back loosely on the chain, and watched in the bathroom mirror as it came to rest above the three ugly black stitches at the top of my sternum.

If the tooth had still been there it would have hung precisely in front of the exit point of the bullet.

As I saw it there were two possibilities; either when I fell to the floor of the pub after the shooting, or during all the struggles to save my life, it had somehow cracked and broken away.

Or there was a second very unlikely scenario, that the bullet in a final act of destruction after exiting my body had hit the tooth and shot it off.

I know this sounds implausible, fantastic even. But the fact was that the tooth that normally sat exactly at the spot where the bullet left me, was no longer there. The fact is also that I had not noticed it since the night of the shooting and I didn't know of any other event of sufficient violence to cause its demise.

What's my conclusion? I'll call it an each-way bet, but I know which story I prefer.

Sometime later back in England I switched on the news one night to hear of a tragedy that had unfolded in Florida, where a couple of young British newlyweds had been attacked in their rental vehicle by some car-jackers. During the struggle the criminals had fired their guns and both the husband and wife had been shot.

The husband very sadly died, and his wife lived.

The next day a story appeared in the Sun describing how the metal clasp in the woman's bra strap had taken the impact and deflected the path of one of the bullets, thus saving her life while her husband tragically died. I think the headline was; 'Bra Saves Brit From Certain Death', or something like that.

I don't buy newspapers as a rule and didn't have a chance to check the name of the reporter who wrote that story, so I have no idea if it was the same guy who had spoken to me down a crackly phone line in Peebles Hospital, but I have my suspicions.

Since then I have seen several similar stories blazoned across the Sun, all variations on the theme, so I guess it's just one of those stories that keeps on giving.

Sex and death. Always a winning combination.

Chapter 17 - Living it up at the Hotel Americana

Yin yang. The positive and the negative; you need both to make a whole experience.

I have questioned often since the shooting what good came of it and what negatives remain. Some truly wonderful things happened both directly and indirectly as a result of the events of that night, so, was it worth it? Philosophically speaking you can work this a million ways, but it always comes back to the same thing: No it effing well wasn't.

Imagine someone gets run over by a bus, loses a leg, then in the hospital they meet a lovely physiotherapist. They fall in love, get married, have six kids and live happily ever after.

Was it worth losing the leg?

Whatever way you look at it the answer has to be no. They could have met on a train and been every bit as happy and everyone gets to keep their shoes.

The thing with events is they blindside you and give you no choice as to whether or not they occur, only how you deal with the aftermath. For me the most positive part of the whole experience has been the people I have met while negotiating the sometimes rocky road since that night.

I could spend a lot of time talking about how incredible so many people have been, and still forget to mention most of them, so I'll single out a few as they crop up and to everyone else I'll just say thank you.

One such person is Felicity Layton of Europ Assistance, the facilitating company whose purpose was to co-ordinate emergency insurance claims for underwriters. In other words these are the people you call if you lose your prescription in darkest Peru or have a bag stolen in Perth, and they will do their best to get you back on an even keel.

Felicity was the senior legal advisor for foreign claims at the time of the shooting, and was the first person Jenny spoke to when she called my travel insurance company's emergency helpline early that February.

The legal team was based in the leafy Sussex village of Cuckfield in the south of England, which was where Felicity and I met for the one and only time more than a year later. Prior to that she had been just a maternal voice at the other end of the line or an ornate signature at the bottom of a fax. But for the entire time I spent in the Virgin Islands following the shooting and for a long while after, she was a rock.

Legal issues were the beginning of her talents but far from the end, as over those turbulent first few weeks we needed and received help with everything from taxis to takeaways, prescriptions to X-rays, travel tickets, hospital bills and hotel bookings. Whatever it was, from four time zones away Felicity was there, and we were grateful. We may even have pushed it once or twice, but we were young.

Felicity did one other important thing for Jenny and me, by introducing us to the head of Romney Associates, Cyril Brandtford Romney.

Cyril was a man of many hats. As well as running his namesake company and being a sitting member of the Legislative

Council, he was the BVI representative for Europ Assistance and an ex-Chief Minister to boot. It was Cyril who arranged our week at the Hotel Americana located near to Road Town's large marina, and probably also provided the taxi to take us there with one from his own fleet. In the weeks that followed we were to meet with the extremely helpful Mr. Romney many times and in many different guises.

The hotel we had chosen was pleasant enough for our needs and catered mostly for business types. It was hardly the sort of place you would come to the Caribbean to spend a vacation in and most guests were attending conferences somewhere on Tortola or in transit to another island. However we were only to be here for a week and the convenience of the location was the deciding factor.

Much of my time during the stay when not engaging in gentle exercise or sleep was taken pondering the Jenny situation. I felt cruel wanting to end our marriage when Jenny wanted to keep trying, and was very aware of what she stoically must have been going through. With superhuman efforts she kept it all together - job, home, my care - all the time putting a brave face to the world and not letting on to anyone about our personal problems.

Several times I heard people say; 'At least you have each other', when what we were actually doing was bracing ourselves for a possible separation.

Having lunch together one day on our verandah, Jenny and I had a surprise visitor.

I had not of course told my wife of what had gone through my mind as I slipped in and out of consciousness on the trolley at the Spanish Town clinic, waking after a hefty dose of adrenaline to be confronted by my angelic Italian.

Agnes had previously only briefly popped into the hospital to visit me whilst on business in Road Town, literally putting her head around my door, a quick peck on the cheek and a how are you, and she was gone. Today she had more time and joined us for a bit of lunch. As she pulled up a chair at the balcony table I can't imagine for a second that Jenny didn't guess something of my feelings for her, and this only the third time we had ever met did nothing to assuage my passions.

About Agnes.

The only daughter of a wealthy Italian businessman, Agnes was in her late twenties and lived on Virgin Gorda with a young daughter of her own, born of a compatriot soon to be ex-husband who lived back in Europe who knew where.

Agnes's father along with his three business partners owned an exclusive resort half-way between Spanish Town and Leverick Bay, placing Agnes in charge as on-site general manager leaving them free to continue their wheeling and dealing on the continent knowing that their investment was safe in her capable hands.

The resort was called Mango Bay, and took up the entire southern half of Mahoe Bay, a crescent of golden sand with high green hills following the curve of the shore almost totally enclosing it from outside prying eyes.

The beach was protected from annoying day trippers by a mini reef which lay partially submerged along two thirds of the bay, stretching along the chord between the headland points and in places coming virtually all the way to the shore.

In between manicured jungle and lush lawns, secretive holiday villas hid in little private glades, accessed by winding sandy paths that all led inevitably to the one place that connected them - the beach.

The cherry on the icing of this very sweet cake was the main residence and office, which was a long three storey house built up the side of what were effectively the western slopes of Gorda Peak. From its vantage point above the centre of the bay the Caribbean Sea stretched away into the distance, and if you have to work for a living, there are worse views from an office window.

I came to know this place quite well, as on her visit Agnes invited us to come and stay with her when our week at the Americana was up. It was such a generous offer that at first we didn't really know what to say, but eventually a plan was hatched.

We would ask Felicity to cover us for another week's paid recuperation, and rather than stay at the hotel in Road Town, if Agnes could offer us a competitive rate (which she could, being the boss) then we'd transfer from Tortola to one of the beachside villas at Mango Bay, thereafter moving to the guest apartment in the main residence on the hill. This second part of our stay would be free, and last as long as circumstances and our hostess's generosity allowed. At some point in the near future some relatives of Agnes were coming to visit from Italy and if a villa was not available for them, then we would have to step aside and allow them to use the guest apartment, but we were assured by Agnes not to worry as we would cross that bridge when we came to it and a solution would be found that wouldn't leave us homeless.

With a concerted effort by Cyril and some gentle persuading of Felicity, we were given the okay from the insurance company for a week's extra paid convalescence, and all was set.

I had reached a peak meanwhile in my recovery. I recognised it as a peak even then because around half-way through our stay in the Americana my chest began to tighten after nearly two weeks of slow but steady progress. Alongside this I began to feel nauseous, and would feel ravenously hungry whenever I smelt food, only to find that as soon as it was placed in front of me I wanted to vomit. After a couple of days this began to concern me as I wasn't eating, and I needed to keep my strength up to continue moving forward with the healing process.

I mentioned these symptoms several times during the nurse and physio visits, but my fears were brushed aside as merely bumps in the road and informed that I should expect a few setbacks here and there.

This didn't satisfy me. I have always believed that we are responsible for fifty percent of our medical care and should never be entirely comfortable blindly placing our lives in the hands of others. If you listen to your body it will tell you much, and a doctor is, after all, just doing their job, but it is your body and you know when things aren't right.

So after two days complaining of my symptoms, I decided to take matters into my own hands and go back to the hospital to tell my doctors in person what was going on.

I arrived at the hospital alone, Jenny having gone to Virgin Gorda for the day to sort out a few things and to inform Joshua and Mary that unfortunately we would no longer require their apartment. Our religious hosts were none too pleased at losing us so soon into our tenancy, but Mary came over the following day to visit me at the hotel and express her condolences at what had befallen us, and I'm sure they didn't harbour any ill feelings.

I was shown into a room at the hospital where I found Doctor Smith and my two Danish friends, and explained my reasons for this unannounced visit. I was examined, my chest listened to and various things measured and checked.

Nothing untoward was found. I was according to the results progressing adequately, and told that I was well on the road to recovery.

Doctor Smith took the opportunity to take out the drawstring stitch which had sealed the armpit aperture, then short of time he asked a nurse to remove the bullet hole stitches.

The nurse chosen for the task seemed a little hesitant, and it appeared that she was quite inexperienced as she chose to try to cut the nylon thread with scissors rather than use a hooked scalpel. This meant that she had to virtually pull the stitches out in order to find enough free thread under the stitch to angle the point of the blade. The first two she managed this, but the third she couldn't and unbelievably just cut straight through the knot leaving part of the stitch still buried in the front bullet hole. I tried to point this out but she was having none of it and quickly threw the remains in the bin so that I couldn't check the evidence. She then moved onto the stitches in my back and I kept my fingers crossed that she would not make a hash of it with these.

Arriving back at the hotel I went into the bathroom and looking in the mirror noticed a black dot in the middle of the pink flesh in the front bullet wound.

I traced my finger over it and detected a little snagging sensation at my fingertip. I retrieved our medicine kit and took out a pair of tweezers, and carefully in the mirror caught hold of the protruding stitch and pulled.

And pulled.

In all about one centimetre of black wiry thread came out of the hole in my sternum. It just kept coming.

I then wondered if the nurse had made an equally haphazard job of the rear stitches, and took my shaving mirror and tried to angle both mirrors opposite each other in order to see behind my back.

It was awkward, and I had very recent bad memories of twisting my torso too much, but in the end I managed to get enough of a look to satisfy me that the nurse hadn't missed any of them.

In doing this I realised that until now I had not seen the entry point of the bullet, so I took a moment to study it in the double reflection. Twisting my arm behind me I could just about touch the hole with my fingertips. The wound was high up in my upper back, and seemed larger than the bullet's exit hole, which was contrary to everything I had ever heard about entry and exit points in gunshot wounds. It was also far smaller than the fist-sized opening I had imagined was there in those first uncertain minutes after the shooting.

I looked at the reflection of the pink indentation in my upper back, and reflected what an innocent ounce of lead can do.

Chapter 18 - The road to Mango Bay

We returned to Spanish Town and from there to Mango Bay* if not with a spring in our step then most definitely looking forward to the next and hopefully easier phase of our stay in the BVI.

(*Mango Bay was the name of the resort; Mahoe Bay was technically the name of the beach on which it sat, although they were becoming interchangeable.)

Things were not going so smoothly at Jenny's work. The two busiest times of the year and peak tourist seasons in the BVI were and are Christmas and Easter. July and August are generally too hot when only the hardiest sun worshippers venture to this part of the Caribbean, although if you can brave the soaring temperatures there are bargains to be had.

Lent was well underway and Easter approaching, Ash Wednesday having fallen during our stay at the Americana, and Jenny's manager was getting increasingly frustrated at her lack of attendance. I think her boss was clinging to the thought that I might leave the BVI to seek further medical treatment, and Jenny remain to see out her contract without the distraction of a sick husband. To be fair her intuition wasn't too far off the mark as little did she know that due to our marital difficulties this was a very realistic possibility.

It was with some relief then that we were back on Virgin Gorda, and especially from her boss's point of view at Mango Bay, which lay half-way between the two salons on the northern and southern parts of the island so increasing the chance of Jenny being able to maintain a normal work schedule.

I was noticeably losing weight by this time and my new-found strength starting to sap, and this was becoming more and more of a concern. I tried to convince myself that it was no big deal, and passed it off when others commented on my thinning frame as being the result of the exertions of the few short walks I managed to take and other bits of exercise, but I felt inside that there was more to it than that.

Every moment was new territory for me so I didn't really know what to expect on a day to day basis, but something was definitely not right.

Agnes met us at the ferry dock as we stepped off a Speedy Boat and onto the quayside dead on a hot sticky noon. It may even have been the same boat in which I had travelled under different circumstances three weeks earlier, but in the daylight and full of noisy passengers it all looked very different.

At the start of what turned out to be a surreal journey to Mango Bay, firstly we went to Joshua and Mary's house to collect the last of our belongings that hadn't already been moved, and then we drove north out of Spanish Town towards Gorda Peak. We stopped briefly at the International School to pick up Agnes's daughter, who jumped gaily into the back seat alongside Jenny and buckled herself in. Introductions were made and Jenny chatted away with her new friend. I remained nervous about twisting my body so I called out my greeting and kept my head facing firmly forward.

As we left the Valley Agnes had one final stop to make, explaining that it was soon her daughter's birthday, and there would be a children's party later that week at the house for which she needed some provisions. I finally after consciously relaxing my spine turned and saw a beautiful young girl with long sun-bleached curls and one tooth prominently missing in her generous smile. In her hand she held a silver toy plastic revolver which was pointing directly at my chest. She kept her grin which might even have grown impossibly wider and looked at me in a 'Stick 'em up!' gesture.

Nobody really knew what to do at this point, as the little girl obviously had no clear idea of the reasons behind our visit, and where she had got the toy gun from was also a complete mystery to all including her mother. Agnes from her driving position smiled a little shocked smile and we all burst out laughing, thankfully with no chest tearing for me, leaving her daughter's smirk to change from one of glee to slight confusion as to why the reaction to her little joke had exceeded her wildest expectations.

Perhaps she had picked up comments about shootings etc. from her mother in conversation with visitors at Mango Bay over the past weeks and thought that if this is what adults are talking about then she would join in the fun. Who knows, but it was a comedy moment even if slightly awkward.

We pulled into a small hardware store, Agnes saying over her shoulder as she parked the people carrier that she wouldn't be long as she was just going to pick up some 'aliem' for the party.

I wasn't sure what she could possibly mean, because it sounded like she was going to return in a minute or two with a little green man on her arm, so I asked her to clarify.

Agnes repeated a little curtly that she was buying 'aliem' from the shop and would only be a couple of minutes if we didn't mind waiting. I think our Italian friend was getting a touch frustrated at her inability to make herself understood with what was usually pitch perfect English, as when I asked a third time she almost shouted; 'Aliem! We always have aliem at Italian parties! Don't you?'

With visions of her coming back from the shop with a tentacle wrapped around her shoulder now firmly in my mind and thinking that she must mean a kids entertainer or clown of some kind, and now wondering if there was enough room for another person or creature in the car, Agnes emerged from the shop with a large packet of party balloons and a medium-sized canister of helium with which to inflate them.

I breathed a sigh of relief as I was beginning to think that either the hospital had given me way too many drugs or not quite enough.

On another day I would have hijacked the canister and squeaked out a few songs with the inert gas for some amusement on the journey, but I thought that under the circumstances I had better not.

We continued on uninterrupted now, leaving the tarmac of the main road just before the mountain pass and turning to skirt the hillside with the sea far down below us to the left. We passed some old mining works by the side of the road, and Agnes played tour guide telling us that centuries ago British tin miners from Cornwall had arrived on Virgin Gorda to mine copper, at the time Cornish miners being revered as the best in the world.

As we drove past several long abandoned red-bricked huts and still solid mining towers, we could see periodically lines of smaller towers leading down to the water's edge and continuing quite a distance out to sea, with isolated equally-spaced constructions visible above the surface of the water far from shore.

These marked the locations of deep shafts and tunnels dug under the sea bed where the miners had found a seam of ore and followed it as far as technology at the time allowed. It was quite amazing looking at these lines of ancient crowns poking up above the surface of the sea, and considering that those hardy men and women built all this without the aid of electricity or modern equipment, some even constructed before the age of steam, just utilising the sweat of their brow and some damned fine ingenuity.

Five minutes or so after leaving the main road we turned and drove down through the gate leading to the Mango Bay Resort.

Arriving at a small collection of buildings, to the left I saw a large open-sided lean-to built into the rocks. This served as the garage with space enough for four or five family cars under its corrugated iron roof. To the right of the concrete driveway was the unassuming door to the Mango Bay office. This was also used as a convenient side entrance to the living accommodation, the coffee room at the rear of the office having a dual function as the utility room for the main residence, with another door at the back leading directly into Agnes's huge kitchen and open-plan living area. We walked through the office to the sounds of dogs barking from somewhere nearby, and took in the breathtaking view from her lounge.

Floor-to-ceiling windows ran the entire length of the room, immediately outside of which was an equally long balcony wide enough for a substantial gathering should they ever feel the need. Everything overlooked the bay, from the rocky points to the extreme left and right, to the golden arc of sand below.

To the right we could see lines of low foaming waves breaking over shadowy underwater obstructions - the reef - creating lagoons of placid water in front of it close to the shoreline. A few sailing dinghies and windsurfing boards were drawn up onto the beach underneath some palm trees, an empty hammock gently swaying in the breeze between two trunks by some steps leading down to the sand.

For me Valley Trunk still had the edge, but it was a close call.

On the plus side here we had the advantage of actually living next to the beach, in luxurious surroundings that we could ordinarily only dream of.

We brought our things through into the main house, Agnes carrying our largest suitcase thoroughly emasculating me, and up some stairs accessed from the far end of the balcony leading to the self-contained guest apartment. This was more or less directly on top of the lounge and had its own private balcony and yes, another swinging string bed.

You can't beat a hammock on a hot day, no sir.

Although we were to spend our first week in one of the secluded villas by the shore, we didn't need much to sustain us down there as everything was already provided, so rather than move twice, the bulk of our belongings were placed in the guest bedroom until we returned next week.

The next task was to go down to the beach and find our designated slice of paradise for the next seven days. The meticulously unkempt jungle which the careful eye could see was designed to look all natural weather-beaten charm but probably cost a fortune to achieve, was accessed via a steep straight concrete road running parallel to the front of the house. This dropped perhaps twenty metres with a sharp bend to the left at the bottom leading eventually via a few more twists and turns to the beach, with small lightly gravelled footpaths spinning off along the way presumably to the individual hidden villas.

After having to endure watching the two women fetch and carry and more than a little embarrassed at my feeble condition, I decided that there was no time like the present to get a little premature jump start on some basic hillwalking, and so I manfully said that I did not need to be driven down to the villa, but would make my own way. I brushed off the concerns of my two carers and strolled as nonchalantly as I could manage down the hill, the surface of which had fortunately been ribbed for traction helping prevent my unsteady feet from slipping.

Not surprisingly going downhill was quite easy, the steep gradient meaning that it was more of a controlled descent with the aid of gravity, the biggest problem being putting my feet in front of each other fast enough to keep up and which was more difficult than I remembered.

Agnes had swapped the people carrier for a pick-up meanwhile, and she and Jenny followed me down at a snail's pace in this procession of man leading machine, directions being called out when necessary in thick Italian, until eventually we reached our destination and the point where the vehicle could go no further.

The girls once again did all of the grafting unloading what items we had brought with us, and leaving them on the verandah - it was inconceivable that there were thieves in this private resort - we went back to the road for Agnes to show us around and particularly the beach.

We were joined now by Jano, another Italian from that night at the Bath and Turtle but whom I had never actually formally met (although he had seen me bloodied and the worse for wear). An ex-soldier, Jano was the new maintenance man for the Mango Bay estate, recently arrived and fresh from Europe. He spoke very little English, and had brought Agnes's bilingual daughter along for the walk, as well as two boisterous guard dogs which playfully fought each other as they jogged along beside Jano who they had easily accepted as their latest master.

So began a short tour of the beach, first walking to the northern end then retracing our steps to the southern point where we climbed a rocky path to a bare concrete platform, half-completed as the ground floor of what was designed to be a spectacular room with a view. The previous owners of Mango Bay, Agnes explained, had begun building their dream home here on the bluff between two bays before running into money difficulties and selling up to her father's group of business associates. She confided to us that it was a dream of hers to one day find the time to complete the project and live there with Alicia, my toothless would-be assassin. It would be a hell of a house to be sure, but as I looked around at the cement of the columns and deck which had been exposed to the harsh Caribbean sun and salt spray unprotected by walls and anti-corrosion materials for several years, I questioned whether it was still safe to build on. Agnes brushed me off with a 'I guess they knew what they were doing when they built it' comment, which wasn't really the point.

She then stood on the edge of the platform and pointed to various parts of the bay visible from our viewpoint, indicating in one place a section of sand hidden in the trees about half the size of a tennis court where the beach was missing. A trench about one and a half metres deep at the landward edge, about one metre at the seaward had been removed. Broken palm roots and stranded subterranean grasses stuck out of the fibrous sandy walls, binding them and keeping them from collapsing.

Early one morning a few weeks previously, the businessman owner of the villa behind the scarred landscape (the northern part of the bay was individually owned and subdivided into irregular plots) had turned up with a gang of labourers from one of his construction sites and proceeded to scoop up several lorry loads of sand with heavy machinery and truck it off to a nearby building project. This was irresponsible and highly illegal, but the businessman was 'connected' locally and so untouchable, especially for a female foreign resort manager to attempt to tackle unless Agnes and her father really wanted to annoy the plugged-in neighbourhood bigwig. I had met this builder in my first weeks on Virgin Gorda when I was still looking for a job, it being he who explained to me that the only employment he could reasonably offer would be as a supervisor or construction foreman, which would have meant weeks of paperwork and visa applications, for a job which I wasn't sure if I even wanted, so I had left his office and let it go. He had seemed to me at the time a nice guy, and had a reputation as such, but this assault on the environment of his home island was not such a positive legacy. And all for the sake of a few hundred dollars to import a little more sand, for a guy who was a multi-millionaire anyway.

Later I found out that he had died whilst in command of a backhoe (a small single-man digger used on construction sites) after it toppled negotiating a steep slope a little way up the coast from Mango Bay on another development. The machine had no safety cabin protecting the driver, and when it fell and rolled down the hill he fell underneath it. What the boss of the firm was doing driving the digger is anybody's guess, but probably for the exhilaration of it and a chance to escape the office for some light relief, which didn't turn out as planned.

This loss of beach was currently of major concern to Agnes as due to the prevailing sea currents, the rolling ocean waves had gradually scoured out a section of the southern bay right in front of two of her ocean-fronted villas, in an attempt by Mother Nature to rebalance the beach and fill in the rudely stolen gap.

Eventually the ocean would no doubt replace the lost sand, but for now erosion had undercut some of the foundations of several of her villas and showed no signs of slowing. I asked what she intended to do about this legally, and Agnes said that in practical terms she could do nothing, as although she was in the right, fighting this battle may make some powerful enemies, so it was better to let it go, boiling though this made her feisty Italian blood. One day I was out with Agnes and she saw the offending businessman, calling out across the street; 'Hey, ___, what have you done with my beach?' with a sarcastic smile; returned by a sheepish one and silence.

Tides have little variation in the BVI in comparison with other places on the globe, and the distance between high and low horizontally is only a few metres, vertically usually less than one, so most of the time this trench just under the tree-line was dry. In storm surges though the water would creep up the beach and fill the hole like a half-constructed swimming pool with a quicksand base. The infrequency of this weird sight prolonged Agnes's agony as the natural re-filling process and so the return of the status quo at Mahoe Bay was destined to take a very long time. She could have paid for her own sand to fill in and replace what her neighbour took, but that might encourage more eco-vandalism, so she let sleeping dogs lie and watched as part of her beloved beach gradually slid north bit by bit.

Politics, it's the same everywhere.

On the way back from the point my confidence was up, so as we walked along the beach with me slightly ahead of the group, I broke into a swift jog along the shoreline. I only ran for ten or fifteen seconds, with more braggadocio than brains, braving the shouts from Jenny and Agnes for me to stop and the total indifference of Jano and little Alicia.

I carried on for as long as I thought was wise and then stopped and turned to face the group with a smile countering their worried scowls. It hadn't hurt, and apart from feeling my back noticeably stiffen I felt okay. I was impatient for some tangible evidence of my physical rehabilitation and felt that another milestone in my recovery had been reached, being my first official run.

Later that night as we lay in bed listening to the cicadas in the glade outside our shutters, I felt my chest twinge sharply again, and began to regret my showing off earlier.

The next day I awoke bright and early and whilst doing the washing up at our kitchenette sink I heard the noise of a vehicle trundling down the concrete slope from the main house. I was curious who it might be at this unconscionable hour, so leaving Jenny in bed I quickly threw on a pair of shorts and a t-shirt to go and investigate. It was Jano bringing the dogs down to the beach in the pick-up for a post dawn walk. Why he brought the energetic hounds that couple of hundred metres through the woods in the open back of a truck heaven only knows, but perhaps it was the thought of trudging up the steep slope again after his exercise that brought about this touch of laziness.

I emerged at the side of the gravel road as the vehicle passed, Jano stopping and in pigeon English inviting me to join him.

He parked, the impatient dogs hurdling the sides of the truck before Jano could release the tailgate. As we walked along the beach the emerging sun behind Gorda Peak kept the whole of Mahoe Bay in shadow, including the ocean as far out as we could see save a few telltale orange reflections off the peaks of the farthermost islands beyond the bay.

Alongside us trotted Mango Bay's two four-legged guards; one a pedigree German Shepherd who was second in command in the pack under Jano, and a young Rhodesian Ridgeback mongrel, who was completely nuts.

The normally dead straight tuft of thick black hair that runs from the nape of a Ridgeback's neck to the tail giving them their name, was on this happy unfortunate's back crooked and uneven, in places disappearing altogether before reappearing in clumps and continuing down his spine. This seemed in perfect harmony with his nature, as he leapt high over the trotting Alsatian from side to side, crouching and barking, tempting his older compadre into a game of chase to which the elder dog every now and then relented and joined in.

He was obviously little more than a pup and extremely athletic, being able to jump right over the senior dog from a standing start, and would nip at the Alsatian's heels then dart out of the way of a lightening rebuke as he perpetually harassed his shaggy kennel mate.

Every few minutes he would stop and comically rub the side of his head along the ground apparently attempting to satisfy some terribly annoying itch in his ears. As he stood up straight for the first time right in front of me, staring inquisitively at this new potential playmate, his right ear flopped lazily down while his head remained perfectly still, the left ear standing erect and pointing forwards as he sized me up. He then looked past me and stared out to sea as if he had spotted a potential seaborne invasion that he must protect us all from, before scratching his head again and remembering that he hadn't hassled his buddy for at least ten seconds which he then returned to with aplomb.

Jano made a motion with his hands signifying that there was some sort of a problem with the Ridgeback's ears, and Agnes further explained later that the dog did indeed have an infection, probably caught from the ocean as the dogs loved to swim in the bay, and that the poor creature couldn't seem to shake it off no matter how many times they applied medicinal drops into the struggling dog's asymmetrical ears. He incessantly rubbed the side of his head along the ground whether cement, sand or grass, which probably made things a whole lot worse.

However he seemed happy enough, and full of life as he bounded around on the sand. I wasn't sure how long this younger dog would remain content to be the runt in the pack as I knew this breed, originally being bred to protect livestock from lions in Africa, and they were hard as nails and grew to a formidable size and could certainly take an Alsatian in a fight. What the result of this power struggle to come was, I do not know.

Over the next week the pain in my chest grew worse, and the fever that I had not experienced since Peebles Hospital returned, slowly at first, then with a vengeance.

Waking every morning to the sound of the ocean lapping the shore just metres from our bed, a sea breeze rustling through palm fronds, chirruping birds and chattering insects taking away any feelings of loneliness I might have once Jenny left for the day, made it all too easy to ignore my deteriorating symptoms. When I ventured outside it wasn't a case of seeking the sun but more of seeking shade from it. Even indoors with all the windows and shutters closed tight, somehow streaks of sunlight still managed to find their way in making escape from ultraviolet should you desire it well-nigh impossible.

Most nights we would take Jenny's jeep on the short journey up to the house on the hill, where Agnes would cook and we would sit together on the balcony or in her lounge, watching TV or listening to music. Sometimes guests would come over - most of the residents in the villas seemed to be repeat customers and knew Agnes quite well and vice versa, many coming to join us for dinner or drop in for a coffee before bed.

One evening our own long lost couple from Chicago came to visit us at the villa, bringing some fresh fish that the husband had caught that day on a yacht charter, and he and I prepared and cooked them whilst the girls drank wine. We ate as the sun set on our west facing verandah, sharing stories of poor health with a laugh and a joke, and all was temporarily fine with the world. They had extended their holiday due to his worsening condition, and were flying home to Chicago in a day or two, and we were the only real friends they had made on their trip. As they said goodbye and walked up the hill to where they had parked their car, I worried for them both and what awaited them back at their own waterside home in Illinois.

No-one mentioned the previous job offer, as events had overtaken all of us by this time.

The next morning I could hardly get out of bed, and a worried Jenny went and got Agnes who took the decision that I should come up to the main house immediately and stay there where I could be kept an eye on. And so our stay on the beach ended on a slightly sour note. It had been a week of escapism, with Jenny and I spending what was to be our last quality time together for a while.

It was clear that this severe pain was a wake-up call and the time to get my head out of the sand had arrived. As the day progressed, our first in Agnes's guest apartment albeit a day or two early, I took the time to assess my situation.

There were two issues preventing me from leaving the BVI straight away, one being the physical act of flying in a jet aeroplane which is not permitted for insurance reasons if you have suffered recent lung trauma. For this to be allowed your health must be vigorously checked and a doctor sign a document to the effect that in their opinion the patient will not suffer a relapse and sustain a collapsed lung or other injury during normal passage in a pressurised cabin ten kilometres up in the sky. This is even more crucial in the event of a sudden cabin depressurisation, where the emergency oxygen masks that air hostesses endlessly demonstrate but no-one ever actually thinks they will have to use, are deployed.

On the rare occasion that these masks are necessary, if you have recent severe damage to your chest then the loss in cabin pressure can be debilitating and in a worst case scenario fatal.

The other reason I wanted to stay in the BVI for a little while longer, apart from personal issues between Jenny and me and not wanting to leave this wonderful place and swap it for overcast streets and significantly less naturally joyous people, was that I wanted to see my attacker if not in court, then under court proceedings, and that as yet had not happened. He had been arrested on various charges, some very serious, but then nothing had moved since and the case appeared to be stalling.

The gunman having been in custody since the night of the shooting, had been complaining bitterly about his incarceration, and unbelievably was making moves through a lawyer to be released pending a future trial. He was worried apparently that in prison he could come face to face with some undesirables that he had helped to put away as a serving police officer, and which might not be conducive to his good health. The argument being put forward by his lawyer was that to release him now would be 'for the well-being of himself and his family', which does make one kind of wonder at his grip on reality.

For my part I had given a police statement in the first few days from my hospital bed once I could more or less talk, but I wanted more than anything to give evidence before a court. I was adamant about this as it is far harder to ignore a sworn deposition than a police statement, and I didn't want to go back to England and worry that it was all being swept under the carpet - out of sight, out of mind. Unfounded or not, these were my concerns, and my desire to get my voice heard by a Judge grew steadily until it was of paramount importance.

We no longer had to worry about finances curtailing our stay, as Agnes was being a perfect host, but day by day Jenny was getting more and more frustrated at work, and she needed to stop and begin her own recovery from the emotional trauma of the past weeks. There were actual swearing slanging matches now taking place between Jenny and her boss, and this could not go on much longer.

On the morning of Tuesday 1st of March, I followed Jenny out through the Mango Bay office to her jeep parked under the lean-to. As we said goodbye for the day and she climbed into her red jalopy, I noticed with horror an enormous orange spider slowly making its way up the outside of the driver's door and looking like it had every intention of climbing over the open window to join Jenny for her drive over the mountain to Leverick Bay.

I shouted as Jenny pulled out of the garage and on the third yell she stopped, the kerfuffle alerting Agnes at work at her desk who came rushing out to see what the fuss was about.

I said what I had seen and Jenny nervously opened her door and jumped out onto the concrete, but the hitchhiking arachnid was nowhere to be found. We searched in vain for about ten minutes until Jenny really had to go as she had a client waiting, and eyeing carefully every dark corner of the jeep she gingerly climbed aboard, started the engine and drove off up the road.

I don't know what species it was, having a huge bulbous honey coloured body with no discernible head and long spindly black legs, but I had never seen anything like that monster before.

I had horrible visions of the freeloading passenger crawling across Jenny's lap as she negotiated the tricky mountain pass or leaping from the gear stick onto her hand and scuttling up her arm causing her to lose control on the sheer road, but Jenny was made of strong stuff because off she went, and as she turned the corner for the main road north, I kept my fingers crossed that the freak of nature had jumped out with her outside the Mango Bay office and not got back in.

That evening I was glad to see that my wife returned safe and sound and had even forgotten about the spider incident until I mentioned it.

During the day I had tried calling Doctor Smith at Peebles Hospital to arrange an appointment, but was informed that he was about to travel off-island somewhere to a conference or some such thing, and would not be back for several days. Declining an offer from his secretary to see him for a non-specific date upon his return, Agnes and I broke out the Yellow Pages and scoured the medical section for an alternative interim solution to my chest pain and fever.

The word google in 1994 still meant the sound doe-eyed grandmothers made to newborn babies, so it took a while to find what we were looking for as we let our fingers do the walking. Eventually we came across the name of a private clinic in Road Town, run by a Doctor Robin Tattersall. He appeared to be a jack of all trades in the medical profession, concentrating a lot of his efforts lately on plastic surgery judging by the yellow and black box advert, but my options being quite limited I called anyway and was informed by his secretary that he was an English physician, highly qualified and experienced in many areas of medicine, and she felt sure that he could help.

The Bougainvillea Clinic was owned and operated by him, and seemed quite the place to go if a little sprucing up away from the prying eyes of the paparazzi was what you were looking for. Rich and well-known clients could come and have a discreet nip and tuck, then spend a week or two by the pool which the hospital also had on-site, and go home with their neighbours and work colleagues none the wiser apart from some miraculously tightened sagging eyelids and a slightly less mobile smile.

Doctor Tattersall's assistant on the telephone had heard of me and the shooting, which would have been surprising to be fair if she had not, and spoke for her boss in saying that he would be pleased to see me on the following Thursday, in two days' time.

By now I was using the painkillers which Doctor Smith had prescribed at the hospital at an alarming rate, having first held off on taking them altogether. I felt good knowing that in a day or two I would have a fresh pair of eyes examine me and see if we could get to the bottom of why I was suddenly starting to feel so ill.

For now though some natural endorphins were coursing through my veins. Tomorrow was my twenty fifth birthday, and with Agnes's prompting a party had been planned at the scene of my near demise - the Bath and Turtle in the municipal square in Spanish Town.

There is nothing like a party to keep your spirits up, and I had more reason than most to celebrate. But this was not the end of the good news, because prior to that, on this very evening, we had all been invited - Jenny, Jano, Agnes and I, to a party on Necker, Sir Richard Branson's private billionaire's hideaway lying in the waters north of Leverick Bay.

This would be Jenny's and my first proper night out since the shooting, and what more salubrious way to celebrate than this? We really did need to let our hair down and I think we both deserved it after the month that we'd just had, and for a chance to visit the famed Necker Island where guests would normally pay twenty five thousand dollars per night for the privilege - and that's in 1994 - chest pain or no chest pain, this was one party that I had no intention of missing.

Chapter 19 - Party like it's 1994!

Jenny had worked on Necker Island many times since arriving in the BVI, as it was one of the accounts that her boss ran amongst the other elite client hotels which Virgin Gorda is a-wash with.

Necker itself is a small ultra-exclusive resort that is run both as a family home-away-from-home for the British billionaire entrepreneur Sir Richard Branson, and at the same time there is a second compound of buildings on the island which are rented out on a per-night basis to any who can afford the luxury of your own island for anything from a weekend break to a month-long vacation. If you can take a month off work that is, and the million dollar price tag for such a lengthy stay doesn't faze you.

If one were to name drop on just some of the great and the good, the rich and the famous who have holidayed on Necker, it would be a kiss-and-tell book in its own right, as most of everyone who is anyone has at some point made the little crossing from Virgin Gorda or Beef Island to Necker, or else if time really is of the essence utilised one of the charter helicopters available to transport guests from nearby St Thomas, Puerto Rico or Antigua.

You can walk around the whole island in an hour, and there are secluded private beaches, country walks to take a stroll and pass the time, a few hills to hide behind, and sea to swim or sail in to your heart's content, and for the high - but fair, if you see it those terms - price of a night on Necker, the world is your oyster and nothing is too much trouble for the comfort

216

and delight of the guests ensconced within. Homer Simpson if he stayed would definitely be provided pork chops, at four o'clock in the morning, should his rumbling stomach desire it.

The guests' accommodation is usually booked solid for months or on certain dates even years in advance, and Richard's extended family come and go as they please to the main residence. But every once in a while the place is free of guests, and when this rare event happens (sorry Richard if you ever read this but I have heard that he likes a good party so probably wouldn't begrudge it too much) the staff hold a little (read large) soiree for the friends and colleagues of those who ordinarily do the serving. This then becomes their time to live a little of the life of luxury that they work so hard to provide for others on a daily and nightly basis.

One such event was occurring this very night, and all of Virgin Gorda was buzzing with the prospect of an invitation to attend.

Jenny had been invited, as she was known to be one of the blue-collar workers who actually grafted on Necker. Agnes was invited as she was a well-known personage in those parts and knew everyone likely to be giving out the invitations to such a highly sought-after event. Jano was invited as he would be providing the transport there for Agnes courtesy of his latest toy - a brand spanking new twenty foot Boston Whaler, now moored on the narrow jetty at Mango Bay. And I was invited through Jenny my wife, Agnes my friend, Peter the manager of Necker, Chris the assistant manager, and if all else failed, my old amigo Gatecrasher would probably have had a look-in had any of the others not thought to pick up the phone and put my name down on the list of entrants.

We were all quite excited at the prospect of a night out, but no-one really wanted to show too much exuberance - or perhaps it was just me that was excited and everyone else really was as cool as I was trying to act - as we drove in Agnes's utility vehicle down to the Mango Bay jetty. This concrete structure had been built at the same time as the rental villas and intended for use as a tourist drop-off point, presumably to add a touch of extra exclusivity to what was already a fairly exquisite private resort. In practice though it was rarely used, as it was just as easy to arrive by the frequently running scheduled ferry services that zipped around the islands all day every day, and then taxi from Spanish Town or be picked up by a Mango Bay member of staff in one of their vehicles from the yacht harbour. In the ten days or so that I had been here the only boats that I had ever seen use the jetty were the occasional fishing charter that picked up or delivered guests from their day-sail bookings, and Jano's beautiful sleek and shiny shallow-hulled pleasure boat. It was a magnificent fun-looking craft, with a tight blue canvas awning above a central standing console and steering wheel, with room around the decks to the front, rear and sides for half a dozen people to relax or sunbathe in comfort, or else travel and arrive in style, which was our intended plan for the evening.

It was almost dark when we walked down to the end of the jetty and climbed aboard the boat where Jano was already making final preparations to depart. The glistening white hull shimmered its reflection on the ocean and it all felt so exotic, for a fleeting moment like stepping into a scene from a movie or the life of a person of privilege.

Being the tropics and close to the Equator, sunrise and sunset are very quick, and by 6.30pm the first few stars were already blinking on in the quickly darkening sky. We were soon ready to cast off, Jano with military precision slowly and carefully steering his pristine craft between the sheets of coral which reached up from the seabed dangerously close to the surface, ready to prang a Caribbean newbie's pride and joy if the course sailed was not precise and true. In this task Jano was aided by Agnes, guiding from the bow with her intimate knowledge of the Mahoe Bay waters.

Once clear of the reef we turned to the right and he let out the throttle, building smoothly to a consistent high-pitched roar. As we raced along, the well-crafted lines of the hull deflected the foaming bow-wave safely past us to the sides and rear, so saving me from a liberal dousing and the girls from a major hairdo malfunction. (Their styles for the night had been beautifully coiffured by a hairdresser friend of Agnes who had come over to Mango Bay that afternoon to help make the girls look the business for the party. It didn't require that much work to be honest, as both Jenny and Agnes were no slouches in the looks department, and thankfully I no longer had my shark t-shirt to wear and look like an idiot, which looking back on it was a definite plus.)

The journey to Necker took far longer than I had expected knowing something of the geography of the BVI, and I started to wonder if my painkillers would last the evening. I wasn't so much concerned about the voyage there, it was the return that bothered me. We took a long fiddly and circuitous route around the north-western tip of Virgin Gorda, Jano not being too familiar with the local waters and doubly so at night, when it is extremely easy to lose track of which island is which if you stray too far beyond easily recognisable landmarks. The result of this was that he followed the coast very closely and steered the boat into and around virtually every cove and headland so as not to lose his way.

Finally we entered the North Sound, which was followed by several; 'No, it's this one...' - 'No, it's <u>this</u> one!' arguments between Agnes and Jano in their native shared language, as we peered through the blackness at each subsequent island that we cruised past in the disorienting night. (I knew enough Italian to decipher at least this much of the heated discussions.)

We eventually found Necker's newly-built jetty which had been completed just a few weeks before, and thus which Agnes had never seen but Jenny was able to confirm as belonging to the island.

As Jano cut the throttle and we decelerated sharply, suddenly many other boats loomed up out of the gloom all heading for and loading or unloading groups of people onto the dock, confirming to us that we were indeed at the right place.

The partygoers would then head for the shore, and one of a steady stream of vehicles stop and gather the guests up, driving them up the road to a glowing group of buildings lying a short distance away beyond a high silhouetted pagoda, dominating all on a hill in the centre of the island. There were a few security guards milling around sporting clip-boards and walky-talkies, but they didn't seem to be taking or checking the names of the new arrivals, so perhaps the 'by invitation only' story had just been a ruse to keep the numbers down.

Some of the new arrivals would muck in and help the constantly arriving boats find a space on the jetty to moor up and decant their human cargo. In this spirit Jano stayed behind for a while to help the next batch of revellers pulling up as Jenny, Agnes and I walked down the crowded platform to the shore.

Once there we mingled with a small crowd of locals and waited with them for the next vehicle to drive us up to the party. Agnes appeared to know one or two as she went off to chat, while Jenny and I stood around feeling a little off balance and not knowing quite what to expect next.

When our turn came to leave, we climbed in the back of a large clean pick-up, everybody squeezing tightly together like sardines, which would have been uncomfortable if we had been good friends with our fellow passengers, but as we didn't know them it was fairly awkward too.

A young Islander with presumably his girlfriend sitting on his lap stared at me as we bumped along the unlit road up to the main house, from where we could now hear music coming into earshot and growing until it blared loudly across the night air. I looked over at him, unable to determine his expression, and in the poor light calmly returned his gaze.

'Where you fram?', he drawled in my general direction after a few seconds.

I wasn't entirely sure if this guy was a friend or a foe.

'England', I replied.

It seemed a fair question so I returned it; 'And where are you from?'

'I born here.'

Short and to the point, you had to admire him for that.

He then went on;

'England is the Mother-country of all slavery and you represent that country.'

Thanks for that.

I didn't know what on Earth this guy was talking about, or what had instigated his provocative outburst, but he carried on staring directly at me until I eventually thought it was about time that someone broke the deadlock, and looked away.

In normal circumstances I would have fronted my way through this aggressive uncalled-for situation with a little provocation of my own, just to show that if he wanted some trouble then it would not be as easy as all that to intimidate me, and perhaps make him think twice about continuing. In my weakened condition however and perhaps also due to a general feeling of unease which had come upon me inexplicably as soon as we had left Mango Bay, I became a little nervous and as I turned my head away I mumbled something about slavery having nothing to do with me and that it was all a very long time ago.

Just as he began to deliver his response we arrived at the house, where I quickly got out and Jenny and I moved to get lost in another crowd and left my confused Islander friend back at the van with his own group of partygoers.

Agnes had heard this conversation, such as it was, and she came over and quietly told me that the guy had been drinking, which she seemed sure of even though I had smelt no liquor on him and seen no signs at all of inebriation on his part. Taking Agnes's word for it I tried to forget about the whole incident and just enjoy myself, but decided to keep an eye out for my local friend anyway in case he should choose to conti-

nue the discussion later on. I sincerely hoped that chance would not throw him and I together at the end of the night and
put us in the same vehicle going back to the jetty, and I am pleased to say that it did not. Short of a couple of distant sighti-
ngs of him from time to time at the party, I never came into
close contact with him again and that was just fine with me.
Agnes also said that it would be virtually impossible for him to
start any trouble there, as although the security seemed to me
to be fairly laid back, the people in charge of the island would
not tolerate any such behaviour and without alluding to exactly what or who would stop it, she seemed perfectly confident
that that was the case, and I expect she knew more about the
security of Necker than I did.

The three of us then walked through a large open doorway
and into the main building where the party was already in full
swing, and took in the scene.

My first impression was that there was more booze here
than I had ever seen before in one place in all my life. The only time I had ever come across anything close was shopping in
a French Hypermarket as a booze-hungry teenager. I looked around gobsmacked at the sheer quantity and variety of alcohol,
stacked in boxes, crates and intricate formations of bottles all
around the floor space, creating aisles between them through
which masses of people funnelled like ants.

I would guess that there were several hundred guests there
already, with more arriving all the time. It was hard to be accurate as everyone seemed to be constantly on the move.

A group would exit through one set of doors as others came in, the first lot only to return a few minutes later through
another set of doors on the opposite side, making it very diffi-

cult to keep track. Everyone seemed to be having a good time, calling their hellos and trying to make themselves heard above the booming music, mingling and exploring to see what was what and who was who.

The room was brightly lit, and some of the stacks of crates reached almost to the ceiling creating columns of cardboard and glass which gradually reduced in height as bottles were consumed, the empty case being swiftly removed and the next one down opened and delved into by eager passing hands.

In corners people were schmoozing while they danced and drank. There seemed to be no dress code as such, and scanning the room I saw everything from those dressed to impress suited and booted, to some wearing bikinis and little else, and many in Caribbean khaki and sandals and looking like they'd just stepped off crewing a charter yacht for the day and had no time to shower and change, which was probably the case.

At one point I walked past a long line of people snaking their way through the crowd wearing snorkels, face-masks and flippers, which was nice.

I shouldn't really have been drinking with the painkillers I was taking, but spotting half a case of Cuervo I couldn't resist, and asked Jenny to grab a tall person to pinch a bottle from several balanced on top of a pile of aluminium beer kegs stacked end on end next to us. Locating an appropriate mixer (bitter lemon, if you ever feel like trying it) I proceeded to down one or two, possibly three or four, and felt that lovely warm glow that only tequila does for me.

So we drank, and we talked, and we met old friends and new, and the evening progressed in a pleasant golden blur. The party itself passed as any party does, with the added bonus of being in such exclusive surroundings, and perhaps who knows using a toilet that a member of Royalty may have taken a pee in that very same porcelain bowl.

During the evening I got re-acquainted with lots of people who I knew but had not seen since the shooting, at one point meeting up with Chris the assistant manager of Necker, with whom I had planned to go scuba diving but which was now impossible due to my injuries. One thing that struck me was how virtually everyone had the same reaction on seeing me; first there would be a worried expression, as if they feared I might start bleeding again and drop dead on the spot. That would be followed by cautious inquisitiveness and sympathy, then finally they would invariably just shrug and come up and say; 'Hi Craig, so how are you feeling? Fancy a drink?', and then it was like nothing had happened and we just slipped back into the way it had always been.

Standing chatting with Chris another person joined our group that I hadn't seen at the party until now.

Yvonne, a British diving instructor, had been at the B & T that night, and although we had met before she had slipped my mind until I saw her again now.

I could see as we talked that she had a tangible look of concern in her eyes. The music was loud and the booze had been flowing, but it was unmistakable.

It gradually came out that not only had Yvonne been present at the shooting, but she had been the person cradling my head and holding it up to stop me choking on the floor of the bar immediately after the event, and had been kneeling in my blood throughout those frantic and ultimately successful attempts to save my life. In all the chaos Yvonne had probably been Harry Schoenauer's calmest helper. She had held on to me despite the horrific nature of the situation, and had stayed with me helping in various ways throughout much of the evening of February 2nd, and I had been oblivious to it all, deep in my reverie about Sir Alec Guinness falling on a plunger and bridges exploding as I had been at the time. Yvonne, wherever you are, may all your dives be deep and satisfying.

The conversation became quite enlightening, filling in many of the blanks from that night. Yvonne herself was far too humble to mention what she had done; others did that, as I pieced together some of the missing minutes at last being able to complete the picture.

It turned out that when I had been placed in the back of the taxi leaving the pub (some said police car) Agnes had taken over from Yvonne holding my head for the journey to the clinic on the hill (the Iris O'Neal Clinic - I was finding out lots about the shooting tonight) and that is how Agnes had come to be the person next to my trolley after I awoke with the adrenaline shot.

I wondered that should the situation ever be reversed, would I act in as cool a manner as they all did when saving my life? I can't be sure as I have never been tested but I can only hope.

Later in the evening Jenny and I left the throng and took a wander outside to explore, although Jenny already knew her way around quite well.

The house which I presumed was the private residence was cordoned off, the owner not at home, or it would have been very doubtful if this unbirthday party (I think it was Chris's?) would have been permitted to take place at all.

The trees and scrub between the paths prevented us from seeing much, so we headed down to one of the beaches and took a stroll along the sand, the music of the party still loud in the distance, and as we walked I pondered silently how the other half lived. I believe in capitalism with a conscience, which I think gives a good mix of incentives to succeed and social justice, but when one person owns an island and others starve when there is plenty of food to go around, something is going wrong somewhere. I mused on the failure of governments to deliver opportunity through education and left my conclusions for another day.

At around midnight we returned to the party and gathered up Jano and Agnes, and hopping aboard one of the utility shuttles drove back down to the dock. Our boat was bobbing independently now against the jetty, having been tightly packed-in during the peak party hours. We could see that Jano had been busy when we had left him earlier deploying rope and plastic buffers around his craft to protect it from the comings and goings of others, and he checked it now, lamenting every tiny mark or possible scratch. It looked okay to me, but then again I was slightly drunk.

It was fairly early to be leaving and there were still plenty of people back at the party house, but Chris had said that it wouldn't be a particularly late night, as new guests would be arriving at ten o'clock sharp the next morning, which given the state of the place seemed a very ambitious target for the cleaners. However he declared confidently that he would be ready to greet them on the dockside the next day and that all would be ready for their arrival, and I had to admire his positivity.

Very tired now, I climbed aboard Jano's cosseted craft and dozed off on one of the canvas cushions at the bow, even somehow finding the smooth roar of the engines soothing. The translucent white hull against the rushing black air felt like travelling on board a ghost-ship, distant islands floating slowly past, the twinkling lights of their towns and coastal villages impossible to gauge the distance between us and them.

A salty mist covered everything. Light droplets from the bow spray landing on my face instantly evaporated due to the speed of the hairdryer air, so that when we finally got home and I went to bed without washing my face, the next morning when I looked bleary-eyed in the bathroom mirror, I could still see little reflective jewels of salt dotted all over my forehead and chin from the boat's night passage.

Chapter 20 - Twenty five, and still alive

I decided against an immediate shower and instead grabbed some clothes and headed downstairs with caffeine on my mind. Everyone else was already wide awake and breezing about the main open-plan living area. I saw Agnes busying herself carrying breakfast items to the dining table on the verandah. Another day in paradise.

I mumbled my 'Good mornings' and headed for the kitchen to pour myself a coffee, then made for the balcony where Jenny was sitting in her white uniform eating a bowl of cereal. I promptly walked straight into one of the huge, and I discovered closed, sliding glass patio doors that were of the same size and shape as the rest of the wall of rectangular glass panels that divided the living room from the balcony. Brushing away spilt coffee from the front of my shorts I looked up and could see a tell-tale glittery face-print from the remnants of last night's facial salt reflecting back at me from the middle of the glass at head height, leaving perfect evidence of my clumsiness if any were needed for all to see.

After everyone had finally stopped laughing, which for Agnes took a while, and I was done rubbing my forehead hoping there wasn't a bruise showing and then the window to get rid of the face-shaped smudge, I tried again with a coffee and making a point brought a full bowl of cornflakes out with me too.

I joined the conversation, the main topics of which were the two parties; last night's frivolities on Necker and the upcoming birthday bash for me tonight...

My birthday!

It was my fault and no-one else's that I had received no congratulations yet, by giving my fellow housemates the gift of laughter before they had a chance to think.

They all wished me a Happy Birthday now, and cards came out and a few presents too.

Agnes's daughter Alicia had wrapped me a cute little glass trinket on a leather shoelace necklace, presumably prompted by someone to replace my dear departed crocodile tooth. Agnes gave me a bottle of rare Italian wine. Jano gave me a handshake. Cheap but heartfelt. And Jenny had amazingly sourced a replacement for my shredded shark t-shirt with another one from the same range, only this one had a killer whale motif in the same foaming turquoise ocean colour scene. Okay, I was harsh about looking like an idiot in the original; this new one really was a nice top and better than the first version which I had chosen myself if I can say that.

Prior to receiving this clothing, I had been toying with the idea of getting a t-shirt printed for tonight's festivities saying; 'Twenty Five and Still Alive!', across the chest, for my own amusement more than anybody else's. However it was now clear what I must wear this evening, as not to air the killer whale would have been offensive to Jenny's generosity. This was probably a good thing because trying to get a t-shirt printed on Virgin Gorda would I imagine have proved tricky.

Later that morning after Jenny had gone to work I decided to head to Spanish Town on a different personal mission.

Agnes told me that she was going into town on a bit of business, so I hitched a ride with her to the Valley and she left me at the municipal square car park at the back of the Bath and Turtle.

Bypassing the pub and entering the square from a side alley, I walked slowly around the shops facing the inner courtyard, browsing the t-shirt and trinket racks under the covered walkway.

I looked up from time to time, passing a furtive glance in the direction of the restaurant, not quite ready to cross just yet, working my way up to venturing over.

From a shop awning I stood adjacent to the satellite bar, boarded and locked up for the day, sure to be open for business and packed with queuing customers later as it had been on my last visit exactly a month before, also a Wednesday live music night.

The central paved area where the band usually played was bare save a few scattered and empty tables and chairs. On the far side some customers were just sitting down on the long verandah in front of the doorway where I had been shot, checking the menus and getting ready to order their lunch.

Once I had agreed a few days before to have the party here, I had made up my mind without saying anything to anyone that my first sight of the scene of my near demise was something that I wanted to experience alone. I didn't want to walk through that doorway into a half-drunk crowd pretending that everything was fine, a false smile stuck to my face showing due appreciation for every shouted birthday greeting. I crossed and went inside.

Everything in the pub was much the same as it always was. The bar appeared to be closer than I remembered it, the tiles lighter. The side doors were open letting in sunlight and a breeze, gently lifting the corners of the wall decorations away from the vertical, until the low draft could sustain the gravity-defiance no longer and they wafted slowly back down to hug the plaster.

I made a conscious effort to be hyper-aware, studying every crack in the paint, every mark on the grey tiles, every criss-crossing line of grout, searching for the slightest trace of what happened there on the floor right in front of me, but I could find nothing. Not a single speck of dried blood ingrained into some random blob of porous cement remained.

I looked at the wooden bar panels beyond where I judged the bullet must have left me for evidence on the grain of pock-marks or shrapnel, again nothing. Maybe I was looking in the wrong place, or maybe the oak had already been repaired and varnished, I could not tell.

I took a seat at the bar and looked across at the tall table next to where I had been standing and which my two friends had comically dived under, and then noticed a crack on the corner of one of the ceramic floor tiles nearby. Had this been where my head bounced off the floor? I told myself not to be ridiculous.

Two waitresses were staring at me.

As I raised my head one said simply; 'It was you wasn't it?'

I nodded and the other just shook her head. I didn't really recognise them, or at least I thought I might but they were wearing staff uniforms, so it was a bit of a giveaway, and if I had seen them away from this environment and passed them in the street wearing something else, would I have known that they worked here? I didn't think so.

'So you're back then? Did you go to England? How are you doin'?'

They apparently had not heard anything much of my whereabouts since I'd been carried from that place, and assumed that I had returned to England, and was now back here for some reason or other. That would have been a bit of a stretch considering my injuries, but they weren't to know that.

We chatted for a short while, and amongst other things they told me of a rumour which I had already heard one version of, which was that the large kitchen knife that Captain Harry had used to cut away my shark t-shirt, was in fact my knife, which I had brought to the bar, and that I had somehow been mixed up in a love triangle (or was it quadrangle?) with the shooter and may have got what was coming to me.

People do love to talk.

I stayed and ordered a burger and a coke, taking them outside on the shaded verandah, the waitresses soon going back to their work, looking over at me from time to time like I was a ghoulish celebrity.

I was glad that I had come, and as I left I met Rose the American owner getting into her vehicle in the car park. We said hi and exchanged a few words. I said that I would see her tonight, and she didn't let on as to whether she knew we were coming or not.

I left the square and managed to track down Agnes shopping in the town, but she still had some chores to do so I found a taxi and made my own way back to Mango Bay, to relax a little on the hammock between two palm trees alone with my thoughts, and awaiting Jenny's return from work.

.

Chapter 21 - Captain Harry

As day turned to warm starry night Agnes, Jenny, Jano and I climbed into the people carrier and drove to Spanish Town and Virgin Gorda's premier nightspot.

The drink-driving laws were not particularly stringently enforced in the BVI at the time - it may have changed since - but Agnes was not an irresponsible person and if she did end up having one or two alcoholic beverages too many which seemed fairly likely, her silver Mango Bay vehicle would remain in the car park overnight and we would all get a taxi back home later, the car to be retrieved the next day when one of us was sober enough to go and get it.

As we arrived the band was just starting up and the bar soon filled with revellers, in half an hour or so becoming a boisterous but friendly heaving mass of tanned bodies drowned in loud Hawaiian shirts and even louder predominantly American accented voices.

If there are two Americans talking in a crowd anywhere in the world, you can virtually guarantee that these are the voices you will hear and identify rising up above the throng, as lovely though most American people I have come across are, they do seem to operate as a race on the theory that the louder you say something, the more right you must be about whichever subject is currently under discussion. On this night that social faux pas could easily be forgiven, as there were probably more residents of the United States present than any other nationality, closely followed by a roughly equal split of Brits and local Islanders, and then a blend in diminishing numbers of many others from many disparate places.

A large table had been prepared on the verandah for our party within a party, created out of several small tables pressed together in a line, the joins disguised with two or three long white overlapping table cloths. The majority of partygoers at the pub that night had nothing to do with our group, and outside of polite interest and alcohol-enhanced conviviality, they neither knew nor particularly cared about my birthday and what it meant to me, but that was fine as it all added to the atmosphere of the evening and provided a lively backdrop to our celebrations.

Each space around our table was rapidly and from then on permanently occupied with friends and well-wishers, as well as a healthy mix of passers by and foot-sore dancers who just wanted a few moments rest before resuming their position on the now packed dance floor. We talked and we ate and we drank, with no set seating arrangements, and with a constant changing of the table guests. As one person got up to leave and mingle with another crowd elsewhere in the pub, the seat would instantly be filled with another smiling body ready to join in the conversation and so on into the night.

As the evening went on I became increasingly touched that I had this second chance in as many nights to catch up with lots of people, and lost count of the number of Heinekens and Red Stripes which were either placed in front of me at the table or pressed into my palm. I soon found myself with at least two full bottles in front of me at all times and often three, making it impossible to shake people's hands if I went anywhere as they were both permanently engaged in holding the next one and the next. It seemed like everyone including those I didn't know wanted to congratulate me for making twenty five. I didn't mind; I'd rather have a full bottle in front of me than a full frontal lobotomy, and if I had to sacrifice a few brain cells to the party gods to celebrate reaching this landmark, then that was okay with me.

Most people at our table took a turn or two on the floor, a reggae-pop fusion band providing the motivation with a female singer once again, but whom I didn't recognise and so may or may not have been from the band present the night of the shooting. As always a DJ was there too, to take over the musical reins whenever the band took a break, spilt beer sticking the soles of the dancers to the floor, a tangle in motion of brown arms and legs and smiling white teeth.

At one point a young American couple sat down with Jenny and me at the long table, who like many of the people that came over throughout the evening I didn't know from Adam or Eve. We chatted for a while and shared our stories, and in the slightly erratic way of everyone that has had a few too many drinks, the entirely crazy story of the shooting became relegated to a matter-of-fact anecdote and blended seamlessly with their more regular stories of his chiropractic clinic in Minnesota or wherever, and what had brought them both here to the BVI.

It seemed that he liked her, and she wasn't too keen on him, and so in an act of daring or possibly desperation - hope always springs eternal pursuing unrequited love - he brought her here to the Virgin Islands for an all-expenses paid vacation, as 'friends', but obviously in hope of far more, on his part at least. Poor guy; this girl was obviously not interested, and I didn't know whether to admire her for taking him up on his most generous offer of what must have been a ridiculously expensive trip - the BVI are not a cheap holiday destination - when she knew full well that nothing was going to happen between them, or to think of her as a bit of a gold-digger intent on getting what she could before the inevitable rebuff of his advances which was sure to come. She was so attractive that I settled tipsily on the former, and shared jokes with her at first at her suitor's, and then at my own expense, as she gently ribbed me at my fashion sense, hoping that Jenny didn't hear.

Just when I was beginning to think that I had probably had too much to drink, which was usually a dead giveaway that I had, a small commotion led my eyes to a smiling group of people who appeared from the inner pub carefully carrying a large round birthday cake with several sparklers fizzing on the top of it, and a spontaneous round of 'Happy Birthday to You!' broke out. It was Rose in the centre of the crowd carrying the cake, so I guess she did know that I was coming when we had met in the car park earlier.

My appetite had improved temporarily; two days of drinking possibly dulling or at least disguising my feverish symptoms, so I happily tucked into a large slice after the singing and clapping had died down. Something that the alcohol could not mask though was the growing feeling of a lead weight incrementally crushing my lungs, and somewhere through my stupor I chastised myself for being so bloody stupid not being at home tucked up in bed nursing my injuries.

Agnes was sitting next to me and she suddenly stopped talking mid-sentence, and without saying another word got up and disappeared through the crowd into the main bar. She returned a minute later, leading by two or three stretched reluctant fingers a man walking a pace or two behind her. He looked a little uncomfortable, a bottle of beer in his free trailing hand. I didn't recognise him, but I didn't have to, because as soon as Agnes said the words; 'Craig, do you know this guy?', the nuances and mannerisms and features which individually meant nothing all clicked into place.

I don't remember having focussed on his face during the night of the shooting, he being more of a presence and a commanding voice, and if it had not been for Agnes spotting him and dragging him reluctantly over, I would never have known he was here now.

It was Harry Schoenauer, the man who more than any other was responsible for saving my life.

I stood up as he approached. We shook hands and I embraced him, and like all men do when they don't know what to say to one another, I offered to buy him a beer. He lifted his hand to show me a nearly full Red Stripe, and I pointed to the half a dozen open bottles in front of me on the table, and we shrugged and both headed off through the crowd back to the inner bar to add to our respective collections.

I was extremely happy to meet him again, and also a little confused.

What was he doing here? Was this a coincidence? Was this all planned and he a surprise guest of honour at the party?

Nope, it was all just a happy coincidence that Harry was here tonight, just as it had been four weeks previously.

Captain Schoenauer was the skipper of the Sir Francis Drake, a large charter yacht, classified a Tall Ship. In sailing parlance she was technically a schooner, and the similarity between her captain's name and the class of his charge was not totally lost on me, but then again I do see coincidences everywhere.

At the time this vessel toured the Leeward Islands of the Lesser Antilles chain, of which the BVI were the most northerly point, giving an opportunity to those who yearned for it to have a real old-fashioned seafaring experience on their vacation.

She had three tall masts of equal height spaced along the deck, from which hung triangular white sails, and was a truly beautiful ship from right out of the pages of a history book. The current schedule encompassed several of the nearby islands, and on Wednesday evenings the Drake would anchor in the waters off Spanish Town, where the crew and passengers would be invited out by their skipper for a night of revelry at one of the Bath and Turtle's legendary twice-weekly live-band nights.

A month before, Harry had been dining outside on the verandah, and followed the commotion into the main bar, where he saw me in desperate trouble and immediately took control. He was a trained first-aider, which was a requirement for his position, and I thank my lucky stars for all that he was and all that he did, and for serendipity that brought him to me in my hour of need.

After leaving me to the care of the professionals he had returned to his vessel, and calmly made preparations to sail the next morning and continue on with the charter. (Germans; they do love things to run like clockwork!)

The coincidence of our meeting tonight at my birthday celebrations was further exaggerated by the fact that not only was the 2nd of March my first visit back to the scene of the carnage, it was Harry's too. He didn't say why he had not returned since, whether by design or chance, but regardless he was here now.

Adding to this straining of circumstance, in a week or two Harry was returning to Europe to pick up where his life had left off when he decided for whatever reason to spend a couple of years as a charter skipper in the Caribbean. Many people only do this job temporarily, drifting into it through the convoluted paths their lives take, and for most it is a sojourn and when they decide that they have had enough they go back to whatever they were doing before or move on to their next adventure.

If Harry told me that night while we exchanged good wishes and a beer what he did originally and what he was returning to I cannot remember, but perhaps meeting me again was a nice experience for him too, seeing with his own eyes that his efforts and emergency training had not been in vain.

For myself it was a wonderful opportunity to say simply thank you, and deeply cathartic. I now had another shot at life, against all the odds, and I wanted to make it count.

We stood at the oak-panelled bar and talked for about fifteen minutes, right by the spot where he had rendered me first-aid. As our order arrived the two of us looked down at that place on the floor amongst the feet of the constantly moving crowd, and shrugged again and shook our heads in unison at the bizarreness of it all, chinking our bottles in cheers.

There wasn't a lot more to be said really, as we weren't friends as such and no matter how important Harry was to my existence, we were both about to go our separate ways; he back to Germany, and me not sure where. The noise was horrendous and I think I only heard one word in three that he said which must also have been the same for Harry. After a short while I judged it was time to leave, and we shook hands again. With some emotion on my part I turned and left the bar to retake my seat at the table outside, replaced by Agnes who had been standing hovering and wanted her own chance to speak with Harry, I guess on the same subject of shared experiences by two of my primary first responders.

I am not sure if Agnes and Harry knew each other before that night. It was very possible as most residents hereabouts knew most everyone else if only by sight. Jenny also had a chance to share a few words with Harry before he departed which he did soon after our chat, and as the evening drew to a close, we all sensibly climbed into a taxi and made our way tipsily back to Mango Bay and to our weary welcoming beds.

In 1999 the Sir Francis Drake broke her moorings and foundered during the record-breaking storms of the strangely named Hurricane Lenny. She drifted and sank off the coast of St Martin several islands down the Antilles chain, and this illustrious vessel ended its long career memorably as a true character of the seas should. There were no casualties, the ship being laid up in preparation for the approaching storm, and as of 2013 there was still a Facebook page dedicated to this schooner giving something of her history for any who wish to see, encompassing her launch in Germany in 1917 and her first days as a cargo vessel rounding Cape Horn, through World War

II, and up to her sad demise as the reigning white Queen (or was it Knight?) of the Caribbean Sea.

Chapter 22 - Rejuvenated

The next day I set off alone by taxi for the Valley to catch the ferry to Road Town and the Bougainvillea Clinic. I had hoped to catch a lift into town with Jano, whom Agnes before going to bed the night before had designated the 'volunteer' to pick up her car from the Bath and Turtle, but apparently I wasn't the only early riser in the place that day as Jano had already breakfasted, walked the dogs and left for Spanish Town by the time I surfaced. Perhaps his army routine had not entirely left him, but in any case it left me without a ride, and I had to call and wait for a cab before I could join the other travellers wishing to cross on the first boat of the day to Tortola.

I had been under strict instructions to ease back on the painkillers by Doctor Tattersall on the morning of our appointment as he wished to examine me with my senses as little dulled as possible. This would better give him an idea of where exactly I was hurting and could thus describe accurately what I was feeling, both generally and in response to whatever tests he would carry out.

As I bought my ticket and waited on the quayside I pondered how much I should tell him about my recent alcohol consumption. This much mental activity this early made my head spin, and I couldn't work out whether the nausea that crept up the back of my throat was due to a hangover, the sudden reduction in analgesics, or something else.

Riding the ferries of the British Virgin Islands was (almost) always a pleasure. The entire experience from start to finish bristled with the noise and hustle and bustle of human life making it a constant feast for the senses. Queuing with the other passengers to cross the gangplank and take my seat aboard the boat, I could see the crew and ground staff busily loading today's cargo. As usual this included mail that had missed the last ferry yesterday, unaccompanied packages and bags being sent around the islands, items of furniture and the boxed belongings of people moving house, and caged pets extremely unhappy at being dropped on the greasy deck in such close proximity to the scent of diesel and noise of thudding engines overpowering their highly developed senses.

The majority of the people were red-eyed and still struggling to shake themselves from sleep, a significant number dressed in suits with their jackets or handbags slung over their shoulders, reluctantly preparing their minds and bodies for the daily slog in front of a green and black computer screen in Road Town. Several mothers were amongst the crowd too, taking their children across the bay to school or daycare while they continued on to their own workplace on Tortola or one of the other islands.

Most locals generally preferred to find a space inside the passenger cabin as opposed to sitting out on the decks; the prospect of a sea breeze buffeting their faces and salt spray staining their clothes during the voyage being an unwelcome one. There was also the added discomfort of the already severe early sun beating down on their delicate morning necks for the forty minutes or so that the crossing generally took.

To the inexperienced eye taking a seat in the cabin might appear to be the wrong choice, as the stationary ferry quickly became as hot as an oven due to the long rows of minimally adjustable glass windows on either side quickly turning the compartment into a sauna. However if one could tolerate being baked into the plastic chair for the few minutes it took the loading to complete, the sweltering interior would soon cool with a refreshing through-breeze once the boat got moving across the water.

The acceleration on these craft was impressive. Their initial lumbering appearance belied the power of some carefully maintained engines which the mechanics constantly tuned to try to gain a competitive advantage over the rival ferry companies. If five minutes could be shaved off the crossing times this would be proudly displayed on advertising posters all around the islands and the timetables altered accordingly. In this way the departure and arrival times were rarely fixed at say 7.30am or mid-day, but instead looked random and arbitrary, such as 7.10 or 8.45, and you had to keep an eye on the constantly changing schedules because if you turned up one minute late you had better be able to jump as the ferry would already be gunning its engines and slipping its moorings.

The departing vessels would crawl towards the buoy saying 'Limit Ends' where the speed restrictions of the inshore waters ceased, then literally as the stern drew level with the floating sign the motors would explode into life, the bow raise in the water and if you were not sitting down when this happened you were lying down with your coffee and a wet bagel all over you.

For me this was still new and exciting. Commuters seldom take the time to really appreciate what is around them, whether bussing through chaotic city streets or looking out of a smudged ferry window, but I always found this interesting wherever in the world I happened to be.

As a young carpenter in Sydney in the late 1980's, I had my first realisation of this, when Jenny and I (she barely seventeen, me nineteen) rented a flat in a high-rise tower in Potts Point close to the Sydney Opera House.

From the bottom of Macleay Street where we lived, we could easily see that other manmade marvel of Australia, the vast black 'Coat Hanger' Bridge impressively spanning and connecting the two halves of Sydney, high over a natural harbour of deep blue ocean stretching and spidering into a hundred bays and coves.

Living in our part of town required a daily pre-dawn walk through the seedy and sometimes dangerous borough of Kings Cross to catch a train to our respective places of work. Although I travelled all over the city, I was regularly sent by the architectural firm which employed me to the residences of millionaires in the posh Northern Suburbs, to fit handcrafted cupboards for the lady of the house to store her latest collection after a credit card busting trip to the boutiques of San Francisco or Hawaii, which seemed to be the trendy shopping destinations for Sydney socialites at the time. Unless I managed to catch a lift with one of my co-workers, this entailed a journey to North Sydney over the spectacular Harbour Bridge, and I'd cross the vista of Port Jackson, known as the most beautiful city-harbour in the world, regularly at the exact moment of sunrise.

On these mornings my train carriage would trundle on squeaking rails through the still dark cityscape of downtown Sydney, and turning into the bridge approach pass between two identical huge grey stone piers. Entering the maze of black wrought iron cables, belligerent seagulls would wheel around the wide deck fighting over the discarded remnants of the first catch of the day fanning out behind the fishing trawlers on the ocean below.

And then I'd see one of the most amazing sights in the world of architecture; the sun rising over the Sydney Opera House, and the humdrum of the daily commute would instantly evaporate.

At first the paling eastern horizon beyond the harbour mouth would fire pink shots across the sky, illuminating in red the fringes of the tumbling scythed domes grey in the pre-dawn light. Then quickly the whole structure which hooks out over the bay on its own peninsula would turn from fiery red to orange to amber, and then finally dazzling white.

I would turn to look at my fellow passengers with their shiny foreheads and creased clothes to share the experience, and find I was the only one awake and not dozing off last night's excesses to have taken in the sight. The moment would pass and we would be over the bridge, soon enough arriving in North Sydney where our daily toil would begin. Personally I was already set up for the day and could take anything that the city threw at me because the drama of the new morning was safely locked away in my memory, ready to bring out again and relive in my mind's eye anytime I felt fed up.

I looked about me now bouncing over the hard indigo water as we passed the southern tip of Beef Island and soaked it all in.

The deceptively harsh rays burnt the place where my collar touched the skin as I decided to take a seat among the rows of benches on the upper deck. Unlike the locals, I revelled in the salty spray prickling my face and the combined smell of the fresh ocean mixed with the nauseating blend of diesel and exhaust fumes. To me this was exotic and to be savoured if not breathed in too deeply.

I shut my eyes to protect them from the hot air rushing past my face and leaned back in the seat, feeling the sun on my forehead and listening to the rhythmic splashes of the bow-wave hitting the water revolving in time with the rising and dipping of the boat. This was matched by the quickening then lowering tones of the engines as the boat ploughed through the ocean, losing then quickly regaining traction in the water according to the pitch of the vessel against the horizontal surface of the sea.

Sometimes I would hear the sounds of another competing engine build from a faint clatter to a more throaty echo, and opening my eyes see other ferries crossing or overtaking us, some near, some far off in the distance, speeding here and there between the islands, the ocean the life blood and the ferry routes the arteries that brought vitality to each of the island outposts.

Slowing as we reached the natural harbour of Road Town the ferry made its way through the mess of other craft and found its designated space on the dockside. Oily ropes were cast and caught and the vessel pulled tight to the quay. Before the first passenger disembarked a different ground crew were already unloading the appropriate cargo and replacing it with yet more, hurrying to prepare for the next part of the boat's journey either back to Virgin Gorda or on to another port I do not know.

The Bougainvillea Clinic was located conveniently on a street parallel to the promenade just behind the ferry terminal, and was set on the ruins of the old Road Town Fort. It therefore had a commanding view of its surrounds and its surrounds had a commanding view of it, and as the Yellow Pages advert had proudly referred to it by its local nickname, the 'Purple Palace', I found the facility without any difficulty at all.

More a small hospital than a clinic, the building seemed to mimic the design of the original castle, with a battlement facade and several low towers linked by lilac-rendered galleries. Built up a sharp rise it had terraced gardens to the front, shielded from the road by masses of thick bougainvillea vines shaped into long hedges and dressed with permanently blossoming pink and white flowers. The largest of these hidden spaces contained an outdoor swimming pool edged with recliners, and to the side climbed a steep path signposted to the main entrance.

The hospital itself gave the appearance of an old colonial residence, and as I walked into the reception it was clear that some parts of the building had been extensively modernised, some areas keeping the original layout and design and merely adapted to suit its later medical purpose.

The female receptionist signed me in and after checking a paper-clipped file, gave me a slip of paper that Doctor Tattersall had already prepared for my arrival. On this was an X-ray request for images of my chest, back and sides, and the options available for me to carry out this task. A radiography department was seemingly lacking on-site, and I had two choices; I could either leave the clinic and turn right for the short walk to the public Peebles Hospital and have the X-rays done there, which would involve a small fee and possibly a long wait, or I could turn left past the Hotel Americana to a private imaging centre next to the marina. They were both roughly the same distance from the Bougainvillea, but the second option although more expensive could virtually guarantee me an immediate walk-in appointment. Although my insurance company was picking up the tab I would have to pay up front for these sundries, so I had to think about which option to choose but in the end I decided that time was the greater factor, turned left and chose private.

I was still getting back into the swing of mobile life and had neglected in the thirty Celsius heat to bring either a hat or sunscreen, my mind elsewhere when I had been preparing to leave for the day. After the initial downhill walk which built up a nice momentum, half-way to the imaging centre I became aware that my body was streaming with sweat and my face and exposed limbs had that early telltale scalding sensation that brings promises of sunburn to come. Mad dogs and Englishmen may go out in the mid-day sun, but you can add to that stupid English patients who have been travelling long enough to ought to know better.

Reaching the medical centre, also a bright and clean colonial conversion, the X-rays were done with a minimum of fuss and I returned to the clinic as fast as my reduced lung capacity could manage, preferring to risk sweat-saturated clothes which could easily be fixed to burnt skin which would not.

On arrival the staff were waiting for me as I was immediately shown into a bright Victorian parlour in the central tower with high ceilings, carpeted floors and three tall windows on the far wall looking out onto the terraced gardens and Road

Harbour beyond. Each window was open a fraction at the top and bottom to allow a fresh sea breeze to circulate, brilliant sunlight diffused through long white net curtains which sashayed in turn like a slow Mexican wave.

The room seemed to serve several purposes at once; being an office, examination room and study combined. To the right as I entered and adjacent to the farthest window was a hardwood desk, and behind that a red leather-bound chair with carved wooden arms darkened through use. In this chair a man sat reading some journals laid out in front of him on the scratched varnish.

Two smaller less ornate chairs presumably for patients were set out in front of the desk, and along the wall behind was a bookcase filled with a multicoloured array of encyclopedias and medical publications. Opposite this on the wall to my left were various weighing scales, height and body mass measuring instruments, and higher-up eye charts.

There were also some smaller bookcases and shelves less densely packed containing GP's bits and pieces, some in small chromed and plastic cases, some unboxed and gleaming in the sunlight.

In the middle of the space directly in front of me was a wheeled medical trolley, its small rubber feet locked into position at the end of each one of its six spindly legs.

The reader stood up and walked out from behind his desk, not a small man but slim and unassuming, so much so that I had continued looking around the room inquisitively even after I had first laid eyes upon him sitting in the leather chair.

Introducing himself as Robin Tattersall, he had a calming aura, like a person at the top of their game into whose trust you are happy to submit, and I could see how he charmed and disarmed Hollywood types with his endearing manner. He appeared to be in his late fifties or early sixties, with a woolly greying fringe over a pair of neat mottled-grey horn-rimmed glasses. He was dressed casually in a short-sleeved shirt and no tie, and spoke softly and clearly, giving the impression that his voice never wavered by so much as half an octave whatever the situation.

Surprisingly immediately three female nurses came in and joined us; one English, one Dutch and one Islander, and independently busied themselves preparing medical equipment about the room and saying little. I imagined they were here to assist the doctor in the examination to come. This seemed like a bit of overkill and I hoped that I wasn't being charged according to the number of members of staff present; the bill was being forwarded to my insurance company, but I didn't want to spend money for the sake of it.

Doctor Tattersall asked me to sit on the bed and examined me quickly in his shirt-sleeves while I removed mine, asking questions which a nearby nurse noted the answers to on a clipboard. He already seemed to have a very good idea of what might be wrong, even before he inserted the earpieces of his stethoscope and applied the cold round diaphragm to my back and chest. His brisk run-through of this part of the procedure seemed as if he was mainly going through the motions of investigation rather than attempting to deduce much at all.

He spent more time now tapping my ribcage front and back, listening intently and asking me at various times to breathe in, hold my breath, breathe out again or cough on cue. Every now and then he would mark a particular point on my back with the tickling nib of a felt-tipped pen, drawing what felt like a game of Tic-tac-toe.

Asking me to keep my shirt removed for the time being for expediency, I sat on one of the two patients' chairs in front of his desk. Doctor Tattersall removed the X-rays from the cardboard envelope I had brought with me and held them up in turn to the bright sunlight streaming in from the window nearest to him. After studying them briefly he then asked me to take a look, and he pointed out various blotchy white marks on the black and white images which for the life of me I could not make out the significance of but which were crystal clear to him.

He went on that due to my history and symptoms, he'd suspected and the X-rays proved to his satisfaction, that fluid was building up inside my chest cavity, forcing my lungs to contract little by little, reducing their effectiveness more and more each day. This explained the increasing tightening I had been feeling virtually since leaving Peebles Hospital.

I asked if he knew what the fluid was and if the X-ray gave him any more information or clues as to what was going on. The doctor then pointed to the lower parts of my lungs on the images, noting that the bottom of each appeared flat. This seemed perfectly fine to me and exactly what I would have expected, but he asked me to look again more carefully.

On closer inspection I could make out that the shape of the lungs should in fact resemble a pair of angel's wings, with the outer lower corners pointing downwards where they touched the ribcage.

In my case these points were almost invisible.

To Doctor Tattersall it was obvious, but to me not, and I really had to look hard, and in doing so I could just see through a thick white tentacled blur where the bottom tips of each lung ought to be; a good inch and a half lower than their present location. He explained that the flat appearance was due to a buildup of a substance, probably a liquid, both inside and outside of the lungs, thus blunting the corners. In addition to this, there were shadows higher up in the chest.

Hearing the phrase 'shadows' when referring to X-rays and lungs, all sorts of worrying thoughts enter your mind, but in this case he followed by saying these were merely further evidence of fluid also building up around the upper surfaces of the lungs.

This fluid was the cause of my laboured breathing, and it was Doctor Tattersall's hypothesis that it had become infected, and I was now well on the way to being quite seriously ill.

In short this liquid had to be taken out of me, and quickly.

At this Doctor Tattersall gestured for me to return to the bed, where I sat on the edge again and waited. The three nurses continued making final preparations around me, but for what I did not yet know. I was asked to remain as still as possible, and Doctor Tattersall then injected a local anaesthetic into several places in my back, as he did so explaining that the fluid inside me had formed into loculated pockets, some with a very thick consistency, some free-running. The thinner liquids would move around inside the pockets according to whether I was upright or lying down, which would explain why sometimes my breathing was better and sometimes worse as some places were more sensitive to this fluctuating pressure than others. The X-rays had given an indication of where these pockets were, and his stethoscope and careful ear had narrowed it down to several main locations, and it was his intention now to go into my back with whatever implements were appropriate and draw out the fluid.

I watched with trepidation building to horror as Doctor Tattersall produced an enormous syringe from a drawer. The needle was so big that I thought for a moment he would smile and say; 'Fooled you! It's not really this one...', but he didn't.

He was serious. This thing was going in my body, apparently right now.

Shit. And the last couple of days had been so much fun. I guessed this was the price and it was time to pay the piper.

'Where exactly is that going?', I asked, afraid of what the answer was going to be.

'Into your back', was the reply I did not want to hear.

He continued; 'Now if you would be so kind as to sit up straight, and whatever you do, do not move! This is very important; if you move while the needle is in there is a risk I may puncture a lung, which could be tricky.'

Tricky?

Terrific. And there I was worrying about sunscreen.

The needle was 3mm across at the tip (1/8 of an inch). To reach the loculated pockets which were between my lungs and the chest wall, the syringe would have to pierce the tough intercostal muscles between the ribs (who knew ribs had muscles?). This required a great deal of forward pressure, and if I can say it blunt force.

If this was the only consideration, then it would just be a matter of gritting my teeth and thinking of England, but that was not all. Once the needle got past the ribs, there were only a couple of millimetres then between the tip and the surface of the lungs, so the physician had to check himself immediately after forcing his way in to avoid puncturing one of them. This required very fine judgement on the doctor's part and no small amount of skill.

Just to make the whole experience as unpleasant as possible, it all had to be done with my torso upright, so that the free fluids could seep down and collect inside my body where they could most easily be extracted. So no general anaesthetic again.

I looked around the room making a mental note where the emergency exit was, and wondered if I had time to make a break for it while the nurses were still distracted.

'Shouldn't I lie down or something? Isn't this a bit dangerous?', I enquired weakly.

'Well, not excessively so', the doctor replied.

Excellent.

I steeled myself in a position that I thought I could maintain come what may, although that was a little hard as I didn't really know what was coming.

Doctor Tattersall angled himself behind me on the other side of the bed. A nurse stood either side of me at my front, each holding and lightly supporting one of my upper arms, the third nurse remaining hovering ready to assist where necessary.

'Are we ready?', Doctor Tattersall asked.

Ready as I'll ever be.

The first thing that I became aware of was a popping sound, each 'pop' accompanied by a brief stabbing pressure in my lower back.

So far, so good. If this was all there was to it, I'd be fine - I had experienced far worse, and much of that quite recently.

I sensed the doctor changing position slightly and moving the angle of the needle inside me, and after apparently bracing himself satisfactorily he gave one final strong controlled push and as the last of the muscle layers was penetrated I felt a thundering whack from a cricket bat in my skull and began to pass out.

The pain was as intense as anything I had so far experienced, including the first time the adhesions had torn at Peebles Hospital. If it had not been for the well-chosen positioning of the two nurses now gripping each of my upper arms I would without a doubt have fallen face forward onto the floor.

'Don't move!' Doctor Tattersall yelled at me at the top of his voice - so much for his imagined calm demeanour - and I remembered through my spinning brain what he had said and what risks there would be if I made the needle jolt. I just managed to hold on to my senses, and the bed. I apologised but I couldn't hear myself speak, and said that I would try to stay still, and immediately felt another massive wave of pain and lurched forwards again, the doctor following my body movements forward so as not to lose the needle's position inside me, and once again yelling at me to keep still.

I couldn't stop myself pulling away, it was just too much. My chest felt like a balloon which the syringe had suddenly popped, and as if all my innards were rushing to escape at once. My body involuntarily jerked and once again almost slipped right off the edge of the bed.

Hurried discussions followed between the nurses and the doctor, of whether to abandon the procedure there and then or try to find a way to continue. Quickly a small shelved free-standing wall cabinet was dragged over to the bed and stood on the floor in front of me. The nurses tried to lift my upper torso and to angle my shoulders and arms over the top to see if it could take my bodyweight and not tip over, but it was totally inadequate being the wrong height, the wrong shape, the wrong everything.

One of the nurses then got a tray-table from somewhere - if it had been in the room earlier I had not seen it - of the kind that can move on its own set of wheels and be raised or lowered on a ratchet, and so able to be slid under a hospital bed.

The tray-table was wheeled in front of me and the shelf unit unceremoniously yanked out of the way, and the flat top raised to more or less my chest height as I sat there swaying. I was told to lean gently onto it, until with help from my two supporting nurses it eventually and a tad precariously took all of my upper bodyweight. My head lay flat on its side with one cheek pressed onto the cold plastic surface, my shoulders slumped and my arms dangling limply over the far edge. My eyes remained open and my strength having failed me I stayed there in that position, feeling and I expect looking like an overdue cadaver.

At least now I couldn't fall, and my body now being secured to his satisfaction, Doctor Tattersall continued with his work.

I wondered why they hadn't thought to make sure I was adequately supported before beginning, and I guess in hindsight Doctor Tattersall hadn't been prepared for the sheer amount of fluid that was inside me desperate to get out.

For the next hour and forty minutes I sat hunched over the tray-table, as the doctor moved the needle around, somehow replacing the sharp point with a thin plastic tube still attached to the syringe*, and withdrawing what he could before periodically changing location and repeating the sequence.

(*This was a trocar needle, a kind of three-way syringe designed to enable fluids to be syphoned off without leaving the metal tip inside your body.)

The syringe filled with fluid again and again, from time to time Doctor Tattersall depositing the partially congealed contents into a glass jar sitting next to me on the bed, similar to the container which I had been connected to at Peebles Hospital.

At first the liquid came out runny and yellow, mixed with long streaks of red semi-coagulated blood, as time wore on getting thicker and darker.

I vomited almost constantly in a slow dribble from my mouth and nose, one nurse's sole job became simply to hold a ceramic bowl next to my mouth and wipe away the drool as it came out. I couldn't move to clean myself up and I didn't want to try, and couldn't care less whether my face was lying in sick or not.

My reaction to all this had come as a bit of a surprise, to me definitely and I think to the doctor and nurses. I had been holding myself together for those past few days, refusing to accept the symptoms as they were being presented to me, instead fending them off with distractions. The nausea, the fatigue, the constant worry of when the next adhesion would tear inside me, plus never really giving my body sufficient time to rest after the massive physical shock of the shooting, all came to a head in that sunny Victorian room.

The tension was now finally being released and telling me to let go, and I visibly shrivelled.

I focussed only in the abstract of trying not to move as Doctor Tattersall targeted several different areas of my back, and I can say that the pain each time he pierced my ribcage was almost but not quite as bad as the first. I could not move so I zoned it out as best I could. It felt as one would imagine it would feel being stabbed with a needle the size of a biro nib, and the anaesthetic, well, it didn't work.

As a further neat little trick, before finally withdrawing the plastic cannula each time, Doctor Tattersall would twist it around inside me like a twizzler, in an attempt to release any loculated fluid nearby that hadn't been free flowing enough to be sucked towards the end of the tube.

I stared sideways across the room and wondered what I had done to deserve all this.

In total one and a half litres of fluid was drawn from me and deposited into the glass jar.

Thick plasters were placed over the needle entry sites, as Doctor Tattersall began to relax a little and explained that although the X-rays had shown roughly where the fluid was, they didn't show how deep the pockets were and so the volume had been difficult to judge. To give an idea an adult male has approximately six litres of lung capacity, and one quarter of this had been taken up outside my lungs but inside the chest cavity with this mix of red and yellow lymph.

He said that he was quite surprised that I had put up with the discomfort for so long, I presume meaning the previous days rather than the last hour and a half.

He then commented that he had not got everything, and as I mentally pleaded for him not to as an afterthought try one more time to get it all, Doctor Tattersall to my great relief in an unsatisfied tone said that was probably enough 'for today'.

I was finally allowed to lie down, and as the table was taken away I let myself crumple onto my side on the mattress without planning where my body fell or adjusting it in any way after it had done so. From then on I did not move a muscle, except I think to smile that this unexpected purgatory was over, for the time being at least.

I think the intention was then for me to be transferred to a ward either on foot under my own steam or perhaps in a wheelchair, but I refused to move.

I merely said in response to the nurses' numerous requests for me to stand; 'I'm not moving', and repeated this until they got the message and gave up trying.

After some discussions amongst the women - Doctor Tattersall if he was there did not join in - the wheels on the bed were unlocked and I was trundled down a corridor into a small two-person ward where an elderly man sat reading a newspaper in a chair by the window. The bandages on his shoulder indicated that this other patient had already had whatever procedure he was here for, and was now recovering in the little luxury of a sunny Bougainvillea suite.

The nurses tried again to sit me up but I was having none of it. I just wanted to be left alone to move in my own time, and in the end they left me to my own devices.

Within a few minutes of the nurses leaving, and still not having budged, I began to notice something amazing.

I could draw almost a complete breath. It was a revelation. The discomfort of the previous couple of hours was nearly forgotten as I carefully at first, then with more confidence breathed and breathed. It was wonderful! I don't know what my room-mate must have made of all this, but he seemed happy to accept me and my supine panting as quite normal, and continued with his crossword sitting in the sun with a smile and a nod at first to me and then to his newspaper.

A short while later a commissary came in and asked what I would like to order for lunch. Being more used to the standard hospital fare of an average UK citizen, it took a while for me to cotton on that this very kind person was offering me the choice of a full menu, and as I looked sideways at it my enthusiasm for a spot of sustenance soon increased considerably.

The choices were virtually cordon bleu, and I asked her what and how much I could order.

'As much as you like, sir, it's all paid for.'

Well the price was right.

She seemed completely unfazed by the fact that I was conversing with her on my side, and I asked then about the drinks options as they didn't appear to be listed.

'Everything is available, sir. If we don't have it we will send someone to get it.'

I liked the sound of this; things were looking up.

I remembered however that for the past two weeks I'd had a repetitive pattern of feeling incredibly hungry, only at the first sight or smell of food to feel sick and hardly be able to eat a bite, so I was cautious about ordering too much.

When the food arrived, I took a couple of long sniffs, checked myself for feelings of nausea - there were none. At this I sat bolt upright and tucked straight in, and it was marvellous. My first truly enjoyable meal in ages, possibly since before I had been shot. Even the freshly cooked fish from our Chicago friends could not compare with this hospital fare, and not just because of the chef's efforts, but because I could taste and breathe and enjoy every last morsel. You can only truly savour something when it has been taken away and suddenly returned, and I ate my fill and ordered seconds.

Afterwards I telephoned Mango Bay and gave a rundown of my adventures to Agnes since I left Virgin Gorda that morning, and left a message for Jenny that I would be staying overnight in the clinic, hopefully to return tomorrow a new man.

In my mind there were still one or two questions unanswered, most prominently where had all this fluid come from and had it stopped now? It obviously wasn't solely the remains of the blood from the shooting four weeks before as Doctor Smith had removed most of that.

I decided to worry about this another day, and ignoring the hot shafts of sun and feeling very altruistic towards my silent room-mate, I didn't ask for the curtains to be drawn and left him to enjoy the afternoon and his crossword and I fell asleep facing the dazzling window without any trouble at all.

I slept for most of the afternoon and night, only awaking in the early hours. The nagging pain that had crept into my dreams and woken me night after night for weeks had gone, and I lay in the quiet darkness and dozed, and I felt okay.

The next morning Doctor Tattersall visited on his rounds, and dealing with my senior friend first, he then came to me and told me that the liquid drawn had shown some early signs of culture growth in their laboratory, but he would need more time to conclude the tests to be certain. As it stood however this indicated that I did indeed have an infection in my chest cavity.

What the source of the liquid was he could not say for sure, as most of the blood in his opinion had been fresh, and definitely not as it would be if it had been inside my chest for a month. He said that as a matter of urgency this must be thoroughly investigated and in facilities more extensive than his, and I should ideally be seen by a specialist on the mainland as soon as possible.

Nothing more to be said or done, I thanked the doctor, dressed and bade goodbye to my elderly brother in arms, and feeling like a completely different person to the emphysemic old crone that had climbed the hill to the clinic only twenty four hours before, I virtually bounded down the path and across the road to the ferry dock.

Boarding the lunchtime ferry back to Virgin Gorda, I took a seat out on the upper deck, and caring little whether I had sunscreen on my face or not, I turned to the bright ball of light, shut my eyes and smiled for almost the entire voyage home.

Chapter 23 - Three wise men

The day of pain and pleasure at the Bougainvillea Clinic served one more major purpose apart from easing my breathing and making me feel human again; it settled in my mind the course I must now take. The time had come to stop prevaricating and get back to England in order to continue with my recovery, which was also bound to bring things between Jenny and me to a head.

I knew that the trial of the gunman would not start for a long while. I had limited experience of criminal proceedings, but had seen enough TV to know that in a situation like this evidence would have to be gathered, lawyers engaged, the prosecution and defence cases prepared and a space made on busy court calendars for the hearings to take place. This could only be many months off, and possibly years, and I had no intention of waiting around in the BVI for that long as there was simply too much at stake regarding my health concerns.

I had already begun exploring the possibility of giving my evidence at a pre-trial hearing, which seemed like it might be the way forward. Not quite as good as being there for the main event, but still an adversarial setting where my testimony would have an opportunity to be recorded and cross-examined, meaning that it would have to be taken seriously and become an inextricable part of the trial proper whenever that happened.

Realistically I was only a minor player in the legal proceedings, and anything I had to say would be more of what is today called the impact statement, but which in the 1990's had not yet been articulated as such. I wasn't even sure if I would be able to identify my assailant if we met again so fleeting was my glimpse of him in the bar. Lots of witnesses could however and had come forward, but many of them were itinerant like me, and the rest didn't have the incentive I had to see this through. All I can say is I felt it was important in my heart to have my day in court.

In the background something was making me uneasy, and I had a suspicion agendas were being hatched back in Road Town which might not necessarily be for my benefit.

There were whispers circulating that it would be far better for all concerned when this matter was laid to rest, and the main tourist and financial industries which relied on safety and security to survive and thrive could get back on track after the unpleasantness of the very public shooting. My continued presence in the British Virgin Islands was not exactly helping these aims and I was a constant reminder to some that all was not perfect in paradise. For these interested parties the day I decided to pack up and leave could not come soon enough.

It was somewhat embarrassing for those in power that I had been shot by a policeman, as this didn't exactly instill trust in potential visitors and investors. People wondering where to take their family on holiday or businesses considering where to put their money may not be so quick to bring either to a place where it wasn't just the criminals who might shoot you, but the cops do too.

I knew that the respite I had been given by Doctor Tattersall's timely intervention would probably prove short lived, as there were obviously things going on inside my body that needed to be dealt with, so I decided now to focus on an agenda of my own before my health problems made free choice impossible.

Returning to Mango Bay with a renewed vitality and vigour, not to mention a sense of purpose which always helps to get the blood fired up, I began bombarding the Attorney General, the Governor, the Commissioner of Police - in fact anyone who I thought could exert some influence on the situation - with phone calls, letters and faxes to try to get a preliminary hearing date set and soon.

Before long I began to receive strange notes in reply, some hand-written, some typed on official headed notepaper from various high offices, at first asking politely how I was and (in my view) feigning sympathy, then ending with surreptitious enquiries about what I was planning to do next, and when did I think I would be leaving the BVI?

One such message was left for me at the Mango Bay office and after I had explained to the relevant person that I would not be happy leaving the Caribbean by aeroplane due to the delicate condition of my lungs, a further note was sent with a schedule attached for a cruise ship just about to dock in Tortola, thereafter heading across the Atlantic to Southampton, and asking if I would like to be on it? Because if so that could easily be arranged...

I could have gone to the press and media and blown the story wide open, of how a tourist can be attacked and all the government can think of is how quickly they can hush it up. This was a sword of Damocles I held over the powers that be, but publicity is a double-edged weapon, so for now I kept that option in reserve.

After much persistent pestering a date was eventually mooted for the hearing to take place; Wednesday the 23rd of March, almost three weeks from my operation at the Bougainvillea. This was just not good enough. The clock was ticking and I wanted action, and these delays posed a great risk to my health. I also couldn't shake the thought that when this date eventually arrived, it might miraculously conflict with another case, or the Judge catch cold, and there would be a further delay and so on until I got fed up, went back to England and washed my hands of the whole affair.

Nevertheless at least I had something positive to work with, and from here I felt that it was just a short step to be able to persuade the court to bring the date forward in view of my circumstances. There were no doubt good people working on my behalf in the government and elsewhere, counterbalancing the faceless types who thought only of themselves and the bottom line, so I determined to rally as much support as I could to my cause. Acting on the theory that it's not what you know but who you know, I decided to take another ferry back to Tortola and pay a visit to my old friend Cyril Romney.

If anyone could help, Cyril could, but would he? He was an ex-Chief Minister, a serious player in the world of commerce, and a nice guy. No doubt he also had vested interests on both sides of this fence.

As always when I entered Mr. Romney's plush offices, I was greeted with a warm handshake and an immediate offer of something to drink (non-alcoholic) which one of his staff obligingly went off to make. He then ushered me into his glass-walled study to discuss what was on my mind. The layout was of an open-plan design, so everyone could see everyone else including the current occupants of the back room where Cyril worked, but conversations although seen could not be heard.

After gladly accepting my usual glass of freshly squeezed orange juice, I explained my problem: I needed my deposition to be brought forward from the tentative March 23rd date, as my return to the UK was now imminent. I didn't want to completely expose my hand and tell him of what precisely had transpired at the Bougainvillea Clinic, at least until I knew where he stood, so I bluffed and told Cyril in no uncertain terms that there was no way whilst I had a breath in my body that I was going to let this matter fade away and be swept under the carpet. I was sticking around in the BVI until my testimony could be heard, and I was prepared to risk all to do so.

Cyril stood leaning against the front of his desk nodding his head thoughtfully as he weighed up all I said.

'I think we should meet someone', he said simply after a few seconds' consideration, and with that he took his office keys and putting them in his pocket asked if I wouldn't mind taking a stroll around the corner with him to Peebles Hospital.

I replied that would be fine, as I wanted to see Doctor Smith anyway to bring him up to date with what had transpired at the Bougainvillea Clinic, and also to speak with him about a medical report to submit to the Court when the time came. So with that we left the cool of his air-conditioned suite and headed out into the blazing heat of a mid-day sun.

Even Cyril who had lived there all his life was perspiring slightly by the time we arrived a few minutes later at the gated entrance to Peebles Hospital. Myself I was absolutely soaked to the skin. Fortunately you dress accordingly if you know what to expect, so my more causal cotton shorts and light shirt quickly dried out, but I marvelled at the way my partner strolled down the dusty street wearing suit trousers, a long-sleeved shirt and leather shoes and wondered how long I would have to live here to reach that level of heat tolerance.

As I stood and steamed in the humid stone foyer, Cyril said he would be back shortly and disappeared down a hospital corridor. I asked a passing attendant if I could speak with Doctor Smith to see if he might be available for a quick chat. I don't know what made me think I could just wander in off the street and meet with the Chief Medical Officer of the BVI anytime I felt like it, maybe it was the casual nature of the Caribbean rubbing off on me, but anyway as the porter went off to find Doctor Smith I took a seat and waited.

After a few minutes a nurse called me into a side room containing a single bed, its headboard against one wall and the foot of the bed extending out into the middle of the floor. There was a second closed door and little else.

Doctor Smith had just returned from his conference and was busy catching up with his regular duties, but told me as he came in that he was glad of the opportunity to see me and give me my first official check-up since I left Tortola.

Into the room immediately behind him walked the two Danish interns, and it was nice to see them again and exchange a few words. They didn't stay for the examination, and as we said goodbye possibly for the last time, I looked at their white faces and wondered if they would ever get a chance to enjoy at least some Caribbean sun before they went home.

Attended to by Doctor Smith and the nurse, my chest was listened to, my breathing checked, bullet holes examined, and he also took a professional interest in the several small thick scabs on my lower back courtesy of Doctor Tattersall.

I tentatively raised the subject of possible infection, paranoid that in some way Doctor Smith would think that I was casting aspersions on anything he may have been responsible for whilst in his care. I had some doubts about my initial treatment; the kids running up and down the wards, the unsanitary glass jar fermenting in my hospital room, but it was my choice and no other's to remain in Peebles Hospital post emergency treatment, as a medevac had been made available in the days after the shooting which I refused. I have to take full responsibility for that decision. If it had been Jenny who had been shot and the roles reversed I would not have listened to her and insisted she accept the transfer to a larger hospital with better facilities in America or wherever, but I recognised that I was not the easiest person to give instructions to and there are pros and cons to that.

The original wound would have been very unlikely to introduce pathogens into my body, as the intense heat of igniting gunpowder launching the bullet from its barrel and the friction of the air usually incinerates all bacteria lingering on either the projectile or a person's skin at the point of penetration. A bullet gets so hot that the lead can actually melt on impact even with soft flesh and pass through a body not in one single entity but exploding into a million microscopic pieces of molten shrapnel, and it is this which often proves fatal to gunshot victims as internal organs are instantaneously shredded leaving toxic lead spread throughout what is left of a person's insides.

The bullet that struck me had been nickel-tipped and was hard as a coin on the outside, so fortunately passed mostly intact right through me. A few small pieces had broken off under my ribcage which the doctor managed to remove with his finger during the emergency surgery (although some metal is still embedded in my sternum and shows up on X-rays to this day).

The high temperature not to mention chipping the odd bone had weakened the nickel to the extent that when it exited my chest and hit the wooden bar of the Bath and Turtle, the softened shell and the lead within had shattered on contact with the hard oak surface. The bits that survived therefore were too small to be worth digging out by a diligent CSI detective and theatrically presented in a plastic bag to a court at a later date, as all that remained were a few tiny granules and some marks just above knee height on a stained bar panel, quickly sanded and re-varnished after the police expressed little interest, and that was the end of that.

As Doctor Smith finished the examination I did what had become a habit whenever we met since that first night; thanked him profusely for all that he had done to the point of discomfort on his part. I couldn't help it; every time I saw him I became a little emotional as it took me instantly back to the operating theatre and the hour I laid awake there, and all that entailed.

He and the nurse left the room saying he would be back in a moment with my notes, and I was left to put on my now dry shirt and await his return. When this was not immediate I at first sat, then lay back on the bed propped up by pillows at the headrest, crossed my arms in front of me, lifted my shoed feet onto the mattress, and scanned the sparse room feeling relaxed and composed.

There was a brief knock at the door to the corridor, and I called out to the person or people on the other side to enter. It opened and in came Cyril Romney with another man behind him wearing grey suit trousers, a white shirt puffed up at the elbows with sleeve garters, and expensive-looking spectacles hanging on a shiny gold chain around his neck. I didn't recognise this other person at first, but something about him looked familiar.

'Hello again Mr. Hartwell,' (Cyril, very formal!) 'this is Mr. Ralph O'Neal, the Chief Minister of the Virgin Islands.'

Okay now I knew him. This was the man who had shown me around the block of apartments in Spanish Town soon after we arrived on Virgin Gorda. The man who I had first seen pensively fidgeting with his keys in his trouser pockets annoyed at my late arrival as I sauntered up the road on a flat-hunting expedition in the Valley. The man I had belatedly realised was not merely a small-time property developer, but a person of very high office and in fact the ruler of this small nation.

Wow. When Cyril pulled strings he yanked the whole loom.

I tried to and I hope succeeded in concealing my surprise, as Cyril Romney, 'Mr.' O'Neal and I talked, them both standing at the end of my bed, Mr. O'Neal with his hands in his pockets as before, and Cyril leaning forward with both palms on the rail above the foot of the mattress. I lay there like an afflicted emperor holding court before my two ministers of state, both of whom spent the entire time nodding sagely, avoiding my eyes and repeating endlessly to each other and to me; 'Terrible. Terrible thing. Terrible thing to have happened. Really!'

We remained there the three of us for a few minutes, not sharing much of any real substance. Mr. O'Neal gave me the distinct impression that he would rather be anywhere else but here in this hospital room with me, and I began to wonder if this was what Cyril had in mind when we purposefully set off from his office an hour or so before.

Not knowing what to say I mentioned that we had already met, meaning 'Ralph' and I, which brought an awkward acknowledgement in response, and me immediately wishing that I hadn't said anything.

Then in walked Doctor Smith without knocking from the second door. He half-looked up from the medical files he was carrying and gave the merest nod to the two Chief Ministers present and an almost imperceptible hello.

The greetings were politely returned, and I understood that if not necessarily friends, these three men of stature were all known to each other and comfortable with their separate positions within the hierarchy of the state. They were all of a similar age, all from the BVI and all ministers in one form or another, so it wasn't all that surprising I suppose.

The unusual meeting over, Cyril and Mr. O'Neal left, Doctor Smith staying to discuss something with me which turned out to be very relevant to the task in hand.

Several years later, Doctor Orlando Smith entered politics full-time, eventually replacing Ralph O'Neal as Chief Minister of the British Virgin Islands. So looking back on that day in Peebles Hospital I had a fleeting moment where a carpenter from Kent held the attention of not one, not two, but three prime ministers, which I don't imagine will ever happen again in my lifetime.

Chapter 24 - Playing politics

What the thinking was behind Cyril and Mr. O'Neal's visit to my hospital bed I cannot say for sure. Was it an opportunity to express sympathy on the current Chief Minister's part? Or a subtle bit of politicking by Cyril Romney to make me real in the eyes of the most powerful person in the state and therefore worthy of consideration?

Honestly, for a bit-player it made me feel important, that I mattered, and that was something. I had a two-fronted battle going on right now with the worlds of health and law and I didn't know much about either, so an ego boost if that's all it was, was definitely welcome. But I suspect there was more to it than that.

The next item on the agenda was to acquire from a recognised medical expert an insurance indemnity allowing me to fly, although in slight contradiction to this also to delay the receipt of that essential document for just long enough so that I could stick around in the Caribbean in order to attend the court hearing hopefully about to be held largely for my benefit. I came to see this as simply a matter of juggling a few facts in the air and not letting them bump into each other or fall to the ground until it no longer altered the outcome.

The one thing of note that Doctor Smith had ascertained during my brief examination was that my lungs were now adequately inflated and the original bullet holes sufficiently healed for me to be able to fly. Granted, I had just been through minor chest surgery at the Bougainvillea Clinic, but my lungs had thankfully survived the ordeal intact, and in his opinion I could leave as soon as I liked.

Medical advice in these situations is that one should wait at least twenty four hours after chest surgery before giving the all-clear just to make as certain as one can that no harm to any vital organs has been done and inadvertently gone unnoticed during the operation. As that period had safely elapsed with no ill effects it seemed that I was good to go. Now time was of the essence, and it was almost a battle of wills to see who would crack first; me and leave the BVI unsure if anyone else had the drive to push this case through to its conclusion rather than a quick plea deal by the accused and a deportation to his home island; or 'they', the secretive powers who definitely did not want the fuss and exposure of a high profile court case dragging on for months and potentially damaging their interests.

Any wind they caught of my enforced departure I was certain would be exploited to the max.

I shouldn't have had to deal with this, and wasn't sure anymore which problems in my life were of my own making and which had been thrust upon me. I had a job to do, and I focussed on that.

As I left the hospital following the examination by Doctor Smith, I decided as far as my dealings with the government were concerned to continue to play for time on the assertion that I was still too weak to undertake an arduous journey home across the Atlantic. I could also if necessary allude to the fact that my chest wall down in my lower back had recently been pierced and so needed further time to recover from that new trauma. But this was clutching at straws and risked contradicting Doctor Smith which I didn't want to do.

Still, I felt positive, and decided to give my badgering of the authorities a rest for a while and see what if anything would transpire from the hospital meeting.

Now all that was left to do was return to that little slice of Italy on Mahoe Bay, eat, swim, doze in the shade on my palm tree hammock, and wait.

I could do that.

Chapter 25 - Licence to fly

Mango Bay was seductive. Living here was like hanging out in a pleasant dream, reality biting whenever I passed under the gate on the road to Spanish Town or picked up a pile of faxes with scratched government seals from Agnes's desk.

While I mulled over my amateur attempts at Machiavellianism on the beach and balconies of our hideaway, I began to notice some symptoms creeping back, reminding me as if I needed it that the clock was still ticking.

After the miraculous improvement in my breathing and general condition since Doctor Tattersall removed most of the liquid constricting my chest, within a few days nausea and shortness of breath returned in the mornings especially, little by little sapping me of my strength. This wasn't really much of a surprise as I knew that my body was far from healed, and the infections although quiet were still presumably there waiting to pounce when my immune system was low or just whenever they felt like it. The bacteria had been robbed of their main food source of a jugful of nutrient-rich liquid inside the warm incubator of my chest, but had not disappeared altogether, and in time were sure to regroup and multiply causing me ongoing problems until they were snuffed out permanently.

It was basically a large irritated wound, oozing lymph and used white blood cells. If this was on the skin it could be wiped away and disinfected, but inside my chest there was nowhere for it to go, so there it stayed encouraging more inflammation. The healthy tissue around my lungs given the chance would gradually reabsorb any unwelcome material and my lymphatic system filter and expel it, but the more fluid there was, the greater the area of inflammation, the less healthy tissue was available to mop up the mess.

The bacteria created toxins which further aggravated everything becoming a vicious circle and if I wasn't careful the right lung particularly could be damaged beyond repair. Both Doctor Tattersall and Doctor Smith had prescribed me short courses of broad-spectrum antibiotics, but they were not targeted and inadequate to prevent further infection, so the first job of a chest specialist when I eventually got to see one would be to identify the specific bacteria and then blast it with the appropriate drug. The consensus was that this would break the cycle and set me on the road to recovery.

Imagining that awful gunk inside my body made me feel quite sick psychologically as well as physically if I ever stopped to think about it, so most of the time I tried not to. No wonder I had felt so crap. I'd believed up until that point this was just my body's response to the shooting and a part of the natural healing process and not instead all that extra nonsense of leaking internal body parts and infections.

Finally more than a week after my visit to Road Town the news I had been waiting for arrived.

A facsimile rendition of an official court document announced that a preliminary hearing in the matter of Regina versus X, had been tabled to take place at 9am Friday the 18th of March at the High Courts of Justice in Tortola. The letter also named the Judge who would oversee the session as Justice Ephraim Georges, a Dominican jurist ironically from the same Caribbean island as the rogue policeman.

On the face of it the March 18th date was only five days earlier than the potential March 23rd date I had previously rejected out of hand, but that had come in the form of a telephone call received late one evening from a police inspector, and although honestly imparted, was hardly something I could hang my hat on.

This had more of a feel of authenticity, and gave me the confidence to get moving and organise my certificate to fly. I considered and dismissed the idea of asking Doctor Smith to do this as I wanted to retain an element of control over both the information it contained and the timing of its delivery, as well as creating some distance between myself and the government. I trusted Doctor Smith implicitly, and had no reason to doubt Mr. O'Neal's motives; these were purely tactics on my part.

So, what to do now?

I first contacted Doctor Tattersall, making out that I was not happy with a certificate issued from Peebles Hospital instead preferring to obtain an independent opinion, but he was off-island somewhere so it was back to the Yellow Pages for some inspiration.

With a bit of lateral thinking I hit upon a plan; why not hop across to nearby St Thomas in the United States Virgin Islands and try to get it done there? Jenny and I knew the island quite well as it was where we'd got married a year before, and we were sure to find an appropriate doctor in Charlotte Amalie.

A few phone calls led me to a Doctor Sidney Comissiong M.D., but he was a hard man to pin down. His secretary informed us that his private clinic was booked solid for the next couple of weeks and that there was virtually no chance of fitting us into his regular schedule, as even his cancellation appointments had a waiting list.

I took this as a good sign as he was obviously a popular doctor, and in the private healthcare systems of America where people watch very carefully where they put their money, a popular doctor is usually a good one (either that or cheap, which he wasn't). As I was about to ring off and reluctantly restart the search for another physician, his secretary suggested a possible solution, that of me coming to the public St Thomas Hospital as an outpatient and presenting myself at the Emergency Room during Doctor Comissiong's next shift. In advance of this she would inform him of my situation and imminent arrival and he could try to see me in the accident and emergency department as long as he wasn't too busy.

This seemed like a gamble worth taking, and in any case I didn't see that I had much choice. Time was short and I really had to get cracking or I was in danger of being in the crazy position of giving my evidence in court on the scheduled day, and then having to wait to leave the BVI until medical clearance to fly was successfully obtained.

In an ideal world I would deliver my testimony and get a cab straight from the court to the airport and home to the UK. This degree of co-ordination would be difficult to achieve, but I was determined to give it my best shot.

So, on Monday the 14th of March Jenny and I took a taxi from Mango Bay and headed south for the local airstrip, situated on the far side of a long tree-covered ridge that separated the Valley from the rocky eastern coastline of Virgin Gorda. As we passed through the outskirts of Spanish Town we recognised ahead of us a small group of hills on the far southern edge of town where could be found Heather's hidden wooden home, and on another adjacent hilltop clearly see the green and white structure of the Catholic Church, which had been the first real landmark that we could identify and get our bearings from as we travelled around the island in the days after our arrival.

We had only met Heather once since the shooting when we'd all had lunch together in the Valley, and it had been a strained encounter with plenty of awkward moments and uncomfortable silences. I got the feeling that she'd had enough of sickness and death with the passing of her dear departed husband, and preferred to restrict her interactions as much as possible to the superficial.

I'm sad to say that after that last meeting we never found an opportunity to share another sundowner with our first island host.

Arriving at the dirt runway we drove over to the single storey reception building which served as the check-in desk, luggage store, taxi rank, and virtually the only shelter from the sun for anyone waiting for a flight. Not much more than a wooden shack, the terminal if you can call it that was a tight fit even for the two regular cashiers sitting side by side behind a faded and chipped Formica counter, and if more than three people entered at once it became positively snug.

Air tickets were usually dispensed to travellers outside through a large double-hatched window on the north-western wall of the building, and whether by luck or good judgement this happened to be the side most often in shadow given that most flights took off in the morning or early afternoon.

We paid our driver, who stayed to chat with the other cab-
bies passing the morning waiting for a fare, then checked in
and collected our tickets having already booked them before
by telephone. After half an hour or so rubbing shoulders with
several other people in the extremely limited shade, a jacketless pilot wearing a blue peaked cap and a crisp white short-
sleeved shirt appeared from inside the building and led us over to a small twin-engined aeroplane lined up with several others on the dry grass at the edge of the runway.

Struggling at the back of the queue, some locals wrestled
with armfuls of cumbersome boxes and packages wrapped neatly in brown paper and tied with string. Some of the mystery
items appeared so large that I wondered how they would ever
get them through the narrow cabin door, and if they did how
they would then squeeze themselves in afterwards and still leave room for the rest of us to breathe.

I felt pretty certain that if the stragglers all chose to sit on
one side of the plane it would be in severe danger of tipping
over on one wing on the runway, or if not and we did manage
to get airborne be forced to fly around in circles until we ran
out of fuel and had to swim the rest of the way to St Thomas.

Our pilot was evidently well versed in such dilemmas, as
he politely directed everyone to various seats of his choosing.
He did this looking over his shoulder from a twisting position
in his own very comfortable pilot's chair. There was no room
aboard for a co-pilot nor stewards or stewardesses.

Once satisfied that we were all safely settled into our correct places and the weight had been evenly distributed according to his experienced eye, he asked that we made sure we we-

re all securely buckled in and donning his headgear ignited the engines. The propellers engaged, and loudly gunning the throttle we bumped over the grass to the end of the runaway.

With a quick burst of acceleration we were airborne almost immediately and the bone-shaking judders of everything inside the cabin instantly adjusted to a serene hum, the engines high-revving but smooth as we climbed steeply above the fast shrinking island of Virgin Gorda.

The issue of my lung damage was not a concern on a short flight like this, as although it felt pretty high, the altitude was never such that it required a pressurised cabin. Propeller-driven aeroplanes which operate on circuitous shuttle runs like this are often not constructed to be completely air-tight and thus are incapable of fully pressurising anyway. St Thomas was not too far away and about the same distance on the other side of Tortola as Tortola was from Virgin Gorda. Looking out across the sea from Mango Bay, if it were not for the green landmass of the BVI's capital blocking your view, the high peaks of the US Virgin Islands would be clearly visible on the south-western horizon.

There was a ferry linking the British and American Virgin Islands, but this took several hours and if the sea was choppy it was by all accounts quite an arduous crossing. If the settlements on the collective Islands were on the mainland and connected by highways, the farthest towns would be an hour apart at most. By air in contrast it took almost as long to climb to cruising altitude as it did to cross the ocean, and just as the plane flattened out in the sky, it would be time to start the descent to the destination landing strip.

We rose in a straight line north, and there is not much in this world as spectacular as the Caribbean from the vantage of a small aeroplane. Flying over the Lesser Antilles on this clear blue day was really something. First we approached the mini-mountain splitting Virgin Gorda in half, the weather beacon and red and white navigational tower at its peak zipping below our wings almost clipping our wheels as we surpassed the summit heading for the North Sound.

The impression I'd got from walking around the skirts of Gorda Peak or driving through the pass to Leverick Bay, had been of a dry but generally green landscape. From up here the mountainside looked barren and sparse with only a few tightly grouped collections of trees and occasional scrub to break up the monotony of otherwise large tracts of brown and grey mis-shapen rocks.

As the north face fell precipitously away the beautiful swe-ep of Leverick Bay suddenly emerged, the windows of hundr-eds of holiday villas perched upon the hillside glinting sharply in the sun, temporarily blinding and forcing me to look away until they passed beneath. Somewhere in amongst the neat ro-ws of sailing boats lined up in the water, no doubt the yacht on which I'd sailed with Heather bobbed up and down tied to its mooring buoy, secured with a knot that may well have be-en tied by my own hands assuming the doctor hadn't found a replacement crew between then and now.

Ahead I picked out Necker, its tall pagoda rising up through surrounding trees distinguishing it from the other islands, tog-ether looking like green and brown rough-edged bacteria floa-ting in a giant Petri dish of Royal blue. Several brightly colour-ed catamarans raced each other in its inshore waters whilst people cheered them on from the beach, and I wondered which star might be enjoying the haven of Necker below.

We floated atop the last of the northerly islands, and levelling off having achieved the required height turned in a broad arc southwards and once more back down over Virgin Gorda. Looking to the right I could see Tortola, and for the first time our destination of the USVI beyond.

We flew now down the spine of Virgin Gorda, defined by the ridge of steep hills ranging from Gorda Peak to the southernmost tip at the Baths. The mountain quickly swept past but we were much higher this time flying directly above Spanish Town, and underneath I spotted my beloved Valley Trunk, just a thin golden line separating green from blue.

There was the verdigris roof of the Catholic Church, rising like a beacon in an Eden of trees, looking out across the sea beckoning followers to make haste and come enter paradise.

In a few seconds Valley Trunk and the hilltop church were behind us, and barely having time to register the tiny boulders of the Baths we were soaring high over the busy ocean.

Long white wakes expanded out across the sea with fast ferries speeding at their head, slower more sedate white triangles crossing in front and behind them.

Banking steeply to the right, Beef Island, the Causeway, the winding Ridge Road then Road Town itself all quickly passed. Another green spine, longer this time then ocean again and a dark misty shape, splitting into two as we drew closer; St Thomas and nearer St John.

As I strained to peer forward out of the cockpit and catch my first glimpse of St Thomas, we began our descent, circling slowly down in preparation for our landing at the Cyril E. King Airport of Charlotte Amalie.

What was my first impression after three months of green and crystal gold and blue?

Concrete.

White concrete, grey concrete. Clean concrete and dirty concrete.

Everywhere hard, flat and devoid of texture aside from scurrying human beings and snaking vehicles.

Peppered across this expanse of cement were aeroplanes, some far larger than ours and emblazoned with colours and painted-on flags, some parked and alone, some taxiing or waiting at huge stop signs for the go-ahead to take off or find their place at a terminal ramp.

There were myriad warehouses, steel-shuttered aeroplane pens, glass fronted buildings and a hundred or more trucks and buses of every type, large and small ranging from one-person luggage trains to huge double and triple articulated low-loaders tracing their way around the unseen lane markings on the ground. Tiny human forms moved between everything, looking slightly pointless as most people's meanderings do when viewed from afar.

The grime of civilisation.

I actually kind of missed it.

The US Virgin Islands are about the same size as their British counterparts, but what a difference. Architecture and man's influence on the land can be every bit as spectacular as nature's if it's done right, and it was completely obvious looking down at the log-jammed highways and grids of houses and offices which side St Thomas thought its bread was buttered.

The signs of industry were everywhere, and although in reality green still dominated beyond the towns, after three months of paradise-like vistas it was quite a shock to my system.

And the noise!

As we drew to a stop and our own engines faded, even before our door opened the whistling of too-close jets filled our tight cabin.

Mango Bay could be so quiet that on occasion in between the shuffling of waves lapping the shore like rice falling in a dry saucepan, more than once I heard the unfeasible sound of tiny scaled feet scratching in the sand as finger-sized geckos flicked past me on the beach, stopping to investigate a dropped breadcrumb from my lunchtime sandwich. That must surely be the definition of peace and quiet - being able to detect the delicate rustling of inquisitive claws pushing aside individual grains of sand, by a lizard out on a mid-day scavenge in the baking sun of a tropical beach.

And now this!

Some sweaty paddle-waving men directed us through the shimmering heat haze to the sliding glass doors of our terminal building, and the formalities of American Customs and Immigration being somewhat laxer pre-9/11, we passed through the border controls quite quickly. Leaving through the main exit past some sorry-looking palm trees abutted by tarmac and paving slabs, we made for the taxi rank and hopped into a cab for the St Thomas Hospital.

Leaving the car park we immediately fell into a long line of stationary cars sitting steaming in a lunchtime traffic jam.

We made slow progress, eventually the traffic easing up as we traversed Charlotte Amalie. Before turning left for the hospital, looking out of the taxi window high up on a wide incline I saw a place I recognised.

Paradise Point; a pleasant establishment with a terraced bar and restaurant, and a view overlooking Charlotte Amalie's cruise dock. It was also the place where not so long ago Jenny and I exchanged our vows witnessed by a few of her cruise ship buddies over a couple of beers and a barbeque.

Jenny followed my eyes and saw it too.

Neither of us said anything as our cab turned into the hospital grounds and the hillside passed from our sight.

Chapter 26 - Doctor Comissiong and the haemopneumothorax

Sidney Comissiong M.D. was the Senior Attending Physician of the St Thomas Hospital and Community Health Center in Charlotte Amalie.

He was aged about forty, with short cropped greying hair, a gravelly voice and a hint of cigarettes about him. Almost all doctors back in the UK had given up smoking by the mid-1990's, and it was also hard to find any back home who managed to find the time to be a sports nut.

Doctor Comissiong was obviously a very fit guy, and carried himself with that confidence as well as a relaxed air that made you think he was just the sort of guy you would want nearby in a crisis.

We first met him, Jenny and I, in the second 'inner' waiting room of the St Thomas Hospital accident and emergency department having first been necessary to negotiate the outer waiting room, which I will describe here.

In England medical treatment is essentially free at the point of use, making healthcare a political football which stumbles along permanently somewhere between the two extremes of triumph and disaster. But in the words of Winston Churchill, it is the best worst system, and thus in my view should never be changed. Healthcare should be owned by and run for the benefit of the people, the same as education and justice, or else the rich get well while the poor stay sick, and that can never be right.

On entering A&E (or the ER for Americans) in a UK hospital we have a simple arrangement; you enter, say what has happened or you think may be wrong with you, and then you wait. In due course you will be seen by a nurse or a doctor and your care will begin. Simple, straightforward, and to the point. To prevent the lengthy waiting times of the past, firm guidelines are in place that require the patient to be seen by a triage nurse within a set period of time to assess whether or not the case is urgent, and then dealt with in A&E or sent onwards for specialist care as appropriate.

Sometimes things go wrong as in any system. Sometimes waits can be excessive, sometimes a patient is not treated well and occasionally has to endure low staffing levels or way too much bureaucracy, but generally it works, and eventually you will be seen, and will almost always receive excellent care whatever the problem may be.

America in the 1990's however was different, because then if you were sick and poor, you suffered. This did give one the incentive to try not to be poor, and perhaps even strive to be rich, but what if you couldn't? What if you had tried and failed, or could not work because you were chronically ill, or chose to spend your life serving others for the good of the community and so not pursue money as a goal in itself?

In the afternoon of Monday the 14th of March Jenny and I alighted from the taxi outside the Emergency Room of the St Thomas Hospital. We didn't have an appointment as such, but knew that our chosen doctor was working a shift that afternoon and if his secretary had been true to her word he was aware that we were coming. We were prepared to wait for as long as it took, my situation not being by any stretch of the imagination urgent, not in comparison to a car accident or heart attack at any rate, as long as in the end I got my precious certificate.

Not knowing the arrival procedure in American hospitals, we walked in, looked around and took a seat.

The room was unimaginatively decorated and aside from a few lacklustre cheap prints on the walls and a couple of children's books and games scattered on the floor, it appeared sparse and unloved. It was about the size of a small classroom, with the same kind of cheap plastic chairs that one would expect to find there lining three of the four orange-painted walls. On the far wall opposite the entrance was a large metal door with a small thick pane of glass at head height buried deep within its very thick mass, and no door handle at all that I could see on this side. To the right of this lay a rectangular wooden counter stretching into the corner of the room, another door behind it presumably leading to the same place that the steel door went. The whole counter was completely enclosed to the exposed side and front with solid sheets of Plexiglas making it about as impregnable as a bank cashier's desk. The screen looked strong enough to be bullet proof, and knowing where we were it may indeed have been.

Behind the desk a woman sat typing, and immediately in front of her on the transparent screen was a grill, of the convoluted type which the only thing that could pass through would be a voice.

Seated around the edge of the stuffy room were six or seven people, all West Indian, all looking tired and bored and as though they had been there a long time. Two or three were children, the rest adults of varying age. Some had wounds on show, some did not, but all obviously needed medical treatment or I guessed they would not be here.

After several minutes twiddling our thumbs waiting for a medical practitioner to appear, and without the woman behind the counter even looking up to acknowledge our entry, I decided to go and see what's what.

I walked over to the desk, and dropping my face to the grill designed for people shorter than me I spoke.

'Hello.' My opening gambit.

The woman looked up. Having ceased typing temporarily and now writing in a notepad she shuffled the pen in her fingers and studied me from the top of her glasses. With her shoulders still hunched over and her elbows on the desk, she gestured with one forefinger to a small intercom button on the counter on my side of the Plexiglas.

'Push...the...button', she mouthed from the other side of the glass.

I did as she instructed.

'Hello', I repeated.

'Can I help you?', she responded with an electronic tinge to her voice.

I explained my slightly unusual reason for being there.

'You want to fly somewhere?', she asked screwing up her face like I was mad/in the wrong place/both.

Concerned that her next offering was to be that this was not a travel agency I decided to head her off with three magic words.

'I have insurance.'

I might just as well have said; 'Open Sesame'.

Not much caring anymore whether I required a coronary bypass or a club sandwich, the fact that I had insurance covering it was good enough for her.

She asked if I had any proof of cover and to hold it up to the glass, and having passed this first cursory inspection she motioned for me to slide the policy through to her. I noticed by the intercom button a thin sliver of space between the counter and the vertical wall of glass, just about wide enough to convey an envelope or folded piece of paper.

The format of my insurance was apparently a little different to what she was used to and maybe not too many Brits came through this way, but America and England share almost the same language, and within a few seconds she decided that my covernote was genuine and thereafter began to take my details down for the hospital entry forms. She then pressed another button hidden somewhere under the desk on her side, and an electronic buzz emanated to my left. The huge metal door next to where I stood jumped open a few inches, and after the motor caught up with the spring it continued to swing smoothly inwards until the opening was wide enough for two averagely built people to walk comfortably through side by side.

This all seemed fairly bizarre to Jenny and me, and as we peered ahead into the white glare it felt more like staring at a wardrobe door about to enter Narnia than a hospital's innards. Still, I was curious to see what lay beyond, so we grabbed our bags and hesitantly stepped forward.

The door wasn't actually steel I reasoned, but probably a heavy wooden fire door encased in a thin sheet of aluminium or some other metal, but in any case the point was clearly made: do not even think about coming in until we say you can!

No sooner we were through I recognised our new location immediately as a regular hospital waiting room.

In total perhaps twenty people sat in several rows of chairs. The patients were from a wide range of ethnicities, and while not necessarily seeming comfortable being in a hospital emergency room, certainly not giving the impression of being abandoned or forlorn.

There was also the conspicuous presence of not one nurse taking triage, but three. They moved around the room leaning in and talking with the seated people, taking notes and politely leading individuals and groups into and out of little curtained-off side rooms.

Several sets of double doors led off in different directions, the only metal sheathing required on them being low down as protection from wayward trolleys. The shiny door we had just passed through now automatically shut behind us with a quiet clunk.

I looked over my shoulder through the little glass panel to the stark orange room on the other side. The receptionist was already no doubt re-engrossed in her typing, the pitiful patients being resolutely ignored by her and the world in general.

I asked one of the triage nurses why there were two waiting rooms, and who those people were on the other side, even though I knew what the answer must be.

'Oh, they don't have insurance,' she said matter-of-factly, and then went cheerfully straight into; 'and what can I do for you, sir!'

This was bonkers. These people needed care, no different to me, so why were they on that side of the door and I was stood here? And why were they all West Indian, like the nurses now attending us, while the patients in the genuine ER room were from a cross-section of society?

There was no time to ponder this as the nurse wanted answers to her questions in order to serve us better, and she had a job to do, as did we, so I put my thoughts about an unfair world to one side for the moment and explained my problem and what I hoped could be done about it.

Eventually the penny dropped and after discussing the matter with one of the green theatre-suited ER doctors, our happy nurse came back and told us that none of the staff present were able to carry out this task, so if we liked we could wait for Doctor Comissiong, who was currently in theatre and would be out shortly.

This was fine with us as that had been our plan all along anyway. I think that some of the other doctors could well have been able to help us had we been inclined to pester them, but it was a busy day in the hospital and we were not an emergency case, so we sat and waited for our man.

And we waited.

And we waited.

Several hours passed, with periodic exploratory trips to the cafeteria and toilets, more to relieve the tedium than anything else, and taken in turns so that we didn't miss the doctor if and when he showed up.

As we alternated people-watching and staring at the walls, I thought about what we had seen in the original outer waiting room and wondered what it said about equality in any system which allows poor and predominantly black people to stay sick, while because we had access to money and insurance, we were dealt with immediately, notwithstanding our current boredom but that was of our own making not the hospital's. All the people of the world own the world's resources equally, and we should be differentiated only by our efforts to excel. An accident of birth alone had put me on this privileged side of the door, and that made me feel very uncomfortable.

Not so uncomfortable that I was prepared to give up my place in the queue, so what did that say about me?

From time to time I asked the nurses, first of one shift then others from the next new set of faces when Doctor Comissiong would arrive, and the answer was always a variation of; 'He knows you are waiting, he will be here shortly but he is verrry busy.'

The afternoon drifted on into evening and the fluorescent lights in the hospital got brighter as the windows outside got darker.

Eventually the story started changing and I was told that Doctor Comissiong was now out of theatre and was 'around somewhere', that he was aware of us, and once again that he would be with us shortly.

We watched the patients slowly displacing around us, the ones that had been there longest breaking off and disappearing through different sets of doors accompanied by a doctor or a nurse, new arrivals taking their place. Some came with grazes on their legs and arms and carrying motorbike helmets (smart) but also wearing shorts and t-shirts (silly), some others had rudimentarily bandaged heads and paint on their overalls and hands (an unstable decorating ladder in their very recent past maybe?) looking a bit fed up that they'd had to stop earning a crust for the day and take a trip to casualty. Many however just wandered in through the buzzing steel door or internally from another part of the hospital hiding whatever ailment they carried as we looked at them and macabrely tried to guess what it was that had brought them here today.

At long last our doctor arrived, who judging by the flirtatious looks the nurses gave him was more than a little popular with the opposite sex. One cooed to us as he walked in, 'Oo, e-everybody likes Doctor Comissiong, he is so-o nice.'

So I guess that's settled then; he was nice and everybody liked him.

Or maybe American women just like doctors, but anyway I have to admit he was kind of a cool guy.

Introductions completed, I quickly explained what I required of the good doctor, and he seemed far more switched on than everyone else we had told our problem to up until that point because he got the gist of it before I had finished speaking.

He said that he was supposed to finish at 4pm, then 6, and then again at 7.30, and now it was almost 10pm, and we had only just begun. Apparently after us he had yet more patients to see. Hearing this we didn't have the heart to complain about our own very long wait as he was obviously having a far harder day than ours.

As we traversed the maze of white passageways towards the examination room we chatted, he asking about my injuries and how they came about, and Jenny and I asking about his life on St Thomas. He said that he played baseball, and was supposed to be coaching that night, but couldn't make it due to his workload. I apologised for adding to that, but not too much as we didn't want to give him the idea of slipping off and leaving us now that we finally had him cornered.

Spotting a crushed soft-pack of cigarettes in his shirt pocket I mentioned that he being a doctor and a smoker surprised me, him also being a sportsman into the mix, and he laughed and said that he had tried to give it up many times but his attempts had so far been unsuccessful.

Along a brightly lit corridor near to our destination we passed a row of identical rooms in the radiology department. Looking more closely they were individually identified by door plaques as each housing a CT scanner, helpfully numbered 1, 2 and 3.

This was both impressive and slightly bewildering to us as Brits. In 1994 Computerised Tomography scanners had only recently become widely available in Great Britain, at the time only large hospitals would have possessed a sole example. But here, in this well equipped but still what could only be described as the medium-sized city hospital of Charlotte Amalie, like the triage nurses when you looked for one you found two more! I was curious about this and asked how it came to be, and Doctor Comissiong explained that the hospital had originally only wanted a pair of scanners, but they managed to find a spare million and a half dollars in the budget from somewhere, so they bought three.

Surely it could not have been that simple?

'Only two of them have ever been switched on', he added as an afterthought as I glanced through a corridor window into the third room. In it I saw a futuristic gleaming cream and chrome machine. It had a long sliding bench and a huge smooth circular wheel positioned vertically at one end. Transparent plastic sheeting still covered the instrument panels as if it had just arrived fresh from the factory and after installation immediately abandoned like the Mary Celeste of tomography.

'I take it you haven't had a 'Cat'-scan since the shooting?', the doctor asked.

'Well, not to worry', he said in response to my headshake, 'I would like to have a really good look inside your chest and see exactly what's going on in there.'

I assumed from this that a CT scan was on the cards.

I had never had one of these before and only knew what I'd picked up anecdotally about what exactly they did. The X-rays they emitted were standard but in high doses, and the images formulated in such a way as to allow a computer to create three dimensional graphics of whichever body part had been scanned.

Furthermore if the software allowed for it the operator could then take this 3-D image and do crazy things with it, such as zooming-in to areas of interest, spinning the picture around to study it from every conceivable angle, and had the capability to measure suspicious growths or different aspects of injuries to the millimetre.

My heart sank. Not that I wasn't a tad excited at the prospect of experiencing what this wonderful machine did, but we were on a tight schedule. I imagined this now meant waiting for an appointment with a radiographer which probably ruled out getting my certificate to fly on this trip to Charlotte Amalie, and we'd be returning to Virgin Gorda empty handed.

It turned out that I was only half-right, as to my huge surprise bearing in mind the late hour and Doctor Comissiong's already ridiculously long day, he led Jenny and I into a clinical room a little way along the corridor from the CT suites and immediately got on the telephone to the on-call radiology team to arrange a scan for that very night.

Now I began to comprehend the benefits of private healthcare. Yin yang again. But what's good for me might be bad for someone else.

I asked Doctor Comissiong about the people I had seen earlier in the outer waiting room just as I had the nurses.

He simply shrugged and said; 'If we (the doctors) have time at the close of our shift we go and attend to a few of them. And we don't charge; we do it because it's the right thing.'

Nice, but it still seemed a bit random to me. Our doctor was obviously a compassionate guy who gave the impression of caring for his patients, but my soul-searching on this subject continued.

He then carried out a quick examination. I had a slight fever, to be expected given everything we knew about my health, but apart from that I was generally okay.

Then we were ready. He took me along to one of the working CT rooms and placed me in the care of the waiting staff.

They asked if I'd ever had one of these scans before, and if I knew what to expect. I replied in the negative and they told me to lay down on the electronic sliding platform.

A cannula was placed in a vein in the back of my hand, and I was advised to brace myself for a burning sensation followed by some slight nausea as a radio-contrast dye was injected into my bloodstream. The liquid was clear as it went in but I was assured that it would show up red on the image.

As the dye entered my bloodstream it felt like lava coursing around my body and was followed by lots of saliva swallowing as I fought off the urge to vomit. I would have described this as just plain nausea without the placating 'slight' in front of it.

I had to wait fifteen minutes for the chemical to take effect after which the technicians departed, leaving me alone lying on my back and staring up at a giant's halo.

The machine whirled to life and the narrow bed rolled slowly under the crown, making ticking and beeping noises all the while (the machine, not me). A voice crackled out from a hidden speaker somewhere, through it one of the technicians periodically reminding me not to move and keeping me informed of how much longer the procedure had to go counting down in thirty-second increments to zero.

The gurney moved backwards and forwards several times, stopping at different locations giving the spinning X-rays plenty of opportunity to get all the data the computer required. Finally having completed its task the generator span to a stop and fell silent. Gently automatically the platform rolled back out so that I could see polystyrene ceiling tiles above me once again, and given the okay to stand up I rejoined Doctor Comissiong and Jenny in the examination room.

One of the radiographers accompanied me back down the corridor and pulling a large plasticised folio from an envelope handed it to Doctor Comissiong.

I caught a glimpse of the image as it changed hands and to my untrained eye it was plain that this was something new and wonderful in the world of medicine to behold, and all I could say was; 'Wow!'

Not only was this the first Cat-scan image I had ever seen close up, it was also the first time I got a real sense of what happened to my body during the shooting.

It was quite honestly amazing - not in 3D but it might as well have been.

Every element of my upper torso was reproduced down to the tiniest speck, like an X-ray machine had woken up one morning, yawned, stretched, looked down at its flabby body and decided to hit the gym and enter the modern world. It was clear, it was coloured, and it was fantastically detailed.

My lungs showed up in transparent orange on the picture, and looking closer I could see a smudge of damaged tissue just behind them to the right of my spine coinciding with where I knew the bullet had entered my back, revealing that although on the outside the skin appeared to be healing quite nicely, out of sight under the surface it was still quite a mess.

Leading inwards away from the entry point trailed a hazy white line, like a cobweb drawn loosely right through my body ending at my breastbone. A perfect black circle at the top of the sternum wide enough to place the tip of a finger in was not there anymore, spoiling the otherwise solid band of white where the fronts of my ribs joined.

It appeared incredibly that the hazy line was the route the bullet had taken and was the computer's representation of the wake of disturbed flesh, and despite being more than a month later was still clearly visible.

Doctor Comissiong then held the thin sheet of coloured plastic up so that both Jenny and I could see, and slowly traced with his finger the path of the bullet, describing from a medical expert's perspective and explaining as he went various points of interest along the way.

With this and the benefit of hindsight I can give an idea of what occurred and some of the repercussions.

After penetrating the skin the bullet first encountered a couple of ribs close to the angle where they joined the spine. Squeezing tightly between them it struck both inner edges, bouncing off and chipping bits of bullet and bone which scattered inwards embedding fragments into the nearby flesh.

This glancing impact with dense matter caused the spinning bullet to deviate from its previously straight trajectory, deflecting it into a quickly-swerving 'S' shape, shifting first to the right then to the left inside my torso like a pinball trying to hit as many high-scoring targets as it could before leaving the playfield.

In the middle of the spine at chest height lie the sympathetic ganglia, a large cluster of nerves stretching out from either side of the spinal cord controlling motor function of the arms, blood supply to each side of the body and the muscular functions of the eye, eyebrow, eyelid and tear ducts. The bullet went through the ganglion on the right side, causing me random problems for years to come. Some of the broken nerves managed to re-route over time, others spluttered on in fits and starts, never quite getting back up to speed. Still others were damaged beyond repair and subsequently those parts of my body were destined never to work properly again.

The least of these nerve issues meant that it was difficult from then on for my right eye to generate water, both to cry and for general lubrication, making the eyeball sensitive to excessive light and unhappily for me exacerbating the dehydrating effects of tequila.

However I'm pleased to say this was not bad enough that I was tempted to stop drinking my favourite tipple. I wanted to keep a sense of proportion; I may have been shot, but let's not panic. Salt, lime and a sting in the back of the throat helps keep life more or less bearable, and it would have to be a pretty serious injury for me to give up the Mexican laughing water.

Next in the bullet's crosshairs was an unfortunately positioned major vein, being summarily severed causing a near catastrophic loss of deoxygenated blood. This poured into my chest cavity and when that filled overflowed onto the floor of the bar.

Immediately following the vein the hot nickel ripped through the upper lobe of my right lung, collapsing that entirely, thereafter actually miraculously travelling in an arc around the outside of my heart, skirting the thoracic aorta (the largest blood vessel in the body) and exiting the sternum just below my neck. It was a party in my chest and everyone wearing lead was invited. I hoped it had fun in there and got to brag to its mates in ordnance heaven with tales of wanton destruction.

Doctor Comissiong finished his grisly tour and not for the first time or the last I heard a medic say; 'You're a very lucky man.'

I began to get a real understanding now of what these doctors meant, and despite my recent focus on the lung damage it was clear studying this image that the main life and death issues on the night of the shooting had not been my lungs at all, but the proximity of the bullet to my spine and heart.

The scan showed that on initial entry the invading metal passed within a quantifiable six millimetres (a quarter of an inch) of my spinal cord. Had it made contact there were only three possible outcomes: I would be paraplegic, quadriplegic, or dead.

Not content with that close shave, it was the distance the bullet missed the thoracic aorta by that really caught Doctor Comissiong's attention.

This appeared quite innocuous and the least destructive portion of the bullet's passage and I said so, but the pokerfaced doctor told me rather dramatically that had the bullet passed two millimetres down or to the left I would not have made it. He elaborated by saying that I would have instantly collapsed, been unconscious before I hit the floor, and if I had been shot in the middle of an ER room with a team of surgeons standing by prepped and ready, there would still be nothing they could do to save my life as the blood is under so much pressure at the aorta that even a nick can cause the heart to virtually explode. And that mate, would be your lot. Do not pass Go, do not stop to collect £200, and no Get Out Of Jail Free this time around. Maybe this was the secret behind the five point palm exploding heart technique.

I knew it had been a close run thing, but damn.

As I stared at this visual timeline and soaked up the information it contained, I got to thinking about the shooting from the gunman's perspective.

I wondered at the physics of it, of his position on the dance floor - according to witnesses five or six metres behind me (fifteen to twenty feet). I thought about the direction which the revolver was pointing, quite a short-barrelled weapon in comparison to some handguns, and I imagined him aiming, looking for his wife running into the crowd, probably not seeing me at all through dozens of screaming running bodies, and pulling the trigger.

The act of firing this 'popular' handgun - a .38 Smith and Wesson - is not as simple as TV would have you believe. I know this first-hand as since then I have fired exactly the same weapon on an indoor range in Arizona. To shoot you have to really yank the trigger back, which is followed by a stiff recoil almost jerking the gun out of your hand. You must then consciously reset your trigger finger, take aim as the gun has now moved, concentrate and instruct the muscles and tendons in your forearm and hand to grip the gun tight and pull hard on the trigger again, and so on each time you let a bullet loose. It looks easy but it is not. Every movement in the sequence must be considered and every action is deliberate and forced.

In short this was not a casual act.

He meant to do it, every part of it.

I found the experience of handling this weapon quite upsetting. I only did so in an effort to understand the event and help myself come to terms with it, and it ended up leaving me with more questions than answers.

I don't know what Jenny was thinking as she looked at the image with me, but Doctor Comissiong had his physician's head on and he suddenly broke the silence in a Eureka moment:

'Ah, here is a pneumothorax! Or possibly a haemothorax.'

A what now?

He pointed to several differently coloured areas around the edges of my lungs, explaining that when the lung separates from the chest lining, that gap has to be filled as nature abhors a vacuum. In a collapsed lung the space is huge as the lung essentially shrinks while the ribcage remains an atrium, in my case filling with blood. As my lungs had expanded in the days and weeks following the shooting they hadn't quite reconnected with the chest wall everywhere, and it was into these gaps that fluid had seeped.

Sometimes air gets trapped in these pockets and this is called a pneumothorax. If just liquid is present that's a haemothorax; both blood and air a haemopneumothorax. (Think heemo noomo thorax and you can't go far wrong.)

It is also known as a pleural effusion, and if bacteria are present an infected pleural effusion, but let's not go there.

Paying attention? I was trying to, but by now it was 11pm and I was exhausted, and Jenny was looking pretty tired too. I wondered sleepily when he was going to get to the point and give me the certificate I had travelled all this way to get.

'I think we had better take a closer look at these pockets and try to get some samples off to the lab.'

Wonderful.

What is it with doctors that they always want to investigate things?

Once more unto the breach, for I guessed what was coming next; Doctor Tattersall had expressed something similar a couple of weeks before, and I'd had better days than that.

I dared to hope that he did not mean to do this tonight, and despite the fact that I needed the certificate I wished again that I was someone else living another life.

However he was in charge, and his mind was made up.

Doctor Comissiong stood up and tossed the CT scan onto his desk. He then went to a cupboard and began gathering various medical implements and piling them up on a silver surgical tray in front of him, one I recognised immediately and seeing it gave me little comfort.

I could give its professional name of a trocar needle; the three-way syringe used to extract fluid from body cavities. It was definitely the same style instrument that Doctor Tattersall had wielded, only this version appeared smaller and more delicate.

It had brightly coloured tags on its various connections and was still wrapped in polythene, appearing to be disposable. I found this reassuring for some reason, plus it's always nice to unwrap new things whatever the occasion.

I wondered how Doctor Comissiong could even be thinking about doing this now, some seven hours after he was supposed to have left for the day - goodness knows what time he had started work. He looked tired but to his credit not so much so that his abilities seemed impaired, and without the merest hint of a wavering hand nor stifling a yawn he quietly went about organising the equipment, attaching one implement to another, disinfecting something here, unwrapping and placing on the tray something there until he was satisfied that everything he required was present and correct.

There was a slight disagreement now as to whether Jenny would remain in the room for the operation. Doctor Comissiong jokingly said; 'He'll be fine, stay and hold his hand!'

Jenny and I had other ideas though and she left to sit in the corridor outside and nurse a coffee until it was over.

I walked over to the gurney in the curtained-off section of the examination room, removed my shirt and lay on my side as instructed, trying to relax and get comfortable. Apparently it wasn't necessary this time to be in a seated position as the fluid was less mobile and hopefully less of it. I didn't have to be told to lie on my right, old hand as I was now and beginning to be able to anticipate what would be required of me in whatever medical situation I found myself in.

Placing the CT scan on the mattress to refer to during the procedure, the doctor weighed his options for the locations of the local anaesthetic, and began with a series of small injections into my back to dull the pain.

While we waited for the skin sensitivity to fade, I was anxious to relate my experiences at the Bougainvillea Clinic, and not to put too fine a point on it how nervous I was right now.

I asked about the size of the syringe, and whether pandering to my fears or it's what he was planning to do anyway, he said that the needle he would be using tonight was a mere two millimetres across, and the local anaesthetic he had just given me was very powerful and not to worry. Aside from a little discomfort as the trocar went in, he assured me that I would be fine.

I must not have hidden my apprehension very well as he then injected a little more local anaesthetic just to be sure. Or at least he said he did; I could feel nothing on my back now which should have been all the reassurance I needed.

The pleural cavity has two membranes, inner and outer. The inner has no pain receptors so you can do what you like with that, but to get through to the space where my effusions were, the outer membrane had to be pierced, and that hurts like hell.

This posed a double jeopardy; firstly the outer membrane doesn't respond well to local anaesthetic as it is deep within the body, so whatever you do it's basically going to hurt. Secondly if you blast the area with so much analgesic that the patient feels nothing, the inner membrane then becomes vulnerable to damage as the physician has little idea which membrane he/she is at and has to rely solely on their skill in sensing pressure at the tip of the needle to determine which layer they have reached and whether they should keep pushing or stop. Puncture the inner membrane and you are one muscle twitch away from a collapsed lung.

The doctor told me he could see clearly from the Cat-scan the gaps around my lungs, where they were, and also how large they were, so could absolutely reassure me that there would be no surprise ending this time when the needle went in such as had happened at the Bougainvillea Clinic. Due to the fantastic detail on the image he could also calculate the best angle of approach, and so require less feeling around inside the chest once there.

Perhaps because I knew what to expect or perhaps because Doctor Comissiong was correct in his reading of the situation, the operation was nowhere near as painful as the previous one on Tortola.

It was absolutely not a pleasant experience, and the popping sensations resonating through my body as the layers of intercostal muscles were pierced one by one with what was still a very large needle were teeth-grindingly disquieting, but I think the smaller size helped me quite a bit in coping.

The 33% reduction in diameter did have one obvious downside though, making it that much harder to syphon off the ever-thickening fluid.

Doctor Comissiong mumbled repeatedly under his breath that he should have used the three millimetre syringe, and he seemed now to become very tired quite suddenly and his veneer of calm assurance noticeably to slip.

I could understand him being a bit crotchety at what was in reality the end of a full double shift, and although I'm sure he was sorely tempted to swap the inadequate trocar for its larger cousin, thankfully he did not do so and instead persevered.

Several times he gave up on a particular site cursing under his breath and moving the needle to another location, sometimes pausing to inject more local anaesthetic, sometimes not. At one point he took to twisting around the plastic tube that followed the needle in just as Doctor Tattersall had done to try to release pockets of trapped fluid near to the needle entry site.

As time went on the operation became more and more uncomfortable, and I began to make my feelings known. Frustrated he pulled the syringe out for the last time, applying substantial sticking plasters to several places on my back and asking me to slowly sit up when I was ready and come over to the desk.

I didn't feel too bad, and after a minute stood and made my way over a bit wobbly to the chair.

Doctor Comissiong held up a phial of dark liquid and looked at it in the way you might look at a rusty paperclip responsible for breaking an expensive washing machine.

It was brown in colour, thick and uniform; not the bloody semi-congealed red and yellow lymph I had previously seen drained from my chest (after the bulk of the blood had gone). In total two hundred and twenty millilitres or not quite half a pint had been removed. However he seemed pleased in the end, and as he hurriedly packed everything away I breathed a sigh of relief that this had not been the disaster it might have been, and if this discomfort was the price I had to pay for getting the insurance indemnity, at least it was over and I was satisfied that I had paid in full.

The brown muck would go off to the lab for analysis, and the only thing on my mind now was to grab Jenny and get out of here. It was way past midnight I felt I could sleep for a week, but that wasn't to be as the Doc told me to my dismay as he filled out the self-adhesive label for the phial that he would need to see me again first thing the next morning. I would then be required to have a quick standard X-ray to make sure all was well with my lungs, before issuing the certificate.

Having little strength to argue and less choice in the matter I agreed, and asked him what we should do now as he may have forgotten in all the fuss but we were not residents of St Thomas and had come from Virgin Gorda, and the flights back home would long since have ceased. Thinking for a moment Doctor Comissiong went to a drawer and dug out a flyer for a nearby hotel where relatives of patients and those convalescing from surgery often stayed, and being the helpful chap that he was he telephoned on the spot and reserved us a room. Tapping his finger on the receiver switch, he read from a garish business card extracted from his wallet and ordered us a taxi too. Talk about good service.

We took leave of our stalwart physician, not knowing whether he still intended to see any other patients or call it a well-deserved night.

I did feel fairly certain and quite understandably so that he would not find the time to treat any of the people I had sat with in that unloved orange outer waiting room on the other side of the hospital those many hours before, assuming any of them were still there. I don't blame my superhuman doctor at all for this, who I had nothing but admiration for at his skill and energy levels this late at night, but still I could not get my head around a system which allows anyone to fall by the wayside in their hour of clinical need.

We climbed into the cab that was already waiting for us at the main hospital entrance and soon arrived at the compact but clean Villa Blanca Hotel, the taxi driver cheerfully telling us on the way that he would never normally work this late as Charlotte Amalie could be dangerous after dark. After delivering us he was gratefully going home to his family for the night.

On the short journey over we listened to his stories of drug gangs and gunfights that he probably usually reserved for wide-eyed newbie tourists, and after checking in we went straight to our room and collapsed together on the double bed. With no luggage except for a couple of small bags and not even a toothbrush between us we lay in silence looking up at the shadows on the ceiling of some palm trees tussling and flexing in the breeze of a nearby courtyard. It was mesmerising watching the kaleidoscopic shapes endlessly merge and separate, so much so that neither of us thought of turning on the small TV.

The bulky air-conditioning unit guarding the window suddenly realised that people were present and began to whirr energetically in the background, threatening to continue all night unless we took affirmative action, but neither of us was inclined to get up and do something about it. We were both too tired to take much notice of its sporadic chattering, and at least it kept the room cool.

With tales of miscreants and violent deeds turning occasional night-time sirens and distant backfiring exhausts into sinister spectres tapping into our fading thoughts, we turned out the one dim bedside lamp that remained on, and quickly fell asleep.

Chapter 27 - Loose ends

The man who didn't seem to require any sleep was wide awake and waiting for us when we arrived at the St Thomas Hospital before 9am the next morning.

A taxi had picked us up from the hotel at 8.30, and I honestly don't know how Jenny and I made it that early considering the events of the previous twenty four hours.

Doctor Comissiong however seemed to have no such qualms about burning the candle at both ends. His bearing may have been slightly diminished and he had perceptible dark circles under his eyes, but other than that he was here and functioning, and apparently fully prepared for whatever a day in the life of a busy ER doctor might bring.

Without pausing to let us slowly warm up to proceedings we were immediately whisked into a side room where Doctor Comissiong himself performed an ultra-sound examination of my back. It seemed that he had been ruminating on what he perceived as his partial defeat of the night before, and now apparently after some rest and recuperation he was ready and raring to go for Round II.

As I wiped away the cold conductive gel from my back and sides he announced with a resolve which allowed no room for discussion that he was going to try again to see if he could draw some more fluid from my chest. The Cat-scan image of yesterday had suggested that the loculated pockets contained considerably more liquid than he was able to retrieve on his first attempt, and my hopes of an easier day ended.

More or less reduced to the status of a medical experiment at this point I just nodded my head and followed him back down the corridor to the same exam room we had been in the previous evening, where I sat and looked on while he once again began to pile implements onto a (new) sterile tray on his desk. I won't distract you with the details of the operation but it unfolded pretty much exactly as it had the night before, except that Jenny chose to remain in the room this time. I didn't mind her wanting to stay as I felt pretty confident of being able to keep my veneer of masculinity intact, and with my upper torso suitably browned with iodine I lay back down in the curtained-off section in the corner of the room and let the battle of the bulges recommence.

Whether the body just gets used to certain level of distress I don't know, but this third (or was it fourth?) such experience in a short space of time continued the trend of it becoming more bearable on each subsequent occasion. It was uncomfortable to be sure, and every now and then briefly intensely painful, but I didn't faint, I didn't yell out, I did pass Go and I did collect £200, and on the whole I gave myself a big fat pass. Every man likes to air his; 'Ahh, it's nothing' posturings to his woman while he might be standing holding a severed digit after a DIY faux pas, when what he really wants to do is scream and run for the nearest emergency room, but I expect Jenny saw right through mine as generally she was a pretty perceptive person and when all's said and done knew me about as well as anyone did in the world.

Doctor Comissiong may not have given himself the same green tick for his performance though, as during the surgery he tried three different locations in my back seeking out elusive pockets of trapped fluid, before eventually capitulating and re-leasing me with little more than a few congealed lumps of br-own phlegm in the bottom of his trocar syringe to show for it.

According to the latest word from the lab the previous da-y's extractions had not yet returned any positive results for the presence of harmful bacteria, but it was too early to tell concl-usively, which given the minimal hours between then and now was not that surprising.

If I were to take a negative view of this, the only result fr-om my perspective was that I had now endured another unex-pected and quite possibly pointless chest operation and none of us were any the wiser for it. However, striving for a glass half-full attitude; you don't know what the result of something is going to be until you try.

The outcome could well have been different, and he was the expert, so grit your teeth, keep your head down and plou-gh-on, and with perseverance and tenacity you'll win through in the end. I didn't blame him for his efforts and was grateful that he was interested enough in my prognosis to at least have given it a go.

My head was still a little fuzzy, so when Doctor Comissio-ng told me that he had reached the limit of what he could do surgically and the certificate to fly would be ready for me to pick up from his private practice tomorrow morning, I was a little too disoriented at first to follow the implications of what he'd said.

When I digested it however and consequentially what it me-ant; that we would now either have to go home and return to

St Thomas the following day or else stay in Charlotte Amalie for another night, I began to get a little frustrated.

I had a court appearance to prepare for in a few days back in the BVI, and we also had all our Caribbean belongings to pack and sort and to make arrangements to leave these islands which had been our home for the past three months, perhaps forever. Although sitting on our hands at the Villa Blanca Hotel or being a tourist in the shops and boutiques of Charlotte Amalie for a day might not sound like too much of a hardship, we had things to do, and this enforced layoff was not helping to get them done.

To be fair a day spent chilling on sultry Coki Beach where we'd gone with the bridesmaids for a pre/post marriage swim on our nuptial cruise was probably just what the doctor would have ordered, and I should have jumped at the opportunity, but I wasn't thinking straight.

Doctor Comissiong had not really factored our non-medical issues into his decision to have another crack at me this morning, and nor should he. Most locals thought nothing of hopping onto a fast ferry or catching a flight around these tiny islands, as people back on the mainland may jump on a bus or hail a cab. Nevertheless we were now in the situation and there was no sense crying over spilt milk. The twenty four hour rule applied to chest surgery and that was all there was to it.

Jenny's and my silent looks at each other must not have gone unnoticed, as Doctor Comissiong attempted to placate us with the strong assurance that he would have his secretary type up the insurance indemnity immediately so that it would be ready and waiting for us to collect when we returned, assuming as we hoped that my lungs were undamaged by today's procedure.

We left the physician with a genuine thank you and wandered outside to discuss what to do next, quickly deciding that staying here another day wasn't an option at all. We had to return to Virgin Gorda and make the best of it. It seemed now that there were two sets of plane tickets to arrange - one for us both to return to the UK following my court appearance, but before that another to come back to St Thomas to pick up this elusive but very necessary certificate.

If when I returned the good doctor tried to take yet more fluid samples from my chest, I may just do something very unmedical with that shiny new trocar needle to persuade him otherwise.

The deposition was due to be heard on Friday, that was three days from now, and with this in mind we stepped up a gear and frantically strained to unscramble our already busy schedule to fit a return trip to Charlotte Amalie into it all.

While our discussions continued we took a cab to the Cyril E. King Airport as the first step of our revised plan of action. There was a minimal tussle at the check-in desk as we tried to explain why we had not taken the return portion of our flights back to Virgin Gorda the previous evening, but with a little gentle arm-twisting the Sunaire ticketing clerk swapped them over as we requested and soon we were flying high over an island-peppered sea back to our original dirt airstrip and 'home'.

When we arrived at Mango Bay on Tuesday afternoon, there was a pile of mixed messages waiting for me on scraps of paper transcribed from telephone calls received at the office, appearing to cast doubt on the March 18th hearing date. Even with my knowledge of the haphazard way of things here I was not prepared for two faxes amongst them, one reconfirming the original deposition date of Wednesday the 23rd of March, the other saying Wednesday the 30th. Neither mentioned the other, nor the previously confirmed date of the 18th, and all came from the same office and were signed by the same illegible court official. Being a Brit I was used to receiving things in triplicate, but more usually they were supposed to contain the same information.

I decided to seek some advice on the best course of action to take. Although Agnes was young she had been here a long time and knew her way around the intricacies of the murky place where government and business collide, so I sat her down, explained the situation and asked what she thought I should do.

She knew most of it anyway, us all living in close proximity in her house and the majority of these notifications and messages having crossed her desk, and I think she had been waiting to give me advice should I ask. No sooner had I finished speaking without pausing for cogitation Agnes looked me in the eye and said; 'You have to see JS Archibald.'

In this comparatively small community there were lawyers aplenty vying for trade, in no small part due to the BVI's enormous financial trust industry stretching its tentacles across the world and based out of sleepy little Road Town.

I already had the names of two attorneys with a view to securing a legal presence in the BVI after I returned to the UK, but one of these had simply been plucked from an international phone book by Felicity Layton in her office back in leafy

Sussex, and the other was a local recommendation from friends who might know what they were talking about, but then again they might not, and may just have been repeating the advice of others.

Agnes however was adamant - if I wanted a lawyer, it was Archibald or no-one.

Joseph S. Archibald QC (later a Doctor of Law) was an Islander, coming originally from another ex-British colony of nearby Nevis. Here Horatio Nelson had been stationed as a newly-qualified sea captain two hundred years earlier, and was where he had met and married his long-suffering wife, Francis, the young widow of a Nevis sugar plantation owner. It was also the unlikely birthplace of Alexander Hamilton (no relation) whose signature joins several others on the American Declaration of Independence as a Founding Father of the United States.

Born amongst such rare company Archie as his friends called him grew into a young hotshot lawyer, called to the Bar in 1960 in Lincoln's Inn, London, after which he returned to the Caribbean and since then had built a big reputation and a very successful legal and financial services firm in his adopted home of Tortola. He was by all accounts not a large man physically but intellectually a heavyweight, and had strong connections and contacts with governments and businesses across much of the Caribbean. He had served as both an Attorney General and a High Court Judge, so knew his way around the world that I had inadvertently been thrust into.

I say murky, because it was. However there is murky and then there is total lawlessness, and the ex-British colonies were generally not that. As such I had strong hopes of being able to achieve my goals of securing the deposition hearing, and longer term of possibly pursuing a civil action for my injuries.

Taking Agnes's advice I telephoned the offices of JS Archibald & Co., and with them already aware of my name as the shooting had been the story of the year so far in the islands, I was immediately offered an appointment the very next day with the man himself.

Prioritising now, I decided to delay my return to St Thomas to pick up the insurance indemnity, reasoning that it was pretty much in the bag and barring disaster would be typed and waiting for me to collect basically whenever I turned up. The required X-ray should be just a formality and a matter of Doctor Comissiong signing and dating the pre-prepared certificate, and I was hopeful that no matter how busy he was, he would find a few minutes to do that for me.

So on the morning of Wednesday 16th March I set off on my now familiar ferry journey to Tortola to meet the man I hoped would help with my legal difficulties, leaving Jenny back at Mango Bay packing and making arrangements for our final departure.

The inevitable split between Jenny and her boss had taken place, which was of no surprise to anyone, so we were both free to concentrate on the tasks in hand.

There was a second purpose for going across to Road Town that day, by way of a couple of goodbyes, as I wanted to stop in and see Doctor Smith one last time and additionally to meet with Cyril Romney, who I would name as a friend. It would also be nice and convenient whilst there to purchase our tickets back to the UK through Romney Associates' subsidiary Travel Plan. It made sense to keep things in-house, and besides I wanted to help Cyril any way I could for the support he had given us in the past few weeks, and a bit of business in the form of arranging our plane tickets was something at least.

The first job of the day however was retaining the services of a top lawyer, and if Agnes was right, and she often was, the guy I was about to meet could very well be the one.

The deceptively large offices of JS Archibald and Co. were hidden above and behind a classical music shop, set back from the main drag half-way along Main Street. Being my first visit it took several passes counting down the building numbers as I went and retracing my steps before I spotted the small brass moniker on a wall adjacent to some concrete steps down one side of the retail premises.

This didn't seem a very auspicious start as I'd imagined based on reputation alone that the international headquarters of the JS Archibald Group would be ostentatious and with a very visible high-street presence. This appeared a bit presumptive on my part, so unsure now what to expect I buzzed the intercom and entered a small reception area with doors leading off it at the far end behind an empty desk. I walked up and waited, wondering who had let me in, and after a few moments a young woman appeared and showed me into a genteel library and conference chamber combined. Here I saw half a dozen people dressed mostly in black huddled deep in quiet conversation at one end of a smooth wooden table so big that it practically touched the narrower walls of the rectangular space.

I was evidently interrupting the tail-end of a lawyers' meeting, and as I entered a venerable man at the head of the table differentiating himself from the others not just because of his superior age but also his clothing - they were wearing dark suits to his casual grey sweater - smiled broadly and said; 'Ah, Mister Hartwell, good of you to join us! If you will just have a seat and excuse us for a moment we are dealing with an urgent last minute matter and shouldn't be too long -'

He then motioned to a line of ornate chairs spaced evenly along the unoccupied end of the table, and politely declining an offer of some refreshments I picked the nearest one and sat down.

The room was air-conditioned to the point of being cold, and I began to feel distinctly underdressed, with my shorts, open-necked t-shirt, sneakers and leather bushman's hat which I placed on the table in front of me next to a pile of foreign broadsheets.

There were several bone china cups of half-drunk coffee and matching saucers containing biscuits that no-one had touched littering the busy end of the table. Seeing this made me feel quite peckish but not wanting to interrupt or contradict myself so soon I took my mind off the pangs by looking around the law chamber and taking in what to me was a new experience.

Lining the walls and completely surrounding me apart from the tall net-curtained windows past the head of the table and a couple of subtle doors, were floor-to-ceiling bookshelves packed with what must have been thousands of legal manuals and encyclopedias. Everywhere I looked, row upon row of neat book covers, their binders decorated with gold leaf and laid out in sequence, Roman numerals numbering them from one to whatever high-digit letter. Joining seamlessly where the upper swathes of green ended, below were yet more lines of black and brown and red similarly sized and ordered leather-bound journals stretching around the room. Many had scraps of paper poking out of the tops and sides with scribbled notes marking out pages and passages, no doubt referencing current or pending court cases.

The decor was pale hardwood; clean, varnished and everywhere. The lighting expensive, the carpet deep.

The room yelled calm sophistication, designed to make the user feel important and the guest awestruck, so much so that maybe they wouldn't look too hard at the bill and realise that they were paying for all this grandeur. Okay I'm not that cynical but it's still true.

I turned to the neatly spread pile of newspapers and noticed the headed sections of a recent copy of the Times (London), as well as a Wall Street Journal and pink FT peeking out underneath, and amused myself catching up on the first foreign press that I'd had a chance to read properly in more than three months.

My initial happiness at being immersed in news from home soon gave way to disappointment as I couldn't really tell if I was reading something that had been written last week, last year or was somehow miraculously a future edition yet to be released.

Same old stories, same old news, same old opinions.

The first crucial tidbit that my eyes locked onto was that Scotland had experienced some unseasonably wet weather. In March.

I stopped right there, remembering that escaping newspapers and endless recycled TV was one of the reasons I left Britain in the first place.

I skipped to the travel section.

The conference concluded, which had been conducted virtually entirely in whispers. The hushed tones were not I deduced because of my invading presence, rather everyone spoke quietly because Mr. Joseph Archibald spoke quietly. Consistent with the serene atmosphere the young advocates packed away their notepads and briefcases and silently filed out, smiling politely at me as they passed. I had the feeling they knew me, or something about me, although I had overheard enough to know that I was not the subject of the meeting I'd been privy to today.

Mr. Archibald stood now and walked smoothly over towards me, his right hand outstretched and having adopted this position on standing not altering his pose until he had processed the entire length of the room to my chair and our hands met. I stood up myself to greet him, and we got down to business.

Not much was discussed in the way of strategy, Mr. Archibald motioning for me to retake my seat but himself instead preferring to stalk the room, gliding around the table, stopping, looking as if he was about to change direction then thinking better of it and going back the way he had just come. His eyes darted left and right all the time like a biological calculator engaged in a complex equation, recently furnished with a new set of batteries giving a couple more volts than the recommended charge.

As he walked he kept repeating; 'This is a big case; it's a million dollars. Absolutely, no doubt about that.'

I hadn't asked and he didn't seem as if he was talking to me at all, but the word 'million' is guaranteed to make you prick up your ears when discussing money. I presumed he meant U.S. dollars.

I didn't actually formally hire Archie that day, a better way of putting it that he accepted me as a client, taking for granted that I had chosen him by virtue of the fact that he existed and I walked through his door. This seemed a slightly off the wall method of hiring an attorney, as if he was a river and I a mere tributary, and by virtue of entering his world I had joined the flow and had no choice but to go along wherever he decided to take me. This made me physically smile, which made him smile his broad confident smile, and that was the contract as good as sealed.

Archie was in his early sixties as far as I could tell, with a bright shiny un-lined complexion adorned with a grey moustache, and neat receding almost white hair. He was well-groomed, his physique compact, his posture measured, and he spoke softly because he had no need to shout. It was obvious that every person in the firm doted on him, and if I ever heard his name mentioned outside those offices it was always with a similar respectful tone whichever echelon of society the person speaking about him represented.

In the fullness of time I got to know the man quite well, the legal ramifications of the shooting rumbling on for a long time to come and in more territories than just the BVI and Britain. For now negotiating the next few days was what concerned me.

The meeting lasted an hour, and I left the company of JS Archibald QC with the comfort of knowing that I had a serious legal player in my corner, and when he told me to return to Mango Bay with confidence and wait by the phone for news of the 'reconfirmed' March 18th hearing date, I believed him.

There was one other subject we touched upon which had recently begun to prey on my mind, but more of that later.

Before leaving Tortola I had two more stops to make, the first being to Cyril Romney who I found working in his office. We sat and drank freshly squeezed orange juice and chatted about the upcoming deposition. I also took the opportunity to purchase our tickets home on very appropriately a British Airways flight, departing the day after the court hearing and flying via San Juan. The big jets didn't fly from Beef Island as the runway was too short, so a transfer at a main hub was always necessary, usually either Antigua or Puerto Rico.

We'd held off buying the tickets until now but I decided to throw caution to the wind and take a punt that things were going to pan out: the insurance indemnity was hopefully already awaiting collection at Doctor Comissiong's office in St Thomas, and Mr. Archibald led me to believe that the Friday court date would be honoured, although until I had the Bible in my hand and heard myself say 'I swear', I'd still call it an even bet.

We had considered the possibility of leaving on Friday afternoon directly from the court, Jenny accompanying me to Road Town along with our suitcases and attending the hearing. Sensibly though we agreed that this wasn't worth the added stress, and being a weekend I wouldn't be able to make an appointment with a UK doctor until the following Monday morning at the earliest, so leaving Tortola on Friday or Saturday was a moot point.

Cyril and I shook hands warmly and took a stroll together to the main entrance lobby of his office building. As I left through the tinted glass doors he called out behind me to be sure and visit him if I ever came back this way, and to remember to tell the folks back in England that not everyone in the British Virgin Islands is as bad as the guy who shot me.

I laughed and replied; 'Of course not, I know that. Anyway, he's from Dominica!'

With that I hit the kiln-hot pavement for the short walk across town to Peebles Hospital.

Doctor Smith was in his small study to the side of the examination room where a week or so before I had held court over my procession of Chief Ministers. A nurse led me straight in where I found him standing leaning against his desk giving orientation to a couple of new interns from Germany this time. He was only too happy to bring me into the conversation as a sort of mobile mannequin, and asked me on the pretext of a quick final examination if he could have a look at the bullet wounds.

I think this was more to show off his handiwork to the student employees than anything else, as Doctor Smith asked me to turn to the side, then face the wall, then to the other side and back again, all the while with the forefinger of each hand pressed firmly into the soft flesh of the bullet holes in my upper chest front and rear and revolving me like a spit roast.

I'm not sure the students took this little display in quite the way that Doctor Smith intended, seeming more as if it gave them strong misgivings about their choice of internship location than being impressed at their new boss's skill with a scalpel.

I don't know why, but their visible apprehension at beholding probably their first patient in the BVI and having the unfortunate distinction of him being a gunshot victim, made me feel quite sorry for them, so I spoke up and reassured them that shootings were very rare here and it was a one-in-a-million event that I had been caught up in.

I made a big show as I left of energetically shaking Doctor Smith's hand and expressing my heartfelt thanks for the tenth time for all he had done. As I did so I thought back to the first time I had seen him, buried in a dog-eared paperback novel in the foyer of the Peebles Hospital, not knowing if he was a janitor or the prime minister.

Funny how life twists and turns.

People rarely get a chance to meet someone who they can hand on heart say; 'That person saved my life'.

I could now point to several, and some I will never know, like the nurse at the Iris O'Neal Clinic in Spanish Town who without guidance from a doctor injected a hefty whack of adrenaline into my bicep forty minutes after the shooting.

Had she not done so at the precise moment she did it is doubtful I would have seen the forty first. But she is anonymous to me, as are many others, and I don't know what to say about that.

I said goodbye to Doctor Smith and his ghostly students, and for the penultimate time to Tortola.

It had been a busy two days, and Thursday 17th March arrived and took me, alone this time, by cab to the little dirt airstrip on the far side of Spanish Town to board another flight to Charlotte Amalie.

Before leaving St Thomas on the 15th Doctor Comissiong had given me a radiology appointment slip. The final checkup and collection of my insurance indemnity was to take place at his private surgery not at the main St Thomas Hospital, and like Doctor Tattersall's Bougainvillea Clinic this did not possess an on-site X-ray machine. The scan therefore had to be carried out at a nearby independent imaging centre, and this was my first port of call after the plane touched down on the bleached concrete of the Cyril E. King Airport.

Armed with the name and details of the radiology clinic which seemed to be a far more common type of business than I ever imagined, I caught a taxi straight from the airport to the address given on the slip. I was exactly twenty four hours late, but reasoned that as a paying customer they would be glad whenever I decided to show up and it was unlikely my tardiness was going to be an issue.

It wasn't, the technician merely glancing at the requisition and asking how many images were required as the order signed by Doctor Comissiong was not specific, so I said a single one will do. I guessed this would be sufficient and didn't see the point in spending more money than I had to for what in all probability would turn out to be a quickly discarded item.

X-ray in hand and with time to spare, I asked the technician for directions to Doctor Comissiong's office, and feeling confident (a man you see; never admit you don't know where you're going) I set off on foot to make my way across this part of the business district of Charlotte Amalie.

The modern multi-storey office complex where Sidney Comissiong worked when not being an ER doctor, had central glass-walled aisles lined on each side with chic commercial suites that were home to everything from accountancy firms to anaesthetists, but apparently not the one thing that I had so far needed that morning - an X-ray clinic.

As promised, the insurance indemnity was there printed and waiting, and dated the day before; the 16th of March. It only required a signature to be complete.

With a few deep breaths for the benefit of a stethoscope diaphragm and a quick check of my X-ray held up to the natural light of his office window, Doctor Comissiong sat back in his chair and started scribbling on a pad he took from an open file on his desk.

As he wrote he spoke, relating a story of a doctoring exploit which he had been involved in a couple of months previously and he thought might be of some interest.

A local gang engaged in a turf war had lured a rival group to a drug deal which turned out to be an ambush. As part of a cold and calculated revenge attack and to serve as a sadistic warning to others, one unfortunate guy from the opposition crew had been taken hostage, and after he was first beaten senseless and lay helpless on the floor they shot him four times from close range, execution style.

The first salvo missed from literally two feet away, demonstrating that marksmanship and criminality don't necessarily go hand in hand.

The next three they made certain of. Point blank and with the barrel of the gun pressing against his skin, they fired once into the side of his body through his upper left arm, the bullet passing through the humerus and his left lung and severing his spinal cord before coming to rest lodged between two vertebrae.

The next shot was its mirror but in his right shoulder this time, shattering the scapula before entering his ribcage, piercing the right lung and also coming to a halt in the backbone, facing its mate like a pair of vertebral earrings.

The fourth and final bullet was fired directly into his groin, travelling through the abdomen and ending its bloody journey lodged in the rear of his pelvis just below the sacrum.

His spinal cord had been severed in three places, and when the medics found him he was, quote, in a 'bad way'.

'He lived then?', I asked incredulously.

'Oh, yes. We saved him, he'll be fine.'

This was obviously some new and strange use of the word 'fine' that I was previously unaware of.

'But he was crippled, he can't walk surely?'

'Oh no, of course not! He's in a wheelchair until he dies. He may regain some partial use of his arms in due course with enough time and therapy. That remains to be seen, but he is alive.'

I suppose the one positive was being a drug dealer he had money enough to pay for his care, and Doctor Comissiong's last words were said with an aplomb of pride which I can just about understand.

Where there is life there is hope, and where there is hope there is life.

It seemed that our business was concluding, and as Doctor Comissiong started shuffling through some other papers on his desk I asked him; 'So, we are okay then?'

He didn't look up straight away as he was scribbling again on the notepad. He then quickly tore off the top sheet and placed it with my X-ray in the file next to him and closed it.

'Hmm? Oh, yes, you are fine. Free to go!'

He smiled and handed me the signed letter which I read carefully and put into an envelope, now meaning that any airline would accept me as a paying passenger. I shook another hand and left, pleased that at last things were coming together.

I had a couple of hours to kill before my afternoon flight for Virgin Gorda as I'd allowed a substantial buffer in case of any last minute hitches, and it was still well before noon as I climbed into a taxi outside Doctor Comissiong's offices ostensibly to head for the airport.

'Hi, and where are we going today, sir?', the cab driver asked.

I thought for a moment.

'Paradise Point.'

Chapter 28 - Paradise Point

So it came down to this.

Sitting on a verandah drinking a beer high up on a dry hillside, looking out across Charlotte Amalie's enormous harbour and cruise terminal.

A beautiful clear St Patrick's Day.

Exactly a year before I had taken a cab up this very same hill, on that occasion attempting to hide a few nerves at the prospect of losing my single status, and now coming full circle here I was again tense at the next big change. The Ides of March had come and gone. Two days late but that's inflation for you.

Cruise ships are an impressive sight close up; a horizontal hotel of steel and glass blotting out the daylight in every direction, rising and falling in a slow invisible circle while it chops compressed water against the quayside.

From a mile away when you see three lined up in a row, one slipping its moorings guided by super-powerful mouselike tug boats, another being gently nudged into the vacated space along the dedicated low concrete jetty, it's actually majestic.

I loved views like this; man's struggle to dominate nature. Vast and arresting as they were, still nothing but gargantuan viewing platforms for the real spectacle - the beauty of the Caribbean.

Same hillside, same view, maybe even the same ships.

I looked for the elegant silhouette of the Westerdam, but she was not among them.

Was this fate showing me a glimpse of order in the chaos, like bringing Captain Harry and me together a month after the shooting on my twenty fifth birthday at the same place we first 'met'? Or were these just coincidences? If you look hard enough for patterns you will surely find them. For myself I believe life does show you which direction to take, it's up to you to keep your eyes open and recognise the signs when they appear, and when they do, to decide then whether to venture down that road or not. I usually risk it.

I watched alone today, just as I had faced death alone, and in my darkest moments, I hadn't thought of Jenny at all.

If life is about anything, it's about sharing. A dream dreamt alone dies with you, shared it lives on.

So what about Jenny and me? What do I do now?

I took another sip of rapidly warming beer.

We had arrived in Virgin Gorda, rocky but together. I could imagine us growing old together, which is one of the ultimate tests of any relationship. And she was a lovely person, a great 'catch', everybody loved her, and so did I.

I certainly had taken the chance when Jenny asked me to marry her (yep, she asked, not a leap year) and somehow it had brought me here today albeit via a fairly unorthodox route.

So if it was all so perfect what was wrong with me?

I turned to look at some noisy Irish guys fooling around in the bar, bedecked with tall oversized green felt hats and bizarrely one dressed as Jesus, complete with loincloth and shawl and a false wizard's beard which he pulled down on elastic around his ears every time he took a sip from his black pint.

The underdressed one was trying very hard to impress one of the barmaids.

Good luck with that mate.

I finished my own drink and headed back through the bar to the car park at the rear, beckoning the first cab driver who looked alert enough to spot me. Jumping in and with a soft clunk of the closing door, I said goodbye to Paradise Point and married life.

Now I just had to tell Jenny.

Chapter 29 - One door closes, another one opens

The de Havilland Twin Otter circled high above Charlotte Amalie, setting itself up for the short journey east. As it did so I looked down and mused on the stories of violence perpetrated on those placid streets, when in reality the so-called haven of the British Virgin Islands had proved far more hazardous to my own health.

As we broke out over the ocean came the realisation that in a couple of days all this blue would be replaced with overcast skies and wet shiny pavements, and it was not a welcoming thought.

I wondered if the pilot ever tired of the view from up here. Amazing yes, but like my old Harbour Bridge commuters, had familiarity taken the edge off the spectacular as he shuttled between the same half-dozen islands as many times as the daylight allowed?

I turned my eyes to the cockpit; the captain was stony faced, but then pilots always are when navigating.

We landed at Spanish Town's dusty airstrip, the plane immediately rounding on the bumpy grass ready to pick up the next batch of passengers. I hopped into yet another cab and headed for home. Mango Bay was where my heart belonged now, but sadly not for much longer.

I walked past Agnes in the office who without pausing in her telephone conversation gestured to another pile of messages on her desk, which I collected and continued through to the open-plan kitchen, there finding Jenny playing with Alicia ahead in the long lounge, the sliding glass panels to the balcony fully open letting the day in.

There had been a brief semi-sarcastic exchange of words about it being our anniversary as we raised ourselves that morning (we still shared the same bed), but no more was said about it that day and I didn't mention where I had spent the afternoon.

'Did you get the certificate?', Jenny asked.

'Yep.'

'Any problems?'

'No. How's the packing?'

And so we continued.

I checked the messages from Agnes's desk. One stuck out immediately. Handwritten in blue biro it read:

'Tomorrow Court 9am.

For Your Evidence.

Call Tonight, Anthony Vieira'

*Anthony Vieira was the Senior Prosecuting Counsel for the BVI government in the criminal case against the gunman.

So Archie had pulled it off. Good on him!

It's strange how this one scrap of paper held more weight with me than all the official faxes and letters combined. However I now felt sure in my bones that it would all take place as scheduled.

Agnes had decided to prepare a meal for tonight as a sort of goodbye to Jenny and I, to be joined by Jano and some friends of hers from Italy who were thinking about opening a restaurant on the Mango Bay site.

We all lent a hand in the kitchen as is the Italian way, although the actual cooking turned out to be a competitive display of culinary dexterity between Agnes and her male restauranteur rival. When he proudly cut off a slice of home-made pizza for Agnes and I to taste, our hostess waited until he was almost out of earshot then returning to chopping vegetables said under her breath; 'I've had better.'

We ate on the balcony and watched the sun go down as we passed the wine and plenty of good cheer. Jano brought out a guitar which I wasn't quite drunk enough to play, and when the mosquitos became too annoying we adjourned inside to continue the party in the cool marble lounge.

There were no especial goodbyes said, nor any attention drawn to Jenny's and my imminent departure, and after again mucking in to clear away the dining things and wine bottles and glasses, we said our goodnights exactly as we had done virtually every night for a month, and as if we would continue to do so forever.

During the evening I had received a phone call as promised from the Senior Crown Counsel, and we discussed the format of tomorrow's proceedings and confirmed times and places.

We had met before I think, but wasn't sure if I could place him, however his voice was distinctive; soft and precise, and I hoped that would be enough for me to track him down and exchange a few words in the morning if he didn't find me first.

I didn't possess a suit in the Caribbean, not imagining that I would need one when I'd left England the previous December, so my court attire was cobbled together from the best of what little I had and the rest borrowed from Jano who was more or less my size.

Over breakfast Jenny asked if I wanted her to accompany me to the court, and I said I preferred not. It wasn't because of our personal issues, it was just that it was going to be a very strange day and I wanted to be able to escape into myself whenever I felt the need and not be distracted by other thoughts and feelings.

At 7.30am I went to the Virgin Gorda Yacht Harbour alone to catch a ferry for Road Town, and my long awaited day in court.

The boat was noisy and packed as usual, and I sat inside but for some reason I didn't sweat. Maybe I was finally getting used to the climate, or maybe it was my body's self-defence mechanism balancing the cortisol and stress hormones, placing me in an enforced state of serenity ahead of this momentous day.

I think it was the latter; I actually felt quite Zen.

This was my moment; the opportunity I had been waiting for to express myself, to tell the world what happened when that man came into my life without warning or invitation.

I focussed on the thought that today wasn't about the gunman, today was about placing on record the reality of the experiences of a gunshot victim, and something of the repercussions; it is not like it's portrayed in the movies. In real life you don't get up again, brush off a few spots of blood, kiss the girl and ride off into the sunset on a Harley Davidson, not right away anyway.

The deposition wasn't about him, it was about me, and that is how I intended to get through it.

This brings me to the last matter Archie and I discussed before I left his office two days before.

As soon as it became a genuine likelihood that the hearing was about to occur, a question suddenly hit me - would my assailant be in court?

And the more I thought, the more it concerned me. Not because I was scared, but because I didn't know how I would react and I didn't want to make a fool of myself, maybe breaking down in the witness stand or becoming angry, or most likely just not being able to think straight and mess up giving my evidence. I wanted so badly to get it right, and this could put me in real jeopardy of derailing everything.

So, before Archie and I parted company, and suspecting that he might think I was a wimp for even mentioning it, I broached this subject and asked for his input.

I needn't have worried because apparently this was quite a common question. Archibald's simple words of advice stay with me to this day, and I keep them for use in other life situati-

'You simply ignore him. When the time comes, just look straight at him without deviating or looking down or away. When you feel it is time to break eye contact and you are comfortable, do so.'

It was about control, and understanding that an opponent is not worth giving your emotion to; you save that gift for the people who matter.

'But what if I find him staring at me at any point?'

'Stare back, without emotion. Return his gaze, then look away when you feel it is right to do so and not before.'

Simple, but I thought good advice, and I was glad to have it in my locker for when the time came.

I didn't want to go in empty handed, so I stopped and bought a newspaper from a street vendor, and now quite close to the court I paid the cab driver off and walked the rest of the way.

As I approached the whitewashed structure with its small dry gardens to the front, I saw several groups of black-robed advocates mingling and talking at the bottom of and on the main entrance steps. I imagined they were going over today's cases, or perhaps they were swapping cricket scores but they certainly looked very serious.

Being just before the start of the court day a slow steady stream of new bodies showed up, similarly attired in black suits and many with long flowing black cloaks. The new arrivals chose and walked up to a particular gathering, shook hands, sm-

347

iled, then went off into little conclaves with their bowed foreheads almost touching and talking in whispers.

There were several courtrooms in the building and I didn't know which was mine, so I made my way up past the huddles of lawyers and entered searching for someone to give me a pointer.

It was cool inside the foyer, the thick walls keeping the innards temperate whatever the thermometer said outside.

Not having any joy I wandered back into the sun. Checking my watch at the top of the steps - 8.50am - I started to get a bit agitated.

A veneer of calm is easily broken, and I felt the sweat begin to drip relentlessly down my sides under my white shirt. I hoped it wasn't too noticeable as I had no jacket to disguise my unease.

Breathe.

I heard a voice I recognised and turned to locate the source and put a face to it. Two men were walking up the steps about to enter the building, one carried a briefcase and wore a grey suit under his own ubiquitous ceremonial cape. I moved over to them and after waiting two or three seconds for the speaker to look up and spot me which he didn't, I somewhat rudely interrupted and proffered my hand to the Senior Crown Counsel.

Anthony Vieira stopped in his tracks and looked at me for a couple of seconds, then his features brightened with comprehension;

'Ah, Mr. Hartwell! I am glad you have made it!'

He shook my hand and we walked into the building together, once beyond the doors his colleague disappearing off I presumed involved in another case.

The government attorney was an instantly likeable chap, with a soothing manner and a slow careful choice of words. He seemed young, perhaps in his mid-twenties like me, and had obviously progressed well in his career to be so high up so fast.

He briefly explained the protocol again, telling me what I should expect and when, and outside the allotted courtroom we stopped and shook hands once more. I asked if the accused would be there and Anthony confirmed that he would. He added 'under guard', perhaps misreading my apprehension.

With that he stepped through a pair of veteran wooden swinging doors and left me alone in the corridor.

As the only witness giving evidence today I supposed the wait wouldn't be too long.

There was a sizeable gap separating the two doors through which muffled sounds could be heard, enough filtering to my ears a few metres away for me to be able to take a good guess as to what was going on inside.

At first there was a mumbling of voices and a constant shuffling of feet, then at an unseen signal the voices all stopped in unison. There was a further scramble of shoe leather on hard parquet flooring and a scraping of chair legs.

A voice then called out in a thick West Indian accent;

'Would all present in the matter of Regina versus _ please rise, and anyone not having business here today please leave the courtroom. This Court of the Royal Virgin Islands presided over by the Honourable Justice Ephraim Georges, is now in session.'

Another movement of feet and chairs followed by a heavy wooden clunk. A stout door opening and quickly closing I guessed.

Ok I thought, we are off...

A few preliminaries were settled, all in legal speak, the relevant lawyers indicating who they were and acknowledging the presence of each other and the accused.

The charges were then read.

In all, eight counts of unlawful activity were laid, the ones I caught being the 'attempted murder of a Lucianne Lafonde of the Valley, Virgin Gorda' and 'letting off a firearm in a public place with intent to endanger life'. The last was one of 'grievous bodily harm to a Mr. Craig Hartwell, of Kent, England'.

I heard the tones of a deep Caribbean voice methodically speaking (the Judge?) and then the lighter inflexions of Anthony Vieira declaring in response to a question, that this special hearing has been brought forward in order to accommodate Mr. Hartwell, who must immediately on the closing of his evidence, return 'this very day' to England for urgent medical treatment on the advice of his doctors.

I was actually going home tomorrow, but close enough.

'And is Mr. Hartwell here present?', asked the Judge.

'He is Your Honour', Anthony Vieira again.

'And is he ready to give evidence?'

'He is Your Honour.'

'Then let him be called to the stand.'

The usher bellowed my name, and immediately one of the double doors swung outwards almost hitting me in the face. A man holding it open at the extremity that its spring would allow, said; 'Mr. Hartwell?' (I was the only person there.)

Taking a deep breath, I nodded and walked in.

Chapter 30 - Face to face

I hadn't been in many courtrooms in my life at that point, and my first impression was of a Victorian science lab similar to those in the school I had attended as a boy.

The ceiling was high, the space in front of me long and rectangular, the doors through which I had entered positioned half-way along the inner of the two longer walls. Tall windows were evenly spaced along the vertical surface opposite, letting in masses of light but seemingly none of the heat. To my left a raised wooden platform and solid-fronted desk combined, stretched in tandem almost the entire width of the room, dipping at the left extremity where two or three steps led down to a closed oak door with a sign on it saying 'Judge's Chambers'.

A heavy-set man sat behind the precise middle of the desk, his shoulders hunched forward, his arms folded on the thick varnished wood, and staring intently at me as I walked in.

Under his gaze I barely noticed the rest of the room, but a quick glance around revealed several rows of low tables arranged across the space perpendicular to the windows and facing the Bench. Seated behind them in cheap plastic chairs were mostly young men and women in suits, some towards the front wearing awkward black robes signifying their seniority in rank if not age.

A single such man was stood behind the first row of tables, his elbows at his sides gathering his cape, his forearms raised in the posture of a schoolmaster about to give a lecture - Anthony Vieira; chief prosecutor and Senior Crown Counsel.

Through my peripheral vision I perceived at the very back of the room to my right were benches and wooden pews upon which were ranged more regularly attired bodies - I guessed the public and media gallery, although apart from the higher Judge's Bench everything else was on the same level.

To my immediate left behind the usher who still stood holding the door was the witness stand. This faced across the width of the room directly towards the foremost dazzling white window, immediately in front of the Bench. So close in fact that a long-armed occupant could probably reach over and touch the hallowed grain.

Anyone giving evidence could thus be seen and heard clearly from the entire court and most especially from the Judge's elevated position just a few metres away.

There was neither a jury nor any dedicated place for one that I could see.

Anthony looked at me, and then at the witness stand, the usher gesturing to the same with his open free hand. Looking around for inspiration but finding none I hesitated for a second then stepped behind and up into the slender wooden box.

A second usher who had been standing guard at the door to the Judge's Chambers now stepped forward and handed me a bible, and still keeping a tight grip of it himself asked me to raise my right hand and swear to tell the truth and every bit of it - I did.

There was a bit of theatre now when Anthony Vieira asked the Judge for permission to bring a chair to the stand, 'in view of Mr. Hartwell's injuries'. We had discussed this outside in the corridor at my request, partly out of a genuine fear for my wobbling legs which despite my much better health still had a tendency to crash every now and then, and I didn't know how long I would have to be on my feet in there. It was also in part I am slightly ashamed to say for the sympathy vote, although who I was expecting sympathy from and why I do not know.

Permission was kindly given by the Judge, whose face then softened visibly as did his overall countenance, which was gratifying to see as he was quite a scary guy.

The original doorman brought me a school chair. I sat, and Anthony spoke.

'Can you state your name please sir, for the record, and where you are from?'

'Craig Matthew Hartwell, from Kent, England, currently staying with friends at the Mango Bay Resort.'

'And where is that?' (He knew, everybody did.)

'That is on Virgin Gorda, sir.'

'Thank you. And Mister Hartwell, can you please tell us when you arrived in the British Virgin Islands, what is your status here, and what is your current employment situation?'

'I am a carpenter, I arrived at the beginning of December last year with my wife - I'm sorry I don't remember the exact date - and she is, or has just finished working as a beauty therapist for Little Dix Bay Beauty Services. I am here as a tourist and have some property back in England which is providing me with some income.'

'Thank you. And Mister Hartwell, can you please now tell us, in your own words, about the events of February the 2nd of this year? Sorry, let me rephrase that - do you recall the night of February 2nd; where you were, what you were doing, who with, and if anything of significance happened to you that night...?'

'Yes...' And so began my tale.

I found it easy to recount in some places, difficult in others.

I tried to be matter-of-fact, but once or twice became emotional, having to stop and take a sip of water and at least once swallowing away a lump in my throat.

When I got to the part about me lying on the floor of the bar and sensing a man approach and stand over me (not mister white-trousers; although he was briefly mentioned in passing), Anthony stopped me and said;

'And Mister Hartwell, do you recognise that man in this courtroom today?'

Like I said I had kept my attention mostly to the front of the room until now, both the Judge and the Senior Crown Counsel splayed at slight angles directly in front of me, but I had noticed on entering what appeared to be an unusual grouping sat behind a table near to one of the rear windows. Something about the silhouetted forms looked out of place, and I had guessed who and what they were without attempting to confirm my intuition.

Three people, two tall seated men in uniform flanking a third central seated figure, not short himself but shoulders slightly slumped, showing just a hint of supplication. Dressed pretty much as I was in brown trousers and leather shoes, jacketless and wearing a white shirt; short sleeves to my long. His skin was dark, his features more familiar to me than I would have liked.

His hands were joined in front of him on the table and I could clearly see his naked wrists, indicating perhaps proudly that he was not wearing handcuffs.

Bizarre as it was, I recognised him. Even though he had just been a shape, a mystical looming presence behind me while my body wracked and bled, somehow the edges of my vision had been working overtime without me realising or controlling it; noting the features, registering the facial shadows, filling in the blanks with the most likely shapes like a police identikit, making up the whole, and telling me who this person was.

Unmistakable.

You can fidget all you like mate, I know who you are.

He actually then smiled at me and nodded, like someone you might see at the bus stop each morning but have never yet spoken to. A regular person; a normal human being, giving away perhaps the merest expression of guilt in his sheepish eyes and slightly upturned mouth. A self-reproachful grin spread across his face, like he had been caught picking up a dollar bill off the floor that he knew didn't belong to him, and as he quietly put it into his pocket realised that someone he had not spotted earlier had silently witnessed the whole thing.

It turned out I didn't need Archie's advice at all. My reactions at seeing him for the first time in any real sense came very naturally.

I looked. I stared even.

I met his childish eyes, not interested in the slightest when or if he chose to look away. I instead chose my moment to break that fleeting contact, and turning my head back to Anthony Vieira, said; 'Yes. That's him. Over there between the two policemen.'

'The record will show that the witness has identified the defendant.'

Were they police or prison officers? Honestly I couldn't tell.

Many people have said to me since the shooting; 'He must have been crazy...!', or words to that effect.

I looked, I saw; I judged.

This person before me was not crazy but a deeply selfish individual, who had been having a hard time in his personal life and he wanted revenge. His intentions were evil and vaguely targeted, and he didn't give a damn who he hurt in the process as long as he got his satisfaction.

I continued with my evidence, being prompted from time to time to expand on a particular theme or to pass over others by the ranking government lawyer.

Anthony then asked me to detail some of my health complaints, and I explained what was motivating my immediate return to the United Kingdom, touching on the fact that I may look well, all things considered, but my ailments were real and extremely serious, and that my recovery was by no means yet certain.

When the prosecutor had finished, he asked me to remain in the witness stand as the defence counsel would like a few words and to ask a few questions based on my testimony.

An older white-bearded advocate rose, and began by sympathising with my bad fortune and wishing me a speedy recovery.

His paternal manner belied his true intentions, as quickly the comforting tone became accusatory;

'Mister Hartwell, isn't it a fact that you knew Miss Lucianne Lafonde, that you were involved in a liaison with her which you knew to be wrong, and you had come to the bar that night specifically to meet her, and that the bloodied knife that was found on the floor of the Bath and Turtle Bar and Restaurant was in fact your knife, and you had brought it to the Pub with the intention of doing harm to my client?'

Here we go. I suppose he had a job to do.

Throw enough mud and hope that some will stick.

'No sir, that is absolutely not true.'

I had heard this rumour several times already, and others like it, so I wasn't all that surprised to have it brought up here today.

To be fair the defence counsel didn't speak for long, and I got the feeling that it was mainly a performance for the benefit of his client, and perhaps more importantly to get some counter arguments down on the record so that he would have something, anything to work with, when the trial proper started.

It seemed as though he was searching for some straws to clutch at, and I almost felt sorry for the guy to have so little to go on. Except that he was trying to get the man responsible for nearly killing me home free, so my empathy was tempered.

I gave myself some small credit for taking these questions calmly and coolly, never once losing my temper, just in a measured tone denying his daft allegations and accusations, resolutely and firmly, never wavering or breaking eye contact, and after about ten minutes, possibly fifteen, he gave up and sat back down with a curt 'No further questions'.

I actually met that lawyer some years later, and he was a gentleman. Just doing his job.

My evidence-giving in total had lasted an hour and a half, and after the Judge asked the prosecutor if he wished to add anything further which he declined, Justice Georges looked over at me, still hunched forward and able to dominate the room with only his clasped hands, said;

'Mister Hartwell, I would like to thank you for coming here today at this 'early' court session. I understand that this has been brought forward to allow you to give evidence and to return to the United Kingdom forthwith for urgent medical treatment...'

'Yes Your Honour...'

'...and I am sure that I speak for everyone here when I wish you a speedy recovery and all the best for you.'

'Thank you, My Lord.' (Wrong title.)

And that was that; Court adjourned.

The Judge closed proceedings by stating that the next hearing was to take place at a date yet to be determined, and he referred with a plaintive smile to Anthony Vieira's earlier assertions that in total fifty witnesses had come forward and a plea had yet to be entered on behalf of the defendant. Justice Georges struck his gavel on the desk (or on a coaster, I could not see), stood, bowed to the standing throng, and walked briskly past the guard and through the oak door to his right. This shut behind him so sharply the resultant burst of air ruffled the front pages of the folded newspaper I'd brought in with me and had been sat on the front rail of the witness stand throughout my evidence. I have no idea why I decided to bring the paper in. It seemed like a good idea at the time.

Everyone in the courtroom was now on their feet, including the accused surrounded by three advocates to his front and the two uniformed men to his rear. It seemed a fairly casual scene as his lawyers looked knowingly at each other and attempted to appear sage, but probably not saying much of note as there was not all that much to be said.

The prisoner seemed to be making an effort to look as if he understood everything and that he was an integral part of the conversation, but it didn't cut any ice from my perspective.

When he did interject he looked uncomfortable and noticeably demonstrative, making more use of his hands in conversation than one normally would, I imagine cramming as much movement into his free arms as he could before the cuffs went back on.

I didn't stay to see this small event happen as Anthony stepped forward and taking me gently by the shoulder directed me through the double doors and out into the corridor.

'Let's walk', he said.

As we made our way outside to the entrance steps I asked what will happen next.

He said that the criminal process would take some time, not least because of the sheer number of witnesses whose statements had not been fully correlated. He suspected that they would all say substantially the same thing, but it had to be gone through methodically in order to build the case thoroughly. It could be many months and at least six before they would be able to move forward to the next hearing, and meanwhile he had other cases, including one today and he'd be going into another court presently to deal with that.

He told me not to worry as they had the matter well in hand. I asked when I'd be hearing from him and if I would be required to attend the rest of the trial, and he smiled seriously and said that was not very likely and my part in the process was now more or less done. He said that the indications were that the defendant was likely to plead not guilty, so it was important that the evidence was carefully gathered, including my testimony today which had been an important part of that, and as and when any significant events occurred, he would keep me informed.

The next morning Jenny and I sat and chatted on the balcony with Agnes and Alicia, and after a lazy breakfast took one last walk along the sweep of Mahoe Bay. I said a silent farewell to my palm tree hammock and curled my toes one last time in the crystal sand, brushing the soles of my feet over the blunted red coral which peeked through the beach surface here and there, wanting to savour and remember every tactile sensation of the place I briefly called home.

I had not returned to my wonderful Valley Trunk since the shooting, and with two pieces of paradise firmly locked away in my memory, I was very sad to be leaving both.

We climbed the steep concrete slope to Agnes's house on the hill, my lungs and legs significantly better than they had been the first time I'd stumbled down the same road four short weeks before. Our suitcases were already waiting by the office door, Jenny and Agnes loading them into the silver Mango Bay people carrier, and without ceremony we all climbed in and drove through the entrance gate and out onto the first unmade section of the road to Spanish Town.

Arriving at the yacht harbour soon after mid-day we stood and waited on the dock, the Speedy Boat staff taking our belongings and stowing them on the lower deck amongst caged cats and boxes of this and that. It came time for our goodbyes, the fast ferry signalling its imminent departure with a long blast of its steam whistle, and Agnes and Alicia hugged us, then turned and walked back to the car and without a backward glance drove out of the car park and away. I thought I just noticed little Alicia turn her head towards us as the people carrier slipped from view, but Agnes did not.

Beef Island was a twenty minute crossing across a bumpy white-flecked sea, which was slightly quicker than the last time I had made this journey. The turquoise of the inshore waters quickly changed to the darker blue of the deep ocean, the ancient volcanic peaks and troughs creating a cauldron of whipping breezes so loved by the sailors who crossed our wake countless times before we slowed and pulled up to the concrete quayside of the BVI's only international airport.

It was a quick ferry turnaround at Beef Island, but this was not a problem as the efficient crew had already unloaded our luggage by the time we crossed the gangplank to the shore. An enthusiastic taxi driver got the jump on his laxer colleagues by gathering all the bags up at once unbidden and shuffled awkwardly over to his vehicle with a sharp look over his shoulder, as if signalling that it was imperative that we followed like a member of the resistance leading us to a clandestine wartime rendezvous.

It wasn't quite that important to us which cab we took for the few hundred metres to the airport terminal (shiny steel and glass as opposed to the wooden shack of Spanish Town). We sauntered behind him, even slowing down a little so as not to overtake and bruise his ego as he waddled forward almost tipping over, trying to rush in case we changed our minds, but being so overloaded it was impossible. Normally the cab drivers here were so laid back. It must be rent day.

The runway was wide, flat and smooth, tarmac in places, concrete in others, but emptier and more sedate than the explosion of life at Charlotte Amalie. The arrival and departure times were staggered, but not infrequent. The aeroplanes larger than those lined up on the grass at Virgin Gorda's airstrip but still relatively small, carrying either intimate groups of wealthy holidaymakers in private planes, or for the rest of us mere mortals longer modern commuter jets with a maximum capacity of up to fifty or sixty travellers.

One such sleek winged cigar landed and several dozen passengers disembarked down a steep set of hastily applied wheeled steps. The descenders were a mix of tired, inquisitive and very pale tourists and darker more jaded locals and business people.

We dug out our tickets - we were to be on the British Airways overnight flight from San Juan, but the first part of our journey was via American Eagle, a regional shuttle airline tasked with scooping up the flotsam of jumbos landing at the main international hubs and delivering them around the Caribbean where the big airliners couldn't reach.

We checked the logo on the tail fin - AM Eagle. It must be ours.

A female announcer (an actual person not a tannoy) called out our flight, and stood by the manual glass doors to the runway checking and tearing boarding passes, and after queuing with the other passengers we filed out onto the blistering hot runway for the short walk across to the plane.

Climbing slowly up the rocking stairs to the whistling sounds of turbines, we took one final look at clear blue sky, and ducking my head I stepped into the freezing interior of the cabin.

At 8.30am the next day, Sunday the 20th of March, the front and rear doors of the Boeing 747 opened, immediately letting in twin shafts of cold air and noise. After shuffling up the aisle, bags and my one casual light jacket in hand and me none the worse for the journey regarding pneumothoraxes and whatever else, we nodded politely at the painted-smile hostesses, turned the corner into the fully enclosed passenger walkway and headed for passport control.

Through the windows of the Heathrow terminal the sky looked broody and lower somehow. It was strange to think that in a place a lot warmer, and not so very far away, the air was still charcoal. It was just before 5am in a quiet Spanish Town. The garbage trucks and their drivers were waking getting ready to rumble down the pre-dawn streets to their collection points, a few dogs were barking and the odd cockerel crowing breaking the otherwise humid silence. The first thin horizontal line of pale blue was appearing over the eastern horizon above the Atlantic Ocean, and somewhere below and far out of sight, was London, and us.

Aftermath

We had been in the Caribbean for ninety six days.

Eventful is one way of putting it, but the drama was not to end there.

The court case, first criminal then civil was to linger on for another twelve years, and that is a story unto itself, involving bankruptcy, health setbacks, judicial intransigence and finally ending in Downing Street and provoking a change in the law in more than fifty countries.

Jenny and me?

Short answer, we split not long after returning to the UK.

There were a few last minute near-reconciliations, but in the end with much acrimony and one too many unpleasant scenes we separated and divorced in January of 1995.

My lungs? They healed, sort of.

On returning to the open arms of the NHS I was eventually categorised and pulverised, sterilised then harmonised, making a decent enough recovery in the fullness of time.

The loculated fluids which Doctors Tattersall and Comissiong released from my chest did turn out to be harbouring a particularly nasty infection known as Clostridium Clostridioforme. Hard to detect, harder to treat, but after emptying the contents of an entire pharmacy into me we finally beat the bug. One quarter of my right lung remains non-functioning scar tissue, but that's okay, I can accept that. There are many other petty health annoyances resulting from the bullet that are too boring to mention, and I console myself with the fact these are mostly invisible, so on the whole can live a pretty anonymous life, and I am grateful for that.

Later that year, one wet October afternoon, the telephone rang in the apartment where I now lived alone in Kent. Through a crackly wire came a soft, measured West Indian voice, the addition of a perceptible time delay giving away a good indication of where the call originated.

Anthony Vieira spoke the first words we had exchanged since standing on the steps of Tortola's courthouse seven months before.

'Mister Hartwell? Hello! I thought you should know that your assailant pled guilty this morning to all of the revised counts held against him, thus negating the need to call any of the other fifty witnesses, and as such he was today handed a sentence of five years' incarceration to be served at the state prison in Road Town.'

Five years? Is that all?

I didn't even know there was a hearing scheduled for today, so far out of the loop I was now.

I asked specifically what the charges were that he had pled guilty to, and was told that all of the attempted murder charges had been dropped in exchange for a guilty plea to the lesser offences, and specifically relating to me he had been convicted of Grievous Bodily Harm, and Wounding with Intent.

I asked the prosecutor what the policy on remission and time off for good behaviour was in the BVI, and further asked him to hazard an educated guess as to what length of time he would actually serve in prison.

'My best guess? Three years. And that is a substantial sentence.'

I don't know who he was trying to convince more, himself or me.

I thanked him for his call and put the phone down, immediately picking it up again to telephone Jenny at her parents' house in the next town and tell her the news.

Jenny burst into tears, not much else was said, and the call lasted less than a minute.

Two years later I found myself walking along Main Street one sunny day in Road Town, there to attend one of the many court hearings that were still dragging on in the civil case, and having adjourned for lunch I'd taken a stroll down to Pusser's Bar on the waterfront for some refreshment.

I was dressed more appropriately this time in a silk suit and looked I imagine a lot different to the semi-invalid in poorly fitting clothes who had attended the deposition hearing a lifetime before.

As I headed back to the court walking in the middle of the thoroughfare - which you could still do then in sleepy Road Town as daytime traffic was almost non-existent - I noticed a group of a dozen or so men walking towards me dressed in dirty red overalls, a solitary grey-uniformed figure in the centre, still part of the group but half a pace ahead of the rest.

There was a gentle camaraderie visible amongst all the men, including the guard, and all seemed at ease and were walking freely with no handcuffs or shackles restraining them.

A prison work detail.

I had never seen one before but it could be nothing else.

The men talked and bantered, with a few laughs and playful jostles as they made their way along in loose formation.

In the brightly coloured crowd my eyes were involuntarily drawn to a face I knew.

Unmistakable.

Now just a few metres away, walking straight at me in the middle of the highway as I was, totally oblivious to the healthy man approaching.

I was just another banker on a business trip to Tortola dealing with some corporate affairs, or a foreign lawyer setting up a trust walking between meetings. Just a tall European in a suit, like so many others he had seen. No-one of any significance to him or his life as an inmate of Her Majesty's Prison, Road Town.

We walked right up to each other and our paths crossed, so close I could have touched him on the arm as I passed by the side of the unchained gang.

I looked into his eyes, but he did not even glance at me let alone register any recognition.

The detail continued in the direction of the harbour, perhaps to repair a drainage ditch or to clean the weeds from the sea wall or whatever semi-useless task was assigned for them that day, probably as much to get the guard some fresh air as any form of legitimate community service.

I continued on too, up Main Street towards the courthouse where the afternoon session was about to begin. Climbing the steps past the huddles of lawyers, I entered and didn't look back.

Maps, Bio and Further Info

Craig Hartwell was born in Kent in a town best known for being the birthplace of the Rolling Stones, and home to a rather large bridge.

Studying as a carpenter, he got the travel bug from an early age setting off to explore the world at nineteen, and hasn't looked back since.

Currently in England, where he lives, always by the water.

Supported Charities:

http://www.sightsavers.org/

There are none so blind as those who will not see.

http://www.rspca.org.uk/home

We are judged by how we treat those who cannot defend themselves.

Follow the story of the book on specially prepared maps of both Virgin Gorda and the Virgin Islands at -

www.the-hyip.com

Also see:

https://www.facebook.com/pages/Sir-Francis-Drake-Tall-Ship/194528464258

Thank you for reading this book. If you have any comments please let me know at -

www.the-hyip.com/contact.html

- giving the date of your purchase and the nature of the enquiry, and I will do my best to get back to you as soon as possible.

Unless I owe you money, in which case the cheque is in the mail.

Now where did I put that sunscreen...

CH

Made in the USA
Charleston, SC
27 December 2013